ALIENATION, CONSCIOUS AND UNCONSCIOUS

ALIENATION, CONSCIOUS AND UNCONSCIOUS

Reflections on Psychoanalysis and Sociopolitical Issues

R. D. Hinshelwood
and Giuseppe Caruso

KARNAC
firing the mind

First published in 2026 by
Karnac Books Limited
62 Bucknell Road
Bicester
Oxfordshire OX26 2DS

British Library Cataloguing in Publication Data

A C.I.P. for this book is available from the British Library

ISBN: 978-1-80013-313-6 (paperback)
ISBN: 978-1-80013-402-7 (e-book)
ISBN: 978-1-80013-401-0 (PDF)

Typeset by vPrompt eServices Pvt Ltd, India

www.firingthemind.com

MIX
Paper | Supporting responsible forestry
FSC® C007915

Karnac Books is committed to a sustainable future for our business, our readers, and our planet. This book is made from Forest Stewardship Council® certified paper.

I (RDH) would like to dedicate the book to therapeutic communities, which have been an inspiration through all my career. They have taught me that there are two sides to every story, and dialogue has to be a respectful means of acknowledging that.

I (GC) dedicate this book to E.

Contents

Part II
Individual psychology with its interpersonal dimensions

Part III
The sociopolitical penetrated by the mental

Part IV
How do we "take action"?

Acknowledgements

My (RDH) interest in the implications of psychoanalysis for political thought was greatly stimulated by learning from, and discussion with, Bob Young over a period of four decades or so, until, sadly, he died in July 2019.

Too many to mention are those who inspired my (GC's) commitments to politics (over the more recent decades friends and colleagues in the World Social Forum, Teivo Teivainen above all), and psychoanalysis (for discretion may they be acknowledged as TW, MLR, RR, and DBB). My deepest gratitude to Bob Hinshelwood, for much more than just this book.

About the authors

Giuseppe Caruso is a psychoanalyst of the British Psychoanalytical Society. He works in private practice in London. As a social theorist he has published widely on global justice movements and cosmopolitanism and, more recently, integrating psychoanalytic insights to explore emotional cycles and leadership in groups. His earlier research involved ethnographic fieldwork with the Shipibo-Konibo people in Peru, leading to a monograph about their traditional medical practices.

R. D. Hinshelwood is a Fellow of the British Psychoanalytical Society and a Fellow of the Royal College of Psychiatrists. He had a long interest in alternative psychiatry and worked as a part-time Consultant Psychotherapist in the National Health Service whilst also running a private practice as a psychoanalyst for more than forty years. Subsequently he became professor in the Centre For Psychoanalytic Studies at Essex University (now the Department of Psychosocial and Psychoanalytic Studies), and is now Professor Emeritus. He has written widely on psychoanalysis and psychoanalysts, as well as comparative psychoanalytic research, the psychodynamics of institutions, and a number of political topics (that make up the contents of this current volume).

Abstracts of the papers

The eleven papers published in this book focus on the relevance of psychoanalysis to political issues, debate, and action. Abstracts of each of the papers are below.

Part I

Paper 1
Projective identification and Marx's concept of Man (1983)

At the level of observation, the social science phenomenon of alienation as described in Marx's early writings corresponds surprisingly with the psychoanalytic occurrence of projective identification. There are various headings of the similarities: Weakening and depletion, Imprisonment, Unconscious phantasy, Sensuous activity, Reciprocity, Control and possession.

Paper 2
Convergences with psycho-analysis (1996)

The powerful influences of the communism of the Russian revolution and the medical development of psychoanalysis have pervaded so much of the history and culture of the West in the twentieth century, but they point to radically different deterministic causes. The many attempts to join up a Freudo-Marxism have been dubious. The failure of the Bolshevik Revolution to spread to the more advanced capitalist countries, such as Germany, led to the recognition that more causes were operative than economic ones. Critical theory originating with the Frankfurt School demanded that cultural causes arising from unconscious sources must be in play as factors modifying the classical communist determinism. Here Raymond Williams' formulation of the conceptual superstructure is noted as a model of convergence.

Part II

Paper 3
The individual and the influence of social settings: A psychoanalytic perspective on the interaction of the individual and society (2005)

This paper describes the internal world as if it were a real place with space and time like the external world. That internal reality gives a special colouring to the external world for all individuals in their own differing internal worlds. Insofar as this internal composite is in fact the identity of the person, it become a template that interprets the external world uniquely for each individual. However, it is an unstable world inside us, which is constantly changed by contact with other minds that can evoke new experiences, and especially ones that originate in that "other" mind via an interpersonal "flow" of emotions.

Paper 4
Social Possession of identity (1988)

Projective identification is discussed as an interpersonal phenomena forming a potential bridging concept between the internal defences and the external relationships. There is a flow of personal experiences between people, sometimes shared and sometimes distorted, even denied. The experience may therefore evolve and evoke as it passes through different persons, and ultimately it contributes to group decisions and actions. Interruption of the flow of communication results in flatness and inauthenticity.

Paper 5
Psychological defences and nuclear war (2002)

War arouses powerful reactions in people, including fear, rage, righteousness, and grief, as well as the defences against these basic emotions that numb the impact of death and fear. There is a common element for everyone involved, and so these internal dynamics tend to be shared across a whole society or nation. This paper focuses on these internal states and how they collect together. It also considers a qualitative difference between conventional war and nuclear war. The fear of loss in ordinary warfare is exaggerated when nuclear weapons threaten a total annihilating destructiveness of everything.

Part III

Paper 6
Ideology and identity: A psychoanalytic investigation of a social phenomenon (2009)

An individual's ideal is formed from the group she is in at the moment. There are two forms of allegiance to a group ideal. One is to aspire to it so far as one is capable, and the other is to adopt it so completely that one becomes identified with it to the exclusion of mistakes, aberrations, and inconsistencies; one has *become* the group ideal. This identification is strongly enhanced in a group situation. It is similar to Freud's diminished ego in the face of a loved object. The process involves narcissistic identification of others as bad, and oneself as good; consequently it involves a false consciousness. These two forms of the ideal are parallel with the distinction between the overvalued idea (defensive) and the selected fact (creativity).

Paper 7
Intolerance and the intolerable: The case of racism (2007)

There are two aspects to racism: first, the social intolerance that sweeps through a society; the second is the internal state that the social attitudes seem to recruit. In general, identity is very fluid, and deeply connected with roles in a social context. Pathological personality structures based on the narcissistic split between positive and negative part-egos can then be externalised by being hooked into social relations based on cultural prejudices. The narcissistically intolerable, internal "badness" meets the external intolerance of a difference.

Paper 8
The function of symbol-formation: Pinning down the ego function (2020)

This paper follows a previous one in the *British Journal of Psychotherapy* in 2018, which examined Hanna Segal's theory of symbol-formation and the various modifications she made to it. In this paper, I argue that we need to examine the specific functions involved in symbol-formation to spot which of them fails. To use one thing (a symbol) to represent another requires a kind of suspension of reality; the capacity to represent means taking one thing *as if* it were really another. There is a double relation to the symbol—which is a mark on a piece of paper and is *also* the thing it represents. I have termed this the "as-if" function that is needed in order to use symbols and representations. It indicates the precise location of the psychotic failure to recognise reality. The as-if quality breaks down and the symbol is mistaken as identical (equated) with the thing symbolised. This addition to Freud's list of ego-functions involved in the reality principle is crucial to the development of representation, and ultimately to the capacity for civilisation.

Part IV

Paper 9
Reflection or action: And never the twain shall meet (2017)

We return to the problem of the convergence between psychoanalysis and politics. They each have their own forms of action. Labour process is cited as an example of social processes in action with a damaging impact on the minds of industrial workers. Primitive mechanisms are discussed as processes that interrupt the clear awareness of those involved in industrial relations. Psychoanalytic "action" is different: it is the thoughtful understanding of the defences that distort reality, validity, or authenticity. The gift that psychoanalysis makes is the knowledge of the unconscious. But one cannot simply apply the psychoanalytic action of interpreting an individual unconscious by applying such interpretations to a social group.

Paper 10
The disappointment of democracy (2021)

This paper is a reflection on the discontents of civilisation and the possibility that democracy itself is disappointing at times. I attempt to pinpoint various features that disappoint with our current notion of democracy, and imply that a vigilance for failures is a necessary antidote to idealisation. I discuss a selection of the disappointments with the plea that modern democracy certainly needs systems of accountability much more than empty promises of freedom.

Paper 11
Political action, psychoanalytic action (2023)

The forms of action in the two domains, politics and psychoanalysis, appear quite different. However, political debate is the first step in politics and depends on the individual's mind to manage representations that discussions are based on. We need undistorted representations for creating potential plans and policies and to exchange them with other minds. This first step, debating, corresponds entirely with the psychoanalytic process. Whereas this first step corresponds to the whole process of psychoanalysis, it is only the first step in politics, which proceeds to a further step of putting into effect the experimental policies conceived in thought.

Introduction: A preliminary discussion

GC: To begin with, Bob, let me start by saying how delighted I am to be having this conversation with you on this important part of your work. Thank you for having accepted to do this with me. I will say only a few words to get us started. This book is not only the celebration of one important aspect of the work of a very inspiring analyst, one whose work—as a clinician, academic, and supervisor—spans five decades (and counting); it is also an opportunity to push your thinking further along paths you have travelled and along some you have only indicated you might have travelled had you had the opportunity. The opportunity has come, therefore, now to review, update, and explore further at least some of your reflections on the relationships between psychoanalysis and politics, between what in psychoanalysis is indicated as internal and external reality (the environment, symbolic and material), between what in the social sciences are indicated as the micro and macro dimensions of human activity and being, the fine grain and the fabric of the human cloth.

Your extensive production of clinical papers, the theoretical studies of the work of Melanie Klein (the canonical dictionary), Wilfred Bion, and, more recently, Herbert Rosenfeld, and your works with and on organisations and therapeutic communities, have attracted wide interest in the psychoanalytic and psychotherapeutic field, in academia, and beyond. Your work is imbued with an acute sensibility to social and political matters even when these are not specifically the direct subject of the paper or book in question. Consider, for instance, how genuinely political is the treatment of the subject matter of one of your most psychoanalytic books, *Therapy or Coercion* (1997), on whether psychoanalysis is transformative or a form of brainwashing. While the volume treats matters of concern for the therapeutic community (and its patients), it says a great deal about mechanisms of propaganda and truthfulness, the application of which is society-wide and the experience and awareness of which is common and diffused (or it would be important that it was as a key political skill). You have produced a series of important papers on political subjects over the past four decades. We collect here eleven of your most inspiring papers, the first published in 1983, the latest in 2023.

In the spirit of psychoanalysis and of your engaged and generous nature, we explore your work further in a series of conversations following each group of papers (we discuss the rationale of the grouping below). The conversation starts indeed now, in this introduction, so that we can observe the mind of the psychoanalyst at work as you, Bob, think with me through some of the key aspects and implications of your work. Let me start by asking you something of your personal trajectory, to help us situate your perspective. How did you become interested in a dialogue between political studies and psychoanalysis? What brought you to consider the need for that dialogue and its use?

RDH: Let me say first that, of course, it is flattering, and inflaming of a personal narcissism, to be asked by you (an academic, but also currently a trainee psychoanalyst), to consider, and reconsider, this selection of papers (chapters) on wider social issues.[1] Unlike many of my colleagues, my path to psychoanalysis was not via psychology or child psychotherapy. My path started originally with my shock at first encountering, as a medical student, the conditions in which suffering human beings were housed in mental institutions. Although I had been acquainted with Freud and Jung from my last year or two at school, my first encounter with a Kleinian psychoanalyst was when advised as a young psychiatrist to read Bion's book on groups (1961). Bion, too, had followed a path to psychoanalysis somewhat similarly via a concern with the inappropriateness of the social institutions for mental health.

[1] What we refer to as chapters, here, are the chapters in this book, but they were, of course, previously published elsewhere mostly as papers in journals. The original references are available in footnotes to each chapter heading.

I was young and idealistic (and now old and unrealistic, I suppose) when I started in psychiatry in 1966. Then there were the old mental hospitals, one of which, Shenley, I worked in for a couple of years. It was the hospital where David Cooper had worked and where he developed Villa 21, a legend then, although I have not heard it mentioned for a long time. I never met Cooper—he had left Shenley by the time I arrived—but his spirit remained. At the time, Ronnie Laing was at his height, and being young and hesitant then, I never met him personally, though I went to some of his talks. This movement in psychiatry took me away from the traditional approach and towards, literally, a communal form of thinking, the therapeutic community movement. I am still in support of The Consortium of Therapeutic Communities (TCTC). It took me into my training in psychoanalysis, in the 1960s. There were very few trainings in psychotherapy, and I came to the view that the Institute of Psychoanalysis was the best at the time. Twenty years later, there were too many psychotherapy trainings, and one of the reasons I started the *British Journal of Psychotherapy* was to help some of them to collaborate together.

In fact, the schismatic fervour of analysts and therapists in general is an instance of the problems of collaboration—a genuinely, I think, political matter. It is more than disagreement. In so many ranges of political activity at a group level, there is intransigence rather than mutual enquiry of each other. And in the world of therapy and professional understanding, that is shame indeed. Nevertheless, whatever the mental belligerence amongst psychotherapists, and the physical belligerence of warfare in politics, there has been over history and from civilisation to civilisation, a persistent, slow progress towards verbal engagement. Whatever happens to our present civilisation, it is likely that the next will progress a trifle further than us. So, my sense is that one important foundation stone of the success of humanity is that we have developed the ability to collaborate more than any of nature's species. I nearly said "perfected a collaboration", but human collaboration is far from perfect, which is why we are looking at these issues and problems. Collaboration unfortunately has the purpose of bringing individuals together in some unifying way—unfortunately, in that the generative move towards collaboration also moves us towards a threat to individuality and personal creativity, and thus a rival destructiveness.

GC: I tend to think of war as one expression of anti-politics … I wonder whether here there might be a way to push you a bit to define politics and the political?

RDH: That's a good starting point. I tend to think of politics in rather broad terms—ever since those slogans from my youth, such as "anatomy is destiny", and "the personal is political" emerged. So anything that we are and do is within a context of others. Anything that we do *together* is political. That might include even being a part of a football team. Some would say that what we do in a social setting is group dynamics, but I think I'd try to restrict that to unconscious processes based on the anxiety–defence structure of the unconscious. Politics is significantly conscious though interfered with by unconscious dynamics.

GC: Recounting your experience at Shenley hospital and your involvement with the therapeutic community movement, you mentioned that it was this engagement that brought you into the psychoanalytic training. How did your engagement with therapeutic communities lead you to want to commit to individual clinical work as well? How did the two strands of your work—therapeutic communities and individual clinical work—coexist in your professional career? I am asking this because there is a way in which I understand what you write as though your engagement with groups required of you, elicited in you, the wish to deepen both your political commitments and to train in psychoanalysis—as if these two things were somehow connected in your experience and in your thinking about it.

RDH: Yes, I suppose that the therapeutic community movement has always been an inspiration that has helped me to look ahead to where I might go. And I am still involved and have given presentations recently at the annual conference of the movement. The presentation, in 2022, was called "Psychiatry upside down", which more or less says everything that was in the presentation. I learned psychiatry in the early 1960s at University College Hospital medical school where it was rather inspiringly taught by a number of people, including Roger Tredgold and Heinz Wolff. And by the time I got my first job in psychiatry, the anti-psychiatry movement of Ronnie Laing and David Cooper was getting into full stride and marching with the swinging London of the 1960s. It was a time of sparkling hope after the post-war austerity (that had lasted until the mid-fifties) and now a new phase in human civilisation was opening up. We thought! The problem with psychiatry then was the psychiatric institutions; they were deeply impersonal, or, as I would later realise, deeply depersonalising. Something personal, and personalising, like therapy or psychoanalysis, seemed essential. Actually, at that time, towards the end of the sixties, there were very few formal trainings in therapeutic work, and most of them emerged in the 1970s. The Institute of Psychoanalysis, however, had been training since the 1920s and was obviously one to consider. The only other one was the Jungian Society which I certainly romanced with, and I had read a book about Jung (by Freda Fordham) in my last year at school. Perhaps what decided me was that I knew that some psychoanalysts had recently been working with these difficult "psychotics"—depersonalised as this diagnostic label implies. That was a factor in deciding for the London Institute, and for choosing a Kleinian analyst—and I started my analysis on Guy Fawkes Day in 1969, when I was thirty.

I had already been aware of Elliott Jaques' work on social defence systems, and I suppose that is still central to my thinking. He was at that time part of the core Klein group. And also, Isabel Menzies Lyth's work which showed the relation of institutional depersonalisation to the anxiety-defence structure in hospitals. I was fortunate to have Isabel as my first training supervisor, and people often think I became interested in institutions because of her influence; but in fact, it was the other way around. I remember one occasion, probably in 1975, sitting in her consulting room for supervision on her not very comfortable furniture. She sat on a rather upright settee with her arm along the back and was twiddling a ring on her left-hand ring finger. I was not at all confident enough to comment on the significance of her ring—I was in my mid-thirties, and she was a rather formidable Scottish woman in her mid-to-late fifties. But she did shortly move to Oxford and married Oliver Lyth, who within a year or two promptly, and very sadly, died.

Eventually, influenced by Bob Young, I began to read Marx and some of the Western Marxists. I had been in a small reading group which included Alicia Etchegoyen and Arturo Varchevker. Arturo had organised it in the eighties, and indeed I went to Nicaragua with Arturo around then, and I had met Marie Langer of the Plataforma group, then in Mexico City. The reading group sought to read around psychoanalysis in philosophy and politics. Bob Young was just starting his career as a psychoanalytic publisher, and he was enlisted to be mentor of the group. He did not count himself a communist/Stalinist but did convince us of the social penetration of values, attitudes, and ideas (including false consciousness) behind everything including science itself. I don't think any of us in that reading group regarded themselves as Stalinist. But my brother did join the Communist Party and was a member until 1990. My family was always loyally Labour, and my grandfather was branch secretary of his union. It was the printers' union and I believe my grandfather worked on the *Daily Herald* before the First World War when it was a campaign newspaper for the Labour Party. So, I have a left-leaning inheritance, which I have not forsaken. I have never really been an activist, however, although I was interested in the civil disobedience campaigns against nuclear weapons around 1960. Indeed, I found some newsreel footage, in the film archives of the University of East Anglia, taken of a protest in Norfolk; there is a moment of some ten seconds or so where I am part of the crowd of protesters. That was the one time when we were taken off by the police in buses to Winson Green prison in Birmingham, where we were on remand for three days and then saw a magistrate who sentenced us to "keep the peace for twelve months". Of course, as we said, what else were we trying to do!

GC: This is a fascinating story, and one with deep roots stretching across decades and, indeed, continents. What you say about the cooperation with Bob Young across disciplines but also across domains of living, so to say, is important as we observe the entrenchment of ideologies of radical individualism and competition (not too distant from versions of the belief in the survival of the fittest) governed by transcendental invisible hands. On the perversion of ideas, you write convincingly in your paper on ideology and identity (see Chapter 6 in Part III).

RDH: You are right, the aim is to create a structure of ideas that could contribute to wider debate, and personal history is only a peripheral interest. Nevertheless, the personal is inevitably the context for giving a pattern to one's understanding of a more general history of cultures and of bodies of knowledge. And vice versa, too; each is a reverberating context for the other—the personal history and the social.

GC: Reading Marx's earlier work, you developed very personal and deeply psychoanalytical takes on some age-old philosophical issues. Incidentally, Bion, whose work you discuss at length, including in a recent book (Hinshelwood, 2023), in *Learning from Experience* (1962) and in other places, wrote about the relationship between psychoanalysis and philosophy. For instance, in *Learning from Experience*, he writes that "psychoanalysis … may be regarded as having a relationship to philosophy analogous to the relationship of mathematics to applied mathematics" (1962 [2014, p. 331]). He writes in very similar terms in "A theory of thinking", and in other places as well. This links, somewhat, to a foundational debate in the history of anthropology between armchair anthropologists such as Tyler and Fraser and a new generation of field anthropologists who claimed the primacy of experience of the other over theorising it by reading secondary sources. What is your take on this relationship and how, if at all, the two disciplines, psychoanalysis and philosophy, can complement each other's perspective on human behaviour and life?

RDH: I am not sure that the philosophical approach is easy for me to grasp. It seems … well, a little alienating! (Is it unfair to say that?) But I love the idea that psychoanalysis is a kind of fieldwork philosophy, and philosophy is an armchair version of psychoanalysis. I think Freud might well have agreed that psychoanalysis had put philosophers out of business. And of course, one respects the fact that the Frankfurt School and their critical theory descendants did attempt to turn to Freud, and especially his structural model. But as Freud always said, that model is a metaphor for the hidden experiences of the unconscious. I hesitate to critique such philosophical use of psychoanalysis. But I will say just a few words about what I got from my reading of some critical theorists. It seems quite difficult for the writers to capture experiences that are *not* alienating/reifying. They use terms like "recognition", "appropriation", etc., and try to capture the abstract meanings of the terms they have chosen. Although the variety of arguments that justify these various terms, and problematise them, suggests that none of them really does the trick. So, there may be significant value in capturing and trying to construct a dimension from alienation to authenticity.

And, of course, above all, it is important to relate the impact of the cultural context to people's experience of themselves and each other. I quite accept that the emphasis on private property, ownership, wealth-possession does create a pressure to see persons as commodities, as Marx observed in such detail. That is, the culture that inevitably derives from capitalist forms of ownership, and the self-seeking and exploitative relations that come out of this, is an important pressure on people's relating to each other in conventionally predictable ways (and as we prepare this book, I am finishing a long and involved text on these pressures, which is due to be published now as *Unconscious Politics* (2024)). I am interested that the industrial "social relations of production" came historically after the period of slavery (I mean, after that period in European history)—instead of buying and selling persons as if trading commodities, industrial relations mean buying a person's time as a quantity of a commodity. There seems to be some historical continuity between slavery and industrial relations, and thus a qualitative continuity.

I think it would be interesting at this point to hear a little about your own journey from your initial interest in psychology through your long diversion into anthropology at university. With your eventual return to psychoanalysis, including how it is that you, like me, need to understand the contribution psychoanalysis can make to politics.

GC: Yes, it is true, my journey to clinical psychoanalysis has been long and it involved a number of detours. My interest in psychoanalysis and in political action, though, was born at the very same time around my mid-teens, when I was a high school student. I became very interested in matters of social justice and some of the people I met then and worked with were involved in the anti-psychiatry movement, were feminists influenced by French feminism, were pedagogues committed to educate for freedom and all, in one way or another, directly or indirectly, were inspired by psychoanalysis. So I think I met Freud and Marx in the short span of a few weeks. One of the things that struck me soon enough, as my interest in political action developed, was the reproduction among social justice activists of disruptive group dynamics that enormously weakened their influence and the spread of their, indeed our, ideas and practices. Often, we felt that these dynamics reproduced the very social malaise we criticised. This also caused personal crises and often depression and hopelessness. In a way, my enthusiastic idealisation of activist groups had met inevitable disappointment. However, I turned (or so I like to think) that disappointment to some use. I began thinking that group dynamics and individual psychologies lead to difficulties and failures of collective action, not only the other way around. I also thought that, surely, living in certain social conditions must have an impact on the psyche and on the structures of thinking of those subjected to appalling living conditions, exploitation, abuse, and domination. I thought that keeping the psychological effects of these experiences separated, split, from the organisation of political action meant a great disservice to both activists and their groups, and their ability to act politically. When it came to choosing a course of study at the end of high school, however, I chose to study anthropology rather than psychology as I had originally thought. Among those with whom I spoke then about the things I was interested the most in, many referred often to other societies around the world that were organised in very different ways to our "Western" ones, and were sometimes more egalitarian and democratic. Many, especially the older activists had travelled to South America, Cuba, Africa, the Subcontinent, and in the Middle East. They described not only different organisations and different ways of doing politics, but also entirely different conceptions of what it means to be humans together. Coming from a rather small provincial Sicilian city, I became interested in gaining a broader perspective on the world and, as anthropologists sometimes say, I set off on the longest road home. I returned to academic work several years after graduating, having worked on traditional healing practices in Peru and on international development projects. When I returned to it, it was to study political activism in an interdisciplinary way or, like I preferred to say, in a transdisciplinary way. It was about a decade ago, while I was delving into the debates in political theory on political representation and (indeed, vs!) prefiguration as the privileged forms of political action, that I returned to my early wish to pursue a clinical training. As we will discuss later, I had begun to conceive of psychoanalytic action and political action as closely resonant. When I met you for the first time at the end of 2015 I thought now this is what psychoanalysis, and your work in particular, can offer to political theory! I also thought, that the political theory I was interested in could use the psychoanalysis of the kind you offered. I also did think then, and do too now, that political theory and practice have much to offer to psychoanalysis. In fact, Freud himself often used political imagery to describe the dynamics in the mind between its different agencies. It seems to me that psychoanalysis and politics the way I understand them are best integrated than separated. Their split is, I think, often a symptom of a divided group dynamic that can indeed be illuminated by that very split and worked through in the process. What I found in your work and in your attitude towards different disciplines, was that, without pretending to put political theorists and philosophers out of business but in a spirit of close collaboration, your kind of psychoanalytic thinking can contribute an experience and therefore a language to speak about what is not alienating, what is (the) political, and, by doing that (this providing a language), you offer both tools to think about but, in the process of collective thinking, to work through pathological social organisations. Not only, and here I'm using Klein's formulations, a theory of paranoid–schizoid thinking and behaving but also of what depressive thinking and acting look like. When we initially spoke about my interest in your work and we started imagining this collection, I mentioned that it lay in the ability to bring to life and to political debate aspects of experience that could not be accessed through political philosophy alone. I also mentioned that, perhaps, psychoanalysis could be seen as a vertex—a perspective, a point of view, in a way similar to Bion's conception of vertices as different vantage points to apprehend human experience. You seemed to me unconvinced that that indication could already be seen in Bion. I now agree that there is also an important limitation in this view as it assumes a firmer position than I wish to hold here in the constructivism–objectivism debate. Here instead, I think it would be interesting to hear your thoughts on Klein's thinking in developing your psychoanalytical and political thinking.

RDH: Thanks for letting us in on a glimpse of your own trajectory and that interesting convergence of psychoanalysis and politics which you make. You are right, that I do think Klein's approach was one of the most focused on the patient's experience. Of course, not only her—Kohut coined the term "experience-near", for instance. But I was struck by Klein's recently published lecture notes:

> If we are not bent on labelling our patients as such and such a type, or wondering prematurely about the structure of the case … then are we ready to learn step by step everything about the patient from himself. (Klein, 1936)

So much of the psychoanalytic literature is about patients who fit our metapsychology. But listening in to our *patient's* "metapsychology" ought really to be our starting point. They come in order that we listen to them, their experiences of pain, conflict, anxiety. There has been a constant debate about whether Klein was an instinct-focused drive theorist. In fact, Klein never used the term "drive" in that technical way. She does use the term "instinct", although exceptionally in the term "Death Instinct"; but she really only means aggression. Klein never talks, anywhere, of "psychic energy", nor does she refer directly to Freud's "economic model". She is one of the earliest who focused on relationships, and who was influenced by the very humanistic Ferenczi, her first analyst, and by Karl Abraham, her second analyst, whom she revered. It also came from her work with children, whose play invariably concerned playing with the relationships between toys.

I may have given a wrong impression about Bion. He certainly took as his perspective to see what he could of the patient's experience. He claims he learned from a teacher at medical school, Wilfred Trotter: "Trotter … listened with unassumed interest as if the patient's contributions flowed from the fount of knowledge itself" (Bion, 1985 [2014, p. 38]). However, Bion deviated into an abstruse metapsychology in the early 1960s, trying to create for psychoanalysis the equivalent kind of schema (using a grid) to the physicists' use of mathematics, as you have just indicated. However, he pulled himself back severely from that and became extremely preoccupied with the way an analyst and an analysand can relate from their separate points of view. So, I do agree that Bion did focus as a matter of principle on experience as much as abstraction, though he veered between the two.

And perhaps you are right, though I had not seen it, that what psychoanalysis may offer politics is to realise that so much comes from experience, as much as from logical debate. Populism seems to imply quite desperate experiences, for instance. But the experiences can be at an unconscious level and thus beyond verbalisation unless we employ psychoanalytic insights.

GC: I agree that the use of psychoanalysis for the purpose of social analysis needs to be cautious and this use needs to be spelled out as far as both intentions and method are concerned. This is so for many reasons, including to resist the colonising temptation that often drives some interdisciplinary enterprises. Psychoanalysis, the social sciences, history, philosophy do not form a single unified and stable pattern. These perspectives, these disciplines, form multiple conceptual patterns and, consequently, multiple objects. I would like to ask you to spell out the conditions of convergence and disjunctions between psychoanalysis and social analysis. You suggest we might think in terms of psychosocial analysis. Can you say more about how you think of the relationship (synthesis perhaps?) of these two approaches?

I wonder whether psychoanalysis can offer unique tools for social analysis regardless of the society one is discussing, whether it can access "universal" underlying patterns (and emotional dynamics) of individual and collective human behaviour. In other words, can psychoanalysis provide a theory of political action (as opposed to reaction, acting out, and enactment)? Let me add that this matter is currently the main focus of my own curiosity and research, and I think that you offer a genuinely psychoanalytic approach to groups, institutions, and societal phenomena including populism, nationalism, racism, paternalism, and democracy.

RDH: I think you put your finger on a really important, and tempting, slippage that psychoanalysts are guilty of. We sometimes (even often) "analyse" society as if it were an individual mind on the couch. And, for instance, there is a tradition from Carl Jung to Earl Hopper to talk of the "collective" unconscious or the "social" unconscious. Incidentally, I think that your original training as an anthropologist would be a great asset in our conversations. I might add that many years ago, I was an impressed reader of Lévi-Strauss and structuralist anthropology, now swamped I understand, by the tide of post-structuralism and postmodernism.

With regard to your question about how our understanding of the unconscious can contribute to the social sciences, I think there are several ways, and they will emerge in the course of reading the papers and discussing them. But fundamentally the unconscious is structured in terms of anxiety and defence. There are indeed basic common anxieties—persecutory and depressive, in technical terms. And there are also, of course, characteristic defences that we all share the use of. What is interesting is when similar anxieties in similar situations erupt amongst the group all together so that we form a collectively anxious culture. Then the anxiety can become so intense it is rendered unconscious for everyone through the assistance of "social defences", as Jaques (1955) and Menzies Lyth (Menzies, 1960) called them. Then the collective anxiety–defence system can interfere extensively in political discussion at the conscious level. Then clear political thinking is inevitably disrupted; it fails and degenerates into the potential for rigid oppositions. This powerful obstacle is the existence of the human unconscious, which by its nature resists becoming available for conscious discussion. This is the major gift that psychoanalysts can offer.

GC: This is very interesting, Lévi-Strauss' extraordinary account of his fieldwork in Brazil has greatly contributed to my choice to study anthropology. It has also, however, taken me from my original plan to study psychology. As it is often said among anthropologists, our discipline is the longest way to go back home. And it has taken me three decades to return to my initial clinical interests. But I digress. Let's pause then here and let's turn to reading your papers in turn. Before doing that, let me briefly describe the structure of the book. The papers in Part I, with their focus on social analysis and Marx set the tone for what follows. Key concepts, such as alienation, reification, symbols, representations, politics, political, projective identification, are introduced in these first two papers. The papers in Part II explore the widened scope of Kleinian psychoanalysis in organisational contexts, both in social movements and in psychiatric institutions. The aim is to show the deeper, even deepest levels of the unconscious with their anxiety–defence structure in organisational and political modes. This work is grounded not only in Klein but also in two of her closest colleagues—Elliot Jaques and Isabel Menzies Lyth. In Part III, the scope of your work extends to even wider contexts as you explore the pernicious effects of ideology in general and racism in particular. Key to understanding how you link the deepest workings of the mind with the widest social phenomena is your paper on symbolism and symbol-formation. In Part IV, three papers on political action and democracy conclude this excursus with matters bridging psychoanalytic action and political action. The reader will find some repetitions in the papers, as they were originally set as separate and standalone works. However, as the core concepts recur, one has the opportunity to see them at work in different contexts. These iterations also show small variations that indicate both their internal complexity and adaptability but also their vitality and proneness to transformations. On infrequent occasions there have been small edits to the papers for the purposes of clarity without any change to the meaningful content. Finally, there is one more note I wish to add in this introduction. While avoiding belabouring here a point that will become apparent to the reader as we read through this collection, I will just mention that there is a striking emerging property to these papers taken together. Something that could be expressed by saying, in a Hegelian way perhaps, that an accumulation of quantity brings about a change in the overall quality of the experience. What emerges from this work, I think, are both a number of positions taken vis-à-vis some of the crucial debates on kinds of human activity, and also an integrated way to frame them. Uncovering, that is, describing in convincing terms, what this emergent position may be, is part of what each conversation aims to do. In a preliminary way, and to ease ourselves into the themes of the first part of this collection, it does not seem to me that your work limits itself to adding together Klein and Marx, but aims at their integration, and at opening up new creative ways to look at the relationship between micro and macro dimensions of the human escaping what, to some, is their incommensurability. From a split position to an integrated one, I would like to say. This could be put differently, if not very elegantly. The parts of this work can be thought of as parts of a complex thought digestive system. Paraphrasing Bion, it is possible to think of the combined works here presented (a body of work) as providing a novel containing thinking structure on social and political matters. The way in which this is done is just as interesting, if not even more interesting, than the outcome of each individual containment moment. And now, on to the first set of papers.

References

Bion, W. R. (1961). *Experiences in Groups and Other Papers*. London: Tavistock. In: *The Complete Works of W. R. Bion, Volume IV* (pp. 95–245). London: Karnac, 2014.

Bion, W. R. (1962). *Learning from Experience*. London: Heinemann. In: *The Complete Works of W. R. Bion, Volume IV* (pp. 247–265). London: Karnac, 2014

Bion, W. R. (1985). *All my Sins Remembered*. Abingdon: Fleetwood Press. Republished in *The Complete Works of W. R. Bion, Volume II* (pp. 5–76). London: Karnac, 2014.

Hinshelwood, R. D. (1997). *Therapy or Coercion: Does Psychoanalysis Differ from Brain-Washing?* London: Karnac.

Hinshelwood, R. D. (2023). *W. R. Bion as Clinician*. London: Routledge.

Jaques, E. (1955). Social systems as a defence against persecutory and depressive anxiety. In: M. Klein, P. Heimann & R. Money-Kyrle (Eds.), *New Directions in Psychoanalysis* (pp. 478–498). London: Tavistock.

Klein, M. (1936). Lecture 1: Guiding principles. In: J. Steiner (Ed.), *Lectures on Technique by Melanie Klein* (pp. 29–41). London: Routledge.

Menzies, I. (1960). A case-study in the functioning of social systems as a defence against anxiety: A report on a study of the nursing service of a general hospital. *Human Relations*, *13*(2): 95–121.

Part I

Setting out the psychosocial divide

These first two, early, papers begin a journey in search of a fluent interchange between the subjective experience of one's own individuality, on one hand, and a grasp of social forms, functions, and dynamics that arise, on the other hand, from a collective of individuals. In Chapter 1, a correspondence between two researchers is noted, as it points to a fascination to be satisfied. How do central concepts of the early Marx and of a later psychoanalytic follower of Freud (Melanie Klein) happen to coincide? This correspondence is studied through selected quotes from both Karl Marx and Melanie Klein.

These correspondences receive more detailed examination in Chapter 2. The rigidity of the model of dialectical materialism is as deterministic as any material science. It has had to be softened by the exceptions of history so that subjective intentions, purposes and social determinism converge in a multifactorial path together.

CHAPTER 1

Marxist and psychoanalytic alienations

Introduction

Having completed my psychoanalytic training in 1976, I turned to reading more widely in social and philosophical writing. First, Nick Manning and later Bob Young persuaded me to consider Marx's writing despite my aversion to Stalinism. But, in particular, Soviet Marxism seemed to consider historical process as simply deterministic. Then progress of capitalism would inevitably result in revolution. I was, however, struck by the early writings on alienation, and this first paper described that surprise. It has led to decades of rumination which culminated ultimately in this book (as well as a parallel argument—Hinshelwood, 2024). I was encouraged by a brief personal encounter with the editor of the journal that published the first paper, Tom Haley, who had been an anthropologist prior to his psychoanalytic training; he confirmed how interesting the point of comparison was that I was describing.

PAPER 1

Projective identification and Marx's concept of man*

Although Melanie Klein first explicitly described the mechanism and fantasy of projective identification in 1946, there were precursors in her own and other analyst's writings going right back to the early days (Freud, 1895). Klein was also impressed that the notion had been available to writers outside the analytic world (Klein, 1955) and she described in detail a short novel by a French American writer, Julien Green. This is an imaginative story with a science fiction plot.

Elizabethan and Restoration drama is full of plots involving changed identities for the purpose of getting access to people or for stealing knowledge about them. The Greeks, of course, who knew everything psychological and expressed it in their myths, were endlessly intrigued by stories of heroes who live in projective identification with their gods from whom they then derive omnipotence.

No doubt projective identification has been regularly rediscovered down through the ages. Perhaps it was therefore with unwarranted surprise that I realised that Marx described an unmistakable and very concrete form of projective identification (Lees & Manning, 1981). It is a

* Hinshelwood, R. D. (1983). Projective identification and Marx's concept of man. *International Review of Psycho-Analysis, 10*: 221–226.

concept that underpins not only his view of man his economic situation but also his view of social forces. He called it "alienation".

The acquaintance that an individual makes with an object is subjectively influenced by fantasies about the object and about its modification by the individual. This is familiar enough in psychoanalytic literature. However, Russell (1946) noted:

> [W]e may interpret Marx as meaning that the process … called the pursuit of knowledge is not, as has been thought, one in which the object is constant while all the adaptation is on the part of the knower. On the contrary, both subject and object … are in a continual process of mutual adaptation. He calls the process "dialectical" … (Russell, 1946, p. 784)

Alienation and projective identification

Marx's early interest in philosophical and psychological matters became overlooked in his increasing concentration on his later economic and political writings. In fact, they were so overlooked that they were only published posthumously some fifty years after his death, in 1934.

In those early writings there appears the following arrestingly explicit passage:

> We shall start from a present-day economic fact. The worker becomes poorer the more wealth he produces, the more his production increases in power and extent … This fact simply means that the object that labour produces, its product, stands opposed to it as something alien, as a power independent of the producer. The product of labour is labour embodied and made material in an object … this realisation of labour appears as loss of reality for the worker, objectification as loss of and bondage to the object, and appropriation as estrangement, as alienation. (Marx, 1844 [1975, pp. 323–324])

I shall now examine the comparability of these adjacent concepts—Marx's alienation and projective identification. I intend to draw out the many common features. These are in my opinion—splitting and projection; depletion and depersonalisation; imprisonment; the unconscious nature of the fantasy; sensuous activity; reciprocity between subject and object; and the effort to control.

Splitting and projection

The quotation from Marx indicates quite clearly in his own terminology the process of splitting. The object "stands opposed" and it is projected, it is "alien" and "independent", yet retains an identity with the worker, it is labour embodied. In other words, products of the person's (worker's) body are felt to have become separated off, to become located as a characteristic of someone else and to continue there as a powerful influence on the person. Klein's description of projective identification is very similar: "In such fantasies products of the body and parts of the self are felt to be split off, projected into mother, and to be continuing their existence there" (1955, p. 142).

Depletion

This kind of projection depletes or depersonalises the ego at the expense of the internal world: "As far as the ego is concerned the excessive splitting off and expelling into the outer world of parts of itself considerably weaken it" (Klein, 1946, p. 8). Projective identification may have a variety of other purposes as well as the expulsion of something bad from the body and the personality. Bodily products may "have the significance of gifts" (Klein, 1946, p. 8); or the intention, in fantasy, may be to project good parts of the personality in order "to keep them safe from bad things" (Segal, 1973, p. 27) that are believed to exist in the internal world. It is particularly when the fantasy concerns the projection of good things that the ego feels weakened and depleted. The loss to the ego and the enrichment and idealisation of the external object is not only familiar in psychoanalysis but is equally so to anyone observing group behaviour (Main, 1975). And this social process is exactly what Marx described in the relationship between the worker and the capitalist. In the following passage Marx is quite explicit that it is not just monetary enrichment but some kind of moral or religious enrichment that is also felt to be projected:

> The more the worker exerts himself, the more powerful the alien, objective world becomes which he brings into being over

> and against himself, the poorer he and his inner world become and the less they belong to him. It is the same with religion. The more man puts into God the less he retains within himself. (1844 [1975, p. 324])

Imprisonment

It is not just the sense of personal depletion that the ego suffers, there are other things:

> Projective identification produces a variety of anxieties. The two most important are these: the fear that an attacked object will retaliate equally by projection: and the anxiety of having parts of oneself imprisoned and controlled by the object into which they have been projected. (Segal, 1973, p. 30)

Marx again echoes this:

> The worker places his life in the object; but now it no longer belongs to him, but to the object … the life which he had bestowed on the object confronts him as hostile and alien. (1844 [1975, p. 324])

And "the worker becomes the slave of his object" (Marx, 1844 [1975, p. 325]). Both projective identification and alienation threaten to arouse the fear that the projected part of the person will be imprisoned in the object and that the object may then retaliate hostilely.

Unconscious fantasy

Projective identification makes its impact on the person as a convincing fantasy of what has happened to his own body and mind—but a fantasy that remains deeply unconscious. Meltzer describes it as "a fantasy function so remote from consciousness, save in fairy tales" (1967, p. xi). Marx, too, is explicit that what he is describing is the power of fantasy, and, of course, that it is an unconscious power: "It is nothing but the definite social relation between men themselves which assumes here, for them, the fantastic form of a relation between things" (1867 [1976, p. 165]) ; and "It is not the consciousness of man that determines their existence, but their social existence that determines their consciousness" (1859 [1975, p. 425]).

Sensuous activity

Both Marx and Klein are concerned with fantasies dealing with the concrete product of sensuous bodily activity. Marx makes an impassioned plea for this against the prevailing "spirituality" of his day deriving from Hegel:

> The chief defect of all hitherto existing materialism is that the thing, reality, sensuousness, is conceived only in the form of the object or of contemplation, but not as sensuous human activity, practice, not subjectively. (1845 [1975, p. 421])

Klein follows the basic psychoanalytic principle that the ego is a body-ego first and foremost and in her very first definition of projective identification she nails the fantasy to basic sensuous bodily activity in the form of the activities around the expelling of the products of excretion:

> [A]nal and urethral impulses [imply] expelling dangerous substances (excrements) out of the self and into mother. Together with these harmful excrements ... split-off parts of the ego are also projected into the mother. (1946, p. 8)

Reciprocity

Alienation appears mostly to refer to the evil ways capitalism is supposed to suck the life out of Man. The object in this view then causes the subject (ego) to become depleted and imprisoned; but in projective identification it is the ego (subject) that is the cause. The difference between alienation and projective identification is, however, only apparent. The initiating agent is not so clear-cut. Going back to his original statements, the interaction between subject and object is quite clearly, as Russell noted, a reciprocal one:

> Though private property appears to be the source, the cause of alienated labour, it is really its consequence, just as the gods in the beginning are not the cause but the effect of man's intellectual confusion. Later the relationship becomes reciprocal. (Marx, 1844 [1975, p. 332])

The primacy of the subject in initiating the projection does then correspond to the concept of projective identification.

Control

Another apparent difference between alienation and projective identification is in the motive for control. In the fantasy, is it the object or the subject (ego) that seeks control? Klein's emphasis is that projective identification is originally an attempt at control by the ego over the object. "These excrements and bad parts of the self are meant not only to injure but also to control and to take possession of the object" (1946, p. 8). This differs from alienation where in the fantasy the object (capitalist) seeks control over all the wealth and power of the subject. However, the difference again is more apparent than real. Projective identification covers a wide variation in the fantasies about expelling parts of the ego into the object. In the above quote from Segal, the ego that seeks to control by projection may feel the object retaliates with a hostile control to match. This leads the ego then to feel in turn under the control of an external object, imprisoned. These varieties of projective identification are then in line with alienation.

Projective identification includes a whole category of different fantasies around the main theme: it is "an overall name for a number of distinct yet related processes" (O'Shaughnessy, 1975, p. 325). It encompasses alienation as one of these processes. In particular, alienation would seem to represent the projection of good parts of the self in an excessive way, perhaps as a form of creative reparation in manual work. The projection does however seem to be associated with considerable projection of controlling and greedy impulses into the object as well, which is then felt to take and expropriate the good parts of the subject.

Freud and Marx

From the point of view of the analyst, it is tempting to speculate about Marx's own psychopathology—was he given to employing this form of projective identification in his own perception and relationship to physical work and bodily activity? However, I think this misses out various other important questions which are raised about the relationship between Marxism and psychoanalysis. And I would like rather to pinpoint some of these while leaving on one side Marx's own personality. A subjective element in his writing may have derived from his own use of projective identification. On the other hand, his own pathology may have meant that he was particularly in tune with the social processes he was writing about. In other words, his own pathology could have made him uniquely a man of his time.

There have been many attempts to reconcile the two great systems for thinking about Man—those of Freud and of Marx. One system, starting from the individual, extends into social phenomena, the other starts with social phenomena and seeks an underpinning in the psychology of the individual. A satisfying bridge between the two has been challengingly elusive. It has become, in recent years, the search for a twentieth-century philosopher's stone.

It seems that the hunt for these links may have been persistently taking the wrong direction. This paper shows that going back to Freud's classical papers, like sticking to the classical Marxist formulations in *Capital*, is not the most productive approach. Developments made by Freud's followers are just as valid in so far as they are real extensions of psychoanalytic understanding. Equally there is no reason to expect a reconciliation to start at the most abstract levels of theory; it is, in fact, more likely that the parallels will appear at the level of basic observation, when both analysts and Marxists are closest to their common subject—man.

Early attempts to link Marx and Freud were handicapped by not having the most pertinent writings of Marx available. The *Economic and Philosophic Manuscripts* were not published until 1934, nearly a century after they were written. However, Freudians who were interested in socialism began to take an interest in the application of psychoanalysis to contemporary society soon after Freud's contribution to social anthropology in *Totem and Taboo* (Freud, 1912–13). Paul Federn (1919) was one of the first. He understood that the oppressive relationship between father and son stamps itself onto society in the form of oppressive patriarchal regimes. He saw that the family pattern created an expectation of social structures so that individuals form their institutions to this model in a kind of repetition compulsion. It was therefore because of this psychological expectation that the old patriarchal societies of Europe were so difficult to overthrow and to replace with new societies based on a sibling model.

Since German society was a fully fledged capitalist one (unlike feudal Russia), it should have been more than ripe for revolution. So, when the Russian revolution failed to trigger off the German revolution in 1917, Marxism had to account for this dissonance. The idea that psychological expectations render a society unprepared for revolution in spite of the right economic conditions, was taken up from the 1930s onwards by the Frankfurt School of "critical theorists" (Held, 1980). It has led (in Western Europe) to a contemporary school of Marxism that has looked particularly to Freud for a psychological framework. Marcuse is the best known member of the Frankfurt School, partly because he did not return to Germany after the exile of the School in the USA during the Nazi period. Marcuse started from Freud's views on historical processes: "every internal barrier of repression is the historical result of an external obstruction. Thus: the opposition is incorporated within" (Freud quoted in Jones, 1955, p. 455). For Marcuse (1955) the internal conflict between id and superego was a reflection and internalisation of the class struggle between workers and capitalists. He saw, pessimistically, that this must be a water-tight cycle in which society creates its new members in such a way as to prolong society's present form through their own unconsciously determined expectations. Reich summarises this view: "Every social order creates those character forms which it needs for its preservation" (Reich, 1933, p. xxii).

Fromm was a peripheral member of the Frankfurt School while it was in Germany, but he too remained in the USA. Although he is constantly interested in the social psychology of Marx, he nowhere shows interest in the particular concept of alienation. His views often contrast Freud and Marx (for example, Fromm, 1968). He derives from Marx the passionate humanism that he finds lacking in Freud's mechanistic views. For him, Marx's psychology is *the* depth psychology and is truly dynamic because it is concerned with relationships. In this way, Fromm shows that the developments of the object relations school of psychoanalysis have passed him by. His emphasis is on personal growth and self-expression—the attempt by the individual to overcome his capitalist heritage. This brought him directly into dispute with Marcuse. One could say that Marcuse was a Marxist who remained loyal to Freud; while Fromm was an analyst who gave his loyalty to Marx. Both found the division between Freud and Marx just beyond their reach to join.

The social nature of man

Alienation is a psychological process that inserts man into particular relationships with his social environment. Projective identification is the primitive forerunner of all social relationships—whether they are massively pathological like depersonalisation, or they are normal, like empathy. It is not surprising that Marxist psychology approaches nearest psychoanalysis when man is seen in the midst of the interplay of his object relations.

Some analysts have come near to using the concept of alienation/ projective identification in their understanding of human societies. Reich, whose familiarity with the Marxist concept may have been only partial, was nevertheless very interested in the socially induced separation of the sexual side of human nature, its reification into a depersonalised object and its commercialisation (see Ollman, 1972). From a quite different angle (a linguistic one), Lacan describes the "alienating identification" (see Lemaire, 1977) as an individual is induced to becoming a symbol of himself within society.

Comparison of the different levels—individual and society—is beset with difficulties as well as illuminations. That such similar observations can result from the study of nineteenth-century capitalist society, and from the twentieth-century psychoanalytic study of children, is impressive. However, it leaves an equally impressive theoretical gap. The spanning of this gap must rely on other observations. Main (1975), for instance, demonstrates the very extensive use of projective processes in large groups—in fact, the larger and more impersonal the group, the more projective mechanisms are resorted to. Other psychoanalysts of the Kleinian school have observed groups of industrial and professional classes at work and have shown the very prevalent use of projective identification and introjective identification in the intergroup and inter-class relations (Jaques, 1955; Menzies, 1960). Those studies show that these defence mechanisms develop collectively in social groups under the pressure of common anxieties that afflict the individuals.

The development of society in any particular era probably generates certain kinds of experiences for the individuals (Lasch, 1978). In turn the individuals' personalities developing in that context generate defence mechanisms against the more anxious experiences. Finally, as a result, defence mechanisms negotiated socially, as Jaques and Menzies Lyth show, promote the development of social forms.

The way the two perspectives interlock may be clarified by considering the physical form of biological organisms. That is a result of both embryological development and of evolutionary history. Two time-scales intersect in the individual (Hinshelwood, 1982). The processes involved in embryological development are themselves changed through selection in the evolutionary history. On the other hand, evolutionary history is made out of the vagaries and mutations of embryological developments (de Beer, 1940). It is the same with the psychosocial form (personality) of the individual. Social historical forces bring out certain features in the psychological development of the individual members of the society—and they inhibit others. We can postulate that capitalist society brings out in the individual personality, the potential for excessive projective identification (alienation). In turn projective identification spurs on the form of capitalist society. In fact, the link between latter-day capitalism and the selection for narcissistic personalities by the dominant cultures has been noted and exhaustively described by Jacoby (1975) and Lasch (1978). Personality development in this way goes hand in hand with the historical development of society. With a particular economic age goes a particular selective pressure for certain personality types. That personality is not just a superstructure based on economic forces as recognised in Sève's term "juxtastructure" (1978, p. 144).

The interaction between the two developments (individual and social) is not self-limiting. Each feeds the other, forming an endlessly turning spiral which inescapably rolls on into social and individual forms that threaten to call down disasters. To step out of this rolling momentum may well seem, to some people, to require a revolution.

The possibility that projective identification/alienation is enhanced as a defence mechanism by the increasing development of a capitalist form of society would go towards explaining the historical changes of presenting symptomatology, for example from hysterical conversion symptoms towards borderline personality disorders over the last hundred years.

Summary

The concept of alienation used by Marx in his early writing, in the middle of the nineteenth century, was not really understood until the middle of this century. This paper shows that alienation has all the characteristics of a form of projective identification. Some of the implications of this for both Marxist theory and for the application of psychoanalytic concepts to social phenomena are explored.

References

de Beer, G. R. (1940). *Embryos and Ancestors*. Oxford: Clarendon Press.

Federn, P. (1919). *Zur Psychologie der Revolution: Die Vaterlose Gesellschaft*. Vienna: Anzengruber Verlag.

Freud, S. (1895). Extracts from the Fliess Papers: Draft H, Paranoia (1950 [1892–1899]). *S. E., 1*: 206–212. London. Hogarth.

Freud, S. (1912–13). *Totem and Taboo. S. E., 13*: 1–162. London. Hogarth.

Fromm, E. (1968). Marx's contribution to the knowledge of man. In: *The Crisis of Psychoanalysis*. London: Penguin, 1971.

Held, D. (1980). *Introduction to Critical Theory*. London: Hutchinson.

Hinshelwood, R. D. (1982). Two community time scales. *International Journal of Therapeutic Communities, 3*: 3–6.

Hinshelwood, R. D. (2024). *Unconscious Politics*. London: Karnac.

Jacoby, R. (1975). *Social Amnesia*. Sussex: Harvester Press.

Jaques, E. (1955). Social systems as a defence against persecutory and depressive anxiety. In: M. Klein, P. Heimann & R. Money-Kyrle (Eds.), *New Directions in Psychoanalysis* (pp. 478–498). London: Tavistock.

Jones, E. (1955). *The Life and Work of Sigmund Freud, Volume 2*. London: Hogarth.

Klein, M. (1946). Notes on some schizoid mechanisms. In: *The Writings of Melanie Klein, Volume 3* (pp. 1–24). London. Hogarth.

Klein, M. (1955). On identification. In: *The Writings of Melanie Klein, Volume 3* (pp. 141–175). London. Hogarth.

Lasch, C. (1978). *The Culture of Narcissism*. New York: Norton.

Lees, J., & Manning, N. (1981). Personality and environment interaction: Recent theoretical developments. Paper given to Anglo-Dutch Workshop on Therapeutic Communities, Windsor, September 1981

Lemarie, A. (1977). *Jacques Lacan*. London: Routledge & Kegan Paul.

Main, T. F. (1975). Some psychodynamics of large groups. In: L. Kreeger (Ed.), *The Large Group*. London: Constable.

Marcuse, H. (1955). *Eros and Civilization*. New York: Beacon Press.

Marx, K. (1844). Economic and philosophical manuscripts. In: *Early Writings* (pp. 279–400). London: Penguin, 1975.

Marx, K. (1845). Theses on Feuerbach. In: *Early Writings* (pp. 421–423). London: Penguin, 1975.

Marx, K. (1859). Preface to a contribution to the critique of political economy. In: *Early Writings* (pp. 424–428). London: Penguin, 1975.

Marx, K. (1867). *Capital*. London: Penguin, 1976.

Meltzer, D. (1967). *The Psychoanalytical Process*. London: Heinemann.

Menzies, I. (1960). A case-study in the functioning of social systems as a defence against anxiety: A report on a study of the nursing service of a general hospital. *Human Relations, 13*(2): 95–121.

Ollman, B. (1972). *Introduction*. In: W. Reich, *Sexpol: Essays 1929–1934*. New York: Random House.

O'Shaughnessy, E. (1975). Explanatory notes. In: *The Writings of Melanie Klein, Volume 3* (pp. 324–336). London: Hogarth Press.

Reich, W. (1933). *Character Analysis*. New York: Noonday Press.

Russell, B. (1946). *A History of Western Philosophy*. London: George Allen & Unwin.

Segal, H. (1973). *Introduction to the Work of Melanie Klein*. London: Hogarth.

Sève, L. (1978). *Man in Marxist Theory and the Psychology of Personality*. Sussex: Harvester Press.

CHAPTER 2

Seeking the synthesis

Introduction

I spent over a decade mulling over the distinctly divergent explanations of the alienating process of projective identification. I was invited by Ian Parker to contribute to a book initially entitled *Psychology and Marxism*, but after the final collapse of the Soviet empire in 1991, it had to be renamed *Psychology and Society: Radical Theory and Practice*. My chapter tried to confront the divergent explanations in social science and psychoanalysis of the alienation described in Chapter 1. Because the comparisons converged at the level of observation it seems imperative that the divergent theoretical explanations had to be compared as a dialectic.

PAPER 2

Convergences with psycho-analysis*

Nor is there the least doubt that these sciences [Marxism and psychoanalysis] are directly opposites. The question is, are they dialectical opposites?
—Strachey, 1937, p. 7

In 1924, only two societies within the International Psycho-Analytical Association were larger than the Russian Psycho-Analytical Society. The Russian Society was sponsored by Trotsky in 1930. A number of Freudian and Jungian analysands returned after the revolution, and there were separate branch societies in Moscow, Kazan, and elsewhere. From 1926, psychoanalysis began to be persecuted and slowly disappeared, being finally outlawed in 1936. During its brief period of success, the society in Moscow established a clinic for the treatment of patients: the State Psycho-Analytical Institute for training psychoanalysts, and an experimental children's nursery called the Psycho-Analytical Children's Home and Laboratory run by Vera Schmidt. The latter was for preschool children run on psychoanalytic lines, contemporary with, for instance,

* Hinshelwood, R. D. (1996). Convergences with psycho-analysis. In: I. Parker & R. Spiers (Eds.), *Psychology and Society* (pp. 93–104). London: Pluto Press.

the Malting House School in Cambridge (see Bridgeland, 1971). To this Moscow nursery, Stalin sent his eldest son, Yakov. Although there was some persisting influence on the work of the Soviet psychologist Lev Vygotsky and his colleague Alexander Luria (Wertsch, 1985), the Soviet interest in psychoanalysis was a blind trail.

Marxism and psychoanalysis are the major dominant influences in thinking about human nature that have informed the Western world during the twentieth century. To find a link between them would be a twentieth-century philosopher's stone. In fact, both frameworks have a good deal in common. From their nineteenth-century origins, both claimed to be scientific—before the present-day definitions of science. They are both anti-metaphysical, and materialist; and, like natural science, they are critical of surface appearances; both are in a sense concerned with false consciousness. And then psychoanalysis is, like Marxism, and unlike positivist science, a dialectical method of thinking. They have been jointly attacked as moral systems (for instance, Popper, 1959) and thus pushed into an unexpected alliance.

However, the really difficult sticking point is that Marxist theory starts from the social environment (the means of production), whereas psychoanalysis looks to the internal events in the individual's psychic apparatus, only later expressed in derivative social formations. Thus, psychoanalysts and social theorists stand gazing in opposite directions. In that back-to-back position, both have limited vision. Marxism has risked becoming a simple economism, as banal as Thatcherism; psychoanalysis risks the danger of a solipsism. The difficulty for psychoanalysis is to understand the processes of collectivisation, whilst Marxism needs a good theory of the individual that goes beyond the needs for material provision.

Psychoanalytic Marxisms

Jacoby (1983) concluded that in the 1930s the attempt to embrace a broad psychoanalysis, one that encompassed social theory as well as individual psychology, was widespread in Europe. Increasingly political, as the Nazis dominated more and more of Europe, many psychoanalysts were "socialists and Marxists". They may even have constituted a "majority of the analysts" (Jacoby, 1983 p. 12). Fenichel was a central figure holding together this network of socialist psychoanalysts, increasingly spread across the world, as they emigrated. Subsequently medicalisation and professionalisation of psychoanalysis has eradicated this radical tradition.

The first generation of Marxist Freudians during the 1920s and 1930s worked against the backdrop of the Stalinisation of Marxism and advancing fascism. In fact, both Marxism and psychoanalysis have moved on since then. Marx had pointed towards, though did not develop, a very much more extensive psychology. This is now much better understood since Marx's early manuscripts were not published until the 1930s.[1] In the sixth thesis on Feuerbach, Marx stated categorically, "the human essence is no abstraction inherent in each single individual. In its reality it is the ensemble of the social relations" (Marx, 1845 [1975, p. 423]). Then the negative reaction to Stalinisation surfaced strongly after the defeat of Nazism, and in the attempts to de-Stalinise Marxism, some thinkers showed interest in importing Marx's psychological approaches into their discourses. The new left sought to include a new version of human beings into a pre-Soviet Marxism. For Sartre, the human subject was an agent within a determining matrix. This new dialectic between self-conscious struggling human nature and a conforming determining history returned to the early Marx. The Frankfurt School has remained a lively inspiration. Marcuse's work attained high prominence temporarily in the 1960s. That strong return to the dialectical method was continued by Habermas (1968) and in the exhaustive history of this topic recounted by Wolfenstein (1993).

The development of the new left has more recently been towards single-issue political campaigns—anti-racism, feminism, and the environment—which has linked Marxists in with non-Marxist campaigners. Some have turned to psychoanalysis, in particular, feminists (Mitchell, 1974) and anti-racists—but each in their own way. The critical stance of psychoanalysis has been recently employed by some political thinkers in a stand against the political complacency of postmodernism (Frosh, 1991; Rustin, 1991).

At the same time, it must be recognised that psychoanalysis has greatly expanded. Contemporary psychoanalytic developments have

[1] However, an edited version of *Theses on Feuerbach* was first published in 1888.

been towards the investigation of the relations between subject and object. Foremost in this has been the work of Melanie Klein and the British schools of psychoanalysis. The important premise of object relations psychoanalysis is that the human being's relations with objects from birth, or soon after, are one of the prime factors in the satisfaction of needs. Of course, the first objects the subject relates to in infancy are not necessarily seen as very accurate versions of them. Nevertheless, it is a potentiality from birth to apprehend in terms of relations between subject and objects. The context of the internal world, in particular the internal society, links the psychological with the social (Menzies Lyth, 1981). The internal society, and the internal complex of relationships that form that society, is regarded as an inheritance in each person. The actual links between the internal and external social relations are complex:

> Individuals may put their internal conflicts [and therefore relations] into persons in the external world, unconsciously follow the course of the conflict by means of projective identification, and re-internalise the course of the conflict by means of introjective identification. (Jaques, 1955, p. 497)

The way an individual is constructed from the continuous flow of projections and introjections is the process studied in the practice of a modern psychoanalysis (Heimann, 1950). The important point is that there is an inherited endowment of a potential for an ensemble of relations with others which comprises an active "internal society". However, it is important to avoid characterising psychoanalysis as the theory of the internal world and Marxism that of the external ensemble of social relations. Psychoanalysis is an attempt to address the interchange. And indeed, Marx describes the internal and the external typically in the following way: "But what distinguishes the worst architect from the best of bees is that the architect builds the cell in his mind before he constructs it in wax" (Marx, 1867 [1976, p. 284]). This distinction is comparable to the psychoanalytic process of turning an internal structure (a "fantasy") into something external—objectification in Marx's terms. So, the idea of the internal society that is current in object relations psychoanalysis is not a novel addition to Marxism. It may, however, significantly amplify that aspect of Marxist psychology. In this way, the external interpenetrates the internal world (of object and subject). So, some recent developments in Marxism have coincided with some in psychoanalysis.

The individual and individualism

More recent interpretations of the link between psychoanalysis and Marxism rest on the instinctual needs of human beings as a material and deterministic given. The instinctual needs the psychoanalyst addresses are comparable to the economic needs of a rather crude Marxist psychology. More recently, attempts to understand the creation of subjective experience and of individual identity have taken up the idea of a material base for human needs.

From a psychoanalytic point of view, the self (ego) may split itself into fragmented bits that do not communicate with each other within the person. They may then be projected into, and then possessed by, external others. Thus, the social context is implicitly drawn into *internal* processes making up the individual psychology of a person. But from a Marxist point of view, it is the pressures of society itself that expropriates part of the self. Despite this back-to-back position on the causation, we might, however, examine the processes picked out by the psychoanalyst in order to gain a purchase on the effects of society on the individual. Perhaps if the modernist dilemma is how to sustain a sense of self, the struggles by which the individual does this, or fails to do this, tell us about the obstacles modern society puts in the way of individuality. Referring to this "crisis" of the self in modern society, Richards (1989) observes of his collection of writers:

> Intrinsic to all the accounts of "crisis" given here is the observation that the external social world is not an inert backcloth to individual enactments of crisis-management. (Richards, 1989, p. 2)

There is a concerted effort on the part of individuals to struggle with the crisis that modern society inserts into their sense of being. It is as if the whole of culture is predicated on the need of individuals to establish a stability, continuity, and permanence to their own sense of self—a feature that has given rise to the popularity of Lasch's term "the culture of narcissism" (Lasch, 1979).

This line of thought leads to a very specific reordering of the dialectic between the individual and society. Now the problems become those forces that dissolve the individual's sense of self, and then those that s/he uses (often generalised into a cultural form) to defend and stabilise the sense of self. This view has the advantage of giving some purchase on the problem that collectivisation poses for psychoanalysis. If all individuals are struggling with much the same sort of attacks on themselves from contemporary social relations, then they will tend to orbit around the same sort of responses to defend themselves. This is one specific instance of the notion that character structure is formed by social structure.

In an extended series of essays, Rustin (1991) brought a Kleinian perspective to bear on many features of cultural and institutional life, including psychoanalytic institutions. Fanon (1952) achieved a use of psychoanalysis in his perspective on racism and colonialism. Feminism particularly has begun to be alive to the potential convergence of object relations psychoanalysis with political campaigns. But how do these approaches coincide with the specifically Marxist project of liberation from economic class determinism?

These particulate emancipatory claims can be grouped loosely into a pluralist venture (Rustin, 1985), but it is one that has a declining focus on class and social relations in general.

Habermas developed a return to aspects of Hegel and reconsidered some of the essentials of psychoanalytic paradigms in dialectical terms. This has been more systematically and comprehensively achieved by Wolfenstein (1993). It does create arresting new views on old psychoanalytic topics: "Marx worked dialectically while Freud thought dualistically" (Wolfenstein, 1993, p. 218)—that is only partially true, and therefore a slightly unfair "dualistic" comparison on Wolfenstein's part. In fact, Freud's view of the id and superego in a system mediated by the ego has dialectical form. A dialectical process can consist of two points of view, two positions, one of which negates the other—by opposing it. However, in so far as they have in common much of the perceptions, apperceptions, and conceptualisations, they are said to penetrate each other—or "interpenetrate". Then, the negation is countered by a negation of the negation; and if the process is truly dialectical the end-result will not be a return to the first position, but to a transformed final position, one which somehow synthesises the originating two. We can take the psychoanalytic example: when the id demands satisfaction it does so with an immediacy. For instance, someone wants to eat because of hunger. This meets a superego that demands that the hunger is ignored because, say, the person is sitting in their psychology seminar, and it is deemed ill-mannered to eat there. The ego has to mediate this; it may judge that the prohibition should be countered by sucking a sweet, which the person has in their pocket—or chewing their pen. But the original demand—to eat—is not returned to without modification.

A great deal of psychoanalysis is concerned with the mediating role of the ego, but the ego is not unaided. One of Freud's (1933b) examples is of the sadist who becomes a butcher. In this instance, we can see that the mediating factor is not just the ego. The ego is assisted, even prompted by certain social channels into which impulses can be diverted. The existence of a butchery trade allows the ego to "find" a transformed synthesis of id impulse and superego prohibition. This is known as sublimation and represents a profound interpenetration of the social into the life of the individual whilst he mediates conscience with desires. In this way, we can come to recognise psychoanalytically the interpenetration of the social and the individual—individual impulses are deeply involved in butchery and the butchery trade can deeply mould the developing character of the individual. The collective presence of a whole group or culture creates a pressure towards social institutions whose psychological function is the channelling of impulses. The proviso is that individuals can and will modify their impulses. Such a mutual confrontation and interpenetration between individual and society is a dialectical process. These psychoanalytic illustrations take the dialectical process into the realm of personality development in the psychosocial matrix.

We need to take away the following from this discussion: a recognition of the need for a jointly informed practice; then an understanding that social structure is replicated in character formation; also the importance of the nature of the individual and the historical relativity of identity; and finally the need to proceed with a broadly dialectical method.

Convergence

I shall now review in brief some further connections: that between Marx's theory of alienation and the psychoanalytic view of projective identification (a form of depersonalisation); and that between Marx's theory of the exchange of commodities and a psychoanalytic description of the dispersal of personal identity.

Marx described the impoverishment of the worker confronted with the extent and power of their created products:

> [T]he more the worker exerts himself, the more powerful the alien, objective world becomes which he brings into being over and against himself, the poorer he and his inner world become and the less they belong to him. … The worker places his life in the object; but now it no longer belongs to him, but to the object … the life which he had bestowed on the object confronts him as hostile and alien. (Marx, 1844 [1975, p. 324])

This process in which the object is in some significant sense a lost part of the subject is reflected in very similar descriptions by Melanie Klein; products of the body and parts of the self are felt to be split off, projected into another, and to be continuing their existence there, and "[a]s far as the ego is concerned the excessive splitting off and expelling into the outer world of parts of itself considerably weaken it" (Klein, 1946, p. 8). The close resemblance between these and other passages from Marx and from Melanie Klein's descriptions of projective identification suggest that both are intent on conveying a common human experience. Some convergence between these two sets of observations has been found (Hinshelwood, 1983; see Chapter 1).

The commodities exchanged in the marketplace in a wage-labouring society have a quality that Marx called a fetish. He was struck by the value that commodities seem to acquire beyond their usefulness. Running besides their use-value is some other value that allows it to have comparison with any other commodity. Marx called this its exchange value.

This common element cannot be a geometrical, physical, chemical, or other natural property of commodities. Such properties come into consideration only to the extent that they make the commodities useful, that is, turn them into use-values. But clearly, the exchange relation of commodities is characterised precisely by its abstraction from their use-values. As use-values, commodities differ above all in quality, while as exchange-values, they can only differ in quantity, and therefore do not contain an atom of value since they are merely different quantities (Marx, 1867 [1976]).

Exchanging commodities results in the circulation of an abstract entity without the characteristics of the original commodity or of the producer of it:

> With the disappearance of the useful character of the products of labour, the useful character of the kinds of labour embodied in them also disappears; this in turn entails the disappearance of the different concrete forms of labour. They can no longer be distinguished, but are altogether reduced to the same kind of labour, human labour in the abstract. (Marx, 18671 [1976, p. 128])

The circulation of commodities implies in a concrete way the circulation of the labourer's activity that has been divested of its personal connection with him. In social groups, a very similar process can be described in which certain aspects of the participant's personal identity can also circulate through the social relations disconnected from himself (Hinshelwood, 1982). The "affective network" is a term coined to mean the network of relationships in which emotions pass from one person to another, losing their personal reference to any particular person. One illustration of this (Hinshelwood, 1989 [see also Chapter 4 in this collection]) described a long sequence of movements of something that has psychological "substance" but is unattached to persons:

> The affective network [of a group] is an exchange system of human emotions and identity, of reified bits of human beings. In this sense affective networks parallel the exchange systems of commodities which are also reified bits of human relation … The losing of parts of human emotions and identity in the affective network compares with the expropriation of surplus value in the labour of economic production. (Hinshelwood, 1989, p. 269)

There is a convergence between the circulation of surplus value and the circulation of what we might call "surplus identity". The network of social relations has this specific property: to allow the exchange and circulation of both material commodities and of aspects of personal identity. Such a network is created and sustained by both the economic system of production, and also the basic conditions of human identity.

These two processes—alienation/depersonalisation and commodity/identity—can be viewed both from an external and from an internal perspective. They are potentially a bridge to link the interpersonal and the intra-psychic, and thus to link Marxism to psychoanalysis. The depletion of the individual due to certain kinds of projective identification is not just an individual process. The depleted parts of the person are found in some other part of the field of social relations, some other part of the institution, and this gives rise to the circulation of parts of the personalities of individuals like commodities within the ensemble of social relations.

Base and superstructure

Together with the convergent oppression/repression, we have discovered a bundle of points of contact between the alternative theories. Of course, the theoretical frameworks which correspond to either side of these points of contact are quite different—the psychoanalytic theory of projective identification and object relations, on the one hand, and the Marxist theory of labour and value, on the other. We now need to consider the way these observations and their respective theoretical frameworks are structured. Both Marxism and psychoanalysis once again coincide in constructing the world in the form of a material base which gives rise to a "non-material" superstructure.

According to historical materialism, the methods of technological production prompt a system of economic and social relations around those methods. Not only that, but other manifestations occur—a legal system that protects ownership of products, rules about labour relations, etc. Families adapt to those methods—for instance, moving from domestic production to urban dwelling around factory production. These social adaptations and relations that are engendered by the methods of production constitute the culture of a society; it is a non-material superstructure. It progresses in a time sequence driven by technical innovations in productive methods and this results in historical progress. This leads to a curious anomaly: human beings make their own history, but at the same time their lives are determined by the history of the methods of production. Their subjectivity—the consciousness of themselves—is distorted to conceal this anomaly, and such false consciousness is ideology; it depends upon the inherent property of the human mind to render awareness unconscious.

Something rather similar happens according to psychoanalysis. The body represents another material "base", an observation noted by Timpanaro (1976). Material production is aimed at the material needs of human beings. The body is the instigator of those needs and therefore of production. Hunger, pain, sexual feelings and so on are the primary stimuli which are inherent in having a human body. The body prompts not only the need for a productive industry, but there is another and parallel sense in which the body is a material base. It is the base from which the mind and its potential for object relations emerge. Freud understood the mind to be a locus of transition in which bodily states appear in psychological form. This may be fairly direct, such as hunger which is readily apprehended and gives rise frequently to straightforward behavioural responses. Other states, especially sexual ones, may have a very different route through to sublimated derivatives in the mind—in the character and behaviour of the person—in their object relations.

If economic activity and bodily experiences create separate theories, they also generate separate superstructures—the world of social relations and the world of object relations, respectively. The upshot of the second part of this paper has been to show that the two superstructures converge. They lean together and coincide at certain points; we have dealt with three of those points—oppression/repression, alienation/depersonalisation and commodity/identity.

We can ask: how is this convergence achieved? How do the two material bases throw up superstructures which converge? What mediates that convergence from disparate origins? It is consistent with Marxist and psychoanalytic theories that it is the individual person themself that mediates the tension between the internal sources of their object relations and the external sources of their social relations, or at least it is the person in a collective manifestation—group, nation, population. There is here a potential to develop a theory of the individual on the basis of mediator of these superstructures. We have then transformed the dialectical problem from the need to understand the mediation between the individual and society to a quite different problem of mediation—the mediation between two superstructures from separate bases.

We might ask: what is such a theory of the individual going to look like? And what can it do? As Raymond Williams argued (1980) the cultural superstructure is not rigidly determined by the economic base: it has a "relative autonomy". The present notion of convergence of the superstructures through the person makes that autonomy more comprehensible if we understand there to be two superstructures, cultural and psychological, which are partially (or wholly) mediated by individuality (i.e. personal identity). Then the influences of one and the other will interpenetrate in a process that is not fully determined by either material base. A field of cultural endeavour opens up between the superstructures, to be explored by the collective individuals. The individual, defined as the struggle to sustain a mediation between the cultural and psychological, pushes the progress of both culture and of character psychology in the process of that mediation. Very likely that struggle between the cultural and psychological superstructures is the process which contributes to the sense of agency (will), and our unique consciousness and self-consciousness.

The field of cultural endeavour opened up by this struggle acquires an architecture which is influenced by both the economic relations of production that is extant at the time, the complex of potentialities within the world of object relations, and the talents of given individuals of the time. From a psychoanalytic point of view, that field grows within it certain channels down which are drawn the various tractable, moulded impulses of human individuals—the butcher held within the mould of his butcher's shop. It would be one implication of this view that no cultural phenomenon can be fully understood without its potentiality as a channel for human outlet, both for the pioneering spirits, and those routinisers that come after.

The complementarity of the two superstructures relies on the capacity of human beings to find social channelling for the diversion of the instincts in modified forms, but within the constraints of unconscious phantasies and within those of the social relations of economic production. The individual with their constructed identity and the social channels will tend to gravitate towards the place where the superstructures converge. The convergences are mediated by the individual and simultaneously construct them.

It is no longer possible to sustain a view of the separated personal identity. The psychoanalytic understanding of the dispersal of the person has dissolved the individual into the network of relations (social relations and "object relations") in which parts of their identity gather. That depletion and insecurity, in contemporary society, may lead to a profound search for a stable untampered identity—a narcissistic search, as Frosh concluded. However, that construction of the individual is itself socially enhanced and channelled, like the butcher's solution to sadistic impulses mentioned earlier, and such social possession of the individual has to be concealed from him in order to be successful.

Clearly, as economic production develops and creates historical pressures to change social forms, so the mediation between superstructures will require continual adjustment and modification. The nature of the individual is therefore historically ground anew between the upper and nether grindstones—one of object relations (bodily base) and one of economics (material production). What then is the scope for a negative practice? It is not enough that psychoanalytic practice liberates the individual; and often, incidentally, it does not. Psychoanalysis can only be revolutionary if it has a much wider effect on self-consciousness, in other words, on the false consciousnesses of whole classes—or on particulate liberatory movements—feminism or anti-racism, as well as political liberation. For this move we have to turn to a psychoanalytic version of group dynamics to consider the points where the social imprint brands the developing individual. The dissolving and constructing processes which occur in the networks of groups have been touched on above (Hinshelwood, 1989), and they suggest that there is no finally formed individual which social processes cannot radically reconstruct through the fluid quality of personal identity.

Conclusion

These have been the reflections of a psychoanalyst, and therefore within a discourse that is, originally, individualistic. However, as a discourse between people it is interpenetrated by the social. Psychoanalysis can be dismissed simply as bourgeois ideology; or as irrelevant because it is merely an analysis of a historical period of bourgeois ideology (late nineteenth century). But psychoanalysis is in fact historically relative, and phases in the development of its theory and practice are instantly recognisable—and also in its cultural location. It therefore warrants examination as a socially related and potentially engaged form of thought—both of its time and examining its time. What psychoanalysis is good at is the content of what is collectivised. It has difficulty with understanding the collective itself, and it is difficult to apply the knowledge which Marxism has of the collective to solve that problem for psychoanalysis. And correspondingly, it is just as difficult to supplement the gap in Marxism with the psychoanalytic understanding of the subjective identity of the individual. Complementarity could exist between the two frameworks, but not without a persisting tension—however that tension is reflected, not just between the conceptual frameworks but within the actually occurring problematics at the superstructural level.

References

Bridgeland, M. (1971). *Pioneer Work with Maladjusted Children*. London: Staples Press.

Fanon, F. (1952). *Black Skin, White Masks*. New York: Grove Press.

Freud, S. (1933b). *Why War? S. E., 22*: 197–215. London: Hogarth.

Frosch, S. (1991). *Identity Crisis: Modernity, Psychoanalysis and the Self*. London: Macmillan.

Habermas, J. (1968). *Knowledge and Human Interest*. Boston, MA: Beacon Press.

Heimann, P. (1950). On counter-transference. *International Journal of Psycho-analysis, 31*: 81–84. Republished in: P. Heimann, *About Children and Children-No-Longer* (pp. 73–79). London: Routledge, 1989.

Hinshelwood, R. D. (1982). Two community time scales. *International Journal of Therapeutic Communities, 3*: 3–6.

Hinshelwood, R. D. (1983). Projective identification and Marx's concept of Man. *International Review of Psycho-Analysis, 16*: 221–226.

Hinshelwood, R. D. (1989). Communication flow in the matrix. *Group-Analysis, 22*: 261–269.

Jacoby, R. (1983). *The Repression of Psychoanalysis: Otto Fenichel and the Political Freudians*. Chicago, IL: University of Chicago Press.

Jaques, E. (1955). Social systems as a defence against persecutory and depressive anxiety. In: M. Klein, P. Heimann & R. Money-Kyrle (Eds.), *New Directions in Psychoanalysis* (pp. 478–498). London: Tavistock.

Klein, M. (1946). Notes on some schizoid mechanisms. *International Journal of Psychoanalysis, 27*: 99–110. Republished in M. Klein, P. Heimann, S. Isaacs & J. Riviere, *Developments in Psycho-Analysis* (pp. 292–320). London: Hogarth, 1952; and in *The Writings of Melanie Klein, Volume 3* (pp. 1–24). London: Hogarth.

Lasch, C. (1979). *The Culture of Narcissism*. New York: Norton.

Marx, K. (1844). *Economic and Philosophical Manuscripts*. In: *Early Writings* (pp. 279–400) London: Penguin, 1975.

Marx, K. (1845). Theses on Feuerbach. In: *Early Writing* (pp. 421–423). London: Penguin, 1975.

Marx, K. (1867). *Capital*. London: Penguin, 1976.

Menzies Lyth, I. (1981). Bion's contribution to thinking about groups. In: J. Grotstein (Ed.), *Do I Dare Disturb the Universe* (pp. 661–666). Beverley Hills, CA: Caesura Press.

Mitchell, J (1974). *Psychoanalysis and Feminism*. New York: Vintage.

Popper, K. (1959). *The Logic of Scientific Discovery*. London: Hutchinson.

Richards, B. (Ed.) (1989). *Crises of the Self: Further Essays on Psychoanalysis and Politics*. London: Free Association.

Rustin, M. (1985). *For a Pluralist Socialism*. London: Verso.

Rustin, M. (1991). Psychoanalysis, racism and anti-racism. In: *The Good Society and the Inner World*. London: Verso.

Strachey, J. (1937). Introduction. In: R. Osborn, *Freud and Marx*. London: Gollancz.

Timpanaro, S. (1976). *The Freudian Slip*. London: New Left.

Wertsch, J. (1985). *Vygotsky and the Social Formation of Mind*. Cambridge, MA: Harvard University Press.

Williams, R. (1980). *Problems in Materialism and Culture: Selected Essays*. London: Verso.

Wolfenstein, V. (1993). *Psychoanalytic-Marxism: Groundwork*. London: Free Association.

Discussion of Part I

Divergent approaches

GC: In the two articles we just read, you discuss some questions that are recurring preoccupations through most of the papers in this collection. They are questions such as, how do individuals interact politically (or otherwise) with others in groups and in broader societies? How do their activities shape (or fail to shape) the political sphere? And, in turn, how are individual behaviours and identities shaped by their position in a wider polity? You discuss how different aspects of human behaviour have been studied from different disciplinary perspectives, how these perspectives might have created a sense of a fragmented object when they perhaps, instead, illustrate the fragmentation of a group endeavour (understanding individual and collective behaviour and motivations). To begin with, I would like to ask you to say a bit more about how you chose to develop your psychosocial approach by combining the psychoanalysis of Melanie Klein with the philosophical works of the early Marx.

RDH: To tell the truth it was really just serendipitous. My sporadic reading of Marx and going back to his writing when he was starting out, presented this striking similarity in observations despite the continuous stumbling to create a convincing and applicable Freudo-Marxism all through the twentieth century. The complicating factor in integrating social science and psychoanalysis is that social assumptions, culture, and politics are in fact the creation of the human mind to which those minds then become subjected. The human being is an individual in the context of those others who make up the social milieu of the moment. And yet, John Strachey (the cousin of James Strachey, and a politician in the Atlee Government in the 1940s) declared: "Nor is there the least doubt that these sciences [Marxism and psychoanalysis] are directly opposites. The question is, are they dialectical opposites?" (Strachey, 1937, p. 7). This elusiveness was no less apparent for Victor Wolfenstein who described:

> The theories [of these separate disciplines] are premised upon diametrically opposed anthropologies, exclusive conceptions of human nature and historical development. (Wolfenstein, 1993, p. 9)

Given these assertions, I was taken aback by the quotes I found from Marx, as I was thinking, at the time, of the Kleinian concept of projective identification. I was teaching in a class of psychotherapy trainees. Think about the striking convergence of this: "The worker places his life in the object; but now it no longer belongs to him, but to the object … the life which he had bestowed on the object confronts him as hostile and alien" (Marx, 1844 [1975, p. 324]), with Melanie Klein's formulation of projective identification on how the ego's "expelling into the outer world of parts of itself considerably weakens it" (1946, p. 8). The alienation of a human person, or a part of them, matched the depersonalisation when someone projects a split-off part of themselves into someone else. These are different perspectives on something so strikingly similar. I was always interested in Galileo taking a telescope and using it as a new instrument for observing the stars. He discovered the moons of Jupiter. He did so because he had used a new instrument. A different way of seeing results in different observed "facts". The two disciplines are different ways of seeing persons.

GC: This is a fascinating illustration to begin this conversation. I want to pick this up right away. Are you suggesting that psychoanalysis is providing us with a tool comparable in revolutionary effect to Galileo's telescope? Can you say a bit more about what kind of instrument psychoanalysis is (or provides us with)?

RDH: I always say that psychoanalysis is the science of the subjective! Maybe that's even more revolutionary than a telescope? But it's the case that the discovery of a new tool of investigation leads to new discoveries of the world we investigate (whether the material world or the subjective one). The James Webb telescope out in space is an example of a new tool observing all kinds of new things for physicists to think about and revise their knowledge.

Psychoanalysis is an instrument for an inward gaze. And that is threatening for our own sense of being a person, so Freud was right to assume its access to our unconscious would be resisted bitterly; nobody wants to know about our own unconscious because by definition it is what we don't want to know about. Of course, that's not the whole story and when the unconscious throws up impossible conflict we resign ourselves to investigating our own selves—with someone we hope will be sympathetic. I have suggested elsewhere that a science of the subjective has to be different from the sciences of matter. Although I would agree that subjective experience emerges from the material world, I would suggest that the principle of causality does not necessarily apply to the subjective; then a principle of purpose might be more appropriate.

GC: To return to the matter of convergence between Klein and Marx, you write about the alienation of parts of the self through exploitation of labour and projective identification in this way: "Alienation appears mostly to refer to the evil ways capitalism is supposed to *suck* [my emphasis] the life out of man. The object in this view then causes the subject (ego) to become depleted and imprisoned; *but* [my emphasis] in *projective* [my emphasis] identification it is the ego (subject) that is the cause". In this formulation there seems to be an opposition (sucking vs projecting) rather than a convergence between Klein's and Marx's conceptions of alienation. Can you say more about this and how these two positions end up converging? I ask you this because I was struck by the possibility that the worker's alienation may be initiated by the worker herself if the comparison with projective identification were taken too literally. How does one reach the position you advocate that, in Marx's words (which you quote), "Later the relation becomes reciprocal"; which here could mean, if I understand you correctly, that the process that Klein and Marx describe are mutually constitutive? You also write that "projective identification ... *encompasses* [my emphasis] ... alienation".

RDH: You are right, there is a discrepancy; the social sense sees the active origin in the society, and psychoanalysis sees the active agent in the internal world of the individual. And in the first paper (Chapter 1) I did confront that with brief quotes from both sides where they did each consider the possibility of both or reciprocal origins. It is merely to be expected that an internally focused perspective like psychoanalysis will see internal causation. But incidentally I did notice Bollas coining the term "extractive introjection" (1987). One can certainly understand that kind of phenomenon when considering say the institutionalisation of vulnerable inmates in the old mental hospitals where they were *reduced* as it were to "vegetables". And the similar emphasis on the external social leads Marx to emphasise the intentions there; and he does in fact describe the process as "reciprocal". In a recent contribution (Hinshelwood, 2024) I dwell quite extensively on the possibility that there is a potential for an interaction in which a social pressure to extract something from the individuals cannot succeed unless there is an internal dynamic that prompts the individuals for defensive purposes to split and project. In other words, there has to be a collusion between social and internal pressures.

GC: I would now wish to raise the question of who or what, in both structural perspectives, is doing the controlling, the dominating; whether it is the ego through split-off parts into the object and over the id and the superego, or the capitalist by imposing the wage dependency and alienating the worker from the products of her labour.

RDH: Well, you are right and various writers have noted that question. Marcuse exploited Freud's idea of the superego as the internalised social authority oppressing the ego. This internal/external correspondence in domination may indeed be a similar reciprocating process where influences from each direction reinforce each other. But most likely the source of control and dominance varies with time, society, and individual. The gearing together of individuals at certain times must surely be a social influence, and indeed the essence of political persuasion/coercion. But at this stage I would prefer to leave it as a possibility of both (or either) internal or external origins.

GC: What is striking in the attitudes you quote above, are the statements of absolute conviction "nor is there the least doubt", and about "opposites" (Strachey) or "directly opposites" (Wolfenstein). I tend to approach with hesitation claims presented as true beyond "the least doubt". However, it is important to establish the foundations of such belief that the psychoanalytical and the sociopolitical are not only different observation points, but so different as to be diametrically opposed. Critical of Wolfenstein's accusation to Freud of being a dualist, you write about "the dialectic between the individual and society". And you add, with Menzies Lyth (1979, p. 61), that "[t]he context of the internal world, in particular the internal society, links the psychological with the social".

RDH: Let me point us in the direction of Bion's idea of vertices as you have mentioned previously, which means simply the various points of view, as it does offer an explanation of why there can be steadfastly different claims at the level of theoretical models, when we are all interested in the same thing. It is an important grasp of how different theories give different meanings to comparable observation.

Of course, Wolfenstein also noted there are significant similarities between the two disciplines. They are both materialist and anti-metaphysics. Popper (1963), who defined the logic of science in terms of empirical positivism, also contributed to pushing Freud and Marx together when he decided that psychoanalysis and Marxism were both pseudo-sciences, and in a completely different category of thought and investigation, although dubious, he thought. These very varied similarities present the engaging temptation to draw the theoretical models of the two disciplines together.

Why and how to converge?

GC: Before discussing "how" a psychosocial field/discipline could contain the convergence of psychoanalysis and the social sciences, another question seems to me to arise: "why" is a convergence between the social sciences and psychoanalysis, useful and desirable? Some social scientists have sometimes remarked on the unhelpful separation of the social sciences (sociology, economics, politics). Is then the claim of a psychosocial discipline, that it can group together social sciences under the leading perspective of the "psycho-"—a convergence of all the perspectives that aim to understand (construct) the same object (human behaviour in groups/societies)? Let me add here that I found the following observation of yours important and I think it might provide further context to the convergence we are discussing here. You write that, "[f]eminism particularly has begun to be alive to the potential convergences of object relations psychoanalysis with political campaigns" and, I would add, with political theory. You also notice Fanon's crucial contribution to debates on psychoanalysis and politics. You seem to suggest that meaningful debates on these matters must rest on feminist and postcolonial foundations as well as psychoanalytical ones. Is this a correct interpretation of your work?

RDH: It would be presumptuous to claim a lead role for psychoanalysis, wouldn't it? Perhaps we should think of a multi-factorial system, personal plus social; although the pre-eminence of psychoanalysis may not be out of the question since the human mind is the basic building block. I would not particularly prioritise feminism or anti-colonialism as I think both have a background in, or depend on, an underlying intention, which in Chapter 2 I described as the social process of commodifying (i.e. depersonalising) individual persons.

GC: Attention to the group, in particular to large-group dynamics, seems to be the necessary step you suggest to take in order to make sense of the convergence you propose between the individual and the social perspective. You notice that such convergence can be mutually useful as "the difficulty of psychoanalysis is to understand the processes of collectivisation, whilst Marxism needs a good theory of the individual which goes beyond the needs for material provision". You write, therefore, of the "very extensive use of projective processes in large groups—in fact the larger and more impersonal the group, the more projective mechanisms are resorted to". Is it the case, in your opinion (and with reference to what we discussed above about projective identification encompassing alienation—in fact, more, you write that "[p]rojective identification is the forerunner of all social relationships") that, in a way, a quantitative accumulation of projective processes become, eventually, social alienation? Something else, somewhat related if perhaps tangentially: some might read some of your work as pointing in the direction of projective mechanisms in groups as a viable explanation, from the perspective of psychoanalysis, of processes of collectivisation. I suggest this with reference to your discussion in Chapter 2 of the dynamics of circulation of emotions in groups and your theorisation, which we will come to in Chapter 4 of the "affective network". It seems to me collectivisation of emotional states has repercussions which can be very material indeed. You even draw a fascinating parallel between surplus value and "surplus identity" as agency is extracted, alienated, from individuals in certain groups. What are your thoughts on this?

RDH: We can probably turn to Chapters 3 and 4 in a moment where this process is exemplified and examined in detail. It has fascinated me that in contrast to today's hyper-individualism, if we really look at what goes on in groups we see the exact opposite, a hyper-socialisation. That transmission around a group came from observations of mine in therapeutic communities, but of course inspired by Freud's (1921c) account of the transmission around a group of the group ideal. That Freudian transmission was in part connected with what Le Bon (1895) called "infection" in groups. It led to my interest in the observation of groups along the line of Esther Bick's observation of infants (Hinshelwood & Skogstad, 2000). And Bion came along, to capture the problem by saying the human being is a group animal at war with his groupishness (Bion, 1950).

GC: This is very interesting! If I understand you correctly, looked at through psychoanalytic lenses, hyper-individualism points at forms of hyper-socialisation, a phenomena of dispersion of the individual into groups. Is that what you have in mind? Can you say a bit more about this?

RDH: Well, I think that there is a strong sense in Western culture of the individual as a stand-alone entity basically in competition with each other. This contrasts with the evidence I see of a very different kind of mutual interchange of aspects of identity and experience that weld us into collaborative units, groups, and societies at very basic levels of our personalities. In other words, the observations of projective identification do not confirm the cultural assumptions about individuality. Much of group therapy involves the observation of the roles people take up as if certain ego-functions come more naturally to some people and other functions to others. A group can sometimes seem like a division of psychic labour, like a team of builders who have different physical functions—bricklaying, carpentry, etc.—in the task of building a house.

GC: Some other convergences show their uncertain profile; the social sciences with probabilistic physics, for instance, the neurosciences and anthropology, and so on. Those attempts are interesting and sometimes inspiring, but do they amount to the kind of binocular vision (neuro-psychoanalysis, for instance, or political psychoanalysis) affording depth of perception that each one-eyed observation would not have? This is an important question for any endeavour to establish a psychosocial field. For instance, one could believe that knowing the behaviour of electrons in an atom does not add to our knowledge of what causes the behaviour of human individuals in groups and societies, although some neuro-scientists and biologists have begun studying the quantum physics of the brain and its implications for our understanding of consciousness. What is then the nature of the convergence of psychoanalysis and social sciences? Let me add that I believe that this question has a direct repercussion on conceptions of change, both individual and social. And you bring this up vividly when you show the difference (and the tension) between Fromm and Marcuse, or between a revisionist and a radical use of psychoanalysis.

RDH: This is an important point, and a very decidedly open question. How much are the various disciplines of science compatible with each other with all sharing the same basic premises (Neurath, 1937). This is known as the "unity of science", a crusading project of logical positivism in the mid-twentieth century, known also as consilience in E. O. Wilson's terms (1998). It contrasts with a quite different approach arranging the various disciplines in a hierarchical order separated by the view that downward causation is not possible so that disciplines are distinct on the common-or-garden basis that the whole is more than the sum of the parts. This goes back to John Stuart Mill (1861) in the nineteenth century. One discipline "emerges" out of another. For instance, the biological law of the survival of the fittest (at the root of evolutionary theory) cannot be predicted from the laws of chemistry as the next discipline below, more basic than, biology. However, the biological law must be based on the laws of chemistry (such as the nature of DNA). So, the laws of evolution cannot be reduced simply to the chemistry of biological organisms even though the biological law still depends on the chemistry. This is known as the theory of emergence (see Kim, 1982).

When it comes to the relations of the laws of the mind based on the physiological laws of the brain or body, we might find the theory of emergence compelling, allowing us to accept that the mind is a "whole" that cannot be reduced to the sum of the brain's neurological parts. Freud accepted this psycho-physical parallelism as developed philosophically by Spinoza and Leibniz but introduced to neurology by John Hughlings Jackson. However, Freud did move in a dissatisfied way from material determinism as if he was plotting functions in the brain, like aphasia, to the world of inexistent entities such as dreams and fantasies. Thus, when we come to the relations of psychoanalysis to social science we have to consider if they combine as a unity or as one (social science) emerging from the other (the metapsychology of psychoanalysis). It would seem most convincing to accept that social science is based upon the human mind but is not reducible to it. When it comes to the human mind (and the emergent social sciences) we have to take account not only of causal determinism but of intentionality as well. Indeed, in social science the link between events might be better regarded as an intention rather than a cause. And this may be true of human psychology as well. Human psychology should not be merely behaviour and its determinants, but as Bruner (1990) claimed passionately, psychology must consider meanings experienced as elements of consciousness.

In both our disciplines we move beyond mere deterministic science and thus it could be argued they comprise together a domain of meanings and intentions. It is very clearly the case, for instance, that Soviet politics moved towards an interpretation of history as deterministic just like a natural science; one thing simply causes another. This appeared to rule out human intention, or perhaps intentions were determined causally by political economy. However, that was evidently untrue as the Bolsheviks in Russia did not inspire revolution in Germany which supposedly was more ready for communism. A re-reading of Marx was essential to instil, as I suggest in the second of the papers, an intentional dimension in human behaviour, and therefore in social behaviour, or politics. Briefly you mention the conflation of neurology with psychoanalysis and this is more problematic, as the guiding principle of neurological psychology is causality, whilst the guiding principle of psychoanalysis (as well as social science) is intentionality.

From a psychoanalytic point of view

GC: Let me ask you about another aspect of the difficulties in establishing convergences and communications across disciplines. This is the matter of the internal divergences among social scientists and psychoanalysts. Neither psychoanalysis nor Marxist social sciences are fields devoid of internal conflicts. Could you say something about the differences among psychoanalysts in their interest in, and takes on, convergences between their discipline and the social sciences?

RDH: Perhaps I can only speak for psychoanalysis here. The capacity, or lack of it, to debate these differences and distortions between us, constitutes politics—the politics of psychoanalysis! Indeed, any project to bring together different points of view is thus a political one in itself. Within the psychoanalytic discipline, differences need to be resolved in terms of observation, evidence, and debate. It would take the form of the intergroup debates and under the influences outlined by Kuhn (1962). Interestingly, the project developed by Tuckett more recently explored exhaustively underlying differences between analysts from different schools (Tuckett, 2009). It is not the same if we are using causality as our main principle or intentionality. The different psychoanalytic schools have a common principle—intentionality. We may share intentionality with social science, I suggest, in contrast to the mechanical causality of the physical sciences.

Not only are we unrestrained in our quarrels with each other, but we can disagree inflexibly on many points of theory and technique, and indeed the role of the external and social influences is a specific disagreement. The bitter exchanges over Melanie Klein's neglect or acceptance of the importance of the external object (the environmental mother) is a case in point.

If one were to look at the dynamics that exist between psychoanalytic groups, we would be inconsistent if we did not consider the anxiety–defence structure at the unconscious level. My understanding is that psychoanalysts themselves can be driven to unconscious defences in order to combat the undermining pressure of uncertainly and the demand "to know". The practice of psychoanalysis is very difficult indeed. It is not only learning about the workings and experience of a mind that is not one's own, but the requirement is to be an authority on that other mind. It is so easy then to become rigid and dogmatic as if one were an infallible authority so that our theories become strict ideologies (see Chapter 6). The slightest deviation demands condemnation and this was true from the very early days when Freud excluded Alfred Adler and Carl Jung.

The demands for certainty that make us rigidly adherent to our theories come from two sources. One is ourselves and the other our patients/analysands. In terms of our own unconscious, we need to help and repair and restore suffering others. We need to be successful professionals and mostly we only have ourselves (and our identity with a psychoanalytic school) to back us. It is not like salaried work where an organisation of some kind has endorsed by interview and appointment that we are sufficiently the authority we are expected to be. We work alone and the only back-up are colleagues, many of whom, from different schools, find us inadequate. From the patient's point of view they have had as a last resort to come to us from their own desperation that they can no longer bear the burdens and conflicts of life that arise so mysteriously from their own unconscious. They put themselves in our hands as the authority that can deal with what they cannot deal with themselves. On the other hand, we end up dealing with their ambivalence and resistances that undermine the very competence we both seek to find in ourselves.

I assume that such pressures do not occur with the same degree of force in the academic world of social science. I vividly remember the sense of relief I found when moving from the conscious and unconscious demands of mental healthcare in the NHS to an academic post of teaching and intellectual researching. The unconscious pressures seemed to be off, and a calmer life ensued. It was quite a striking change-point in my life.

This is not a direct answer to your question. I think that psychoanalysts are so focused on the issues and pressures just described that the challenge of an interdisciplinary psychosocial perspective is felt as outside their experience and competences. Nevertheless, some attention has been given by psychoanalysts to the psychosocial dimensions; for instance the contemporary relational approach building on Harry Stack Sullivan's interpersonal psychoanalysis. And Ian Suttie (1922) was one of the earliest analysts to use the term psychosocial, which he took with him to his eventual work with the Tavistock Clinic (Suttie, 1935) which was devoted to a holistic biopsychosocial holism (Dicks, 1970; Crichton-Miller, 1920).

GC: One central claim of this book is a political claim, indeed, bringing together, mediating, conflictual perspectives. That is politics itself. How this is political is worth discussing further. It is my hunch too that this claim, here referred to as the mediation of social scientific perspectives and psychoanalysis, also widens the scope, the field, of political action—a question that we will discuss later on in the book in greater depth.

RDH: If the success of human culture and civilisation is collaboration together to achieve something *as a community*, it must entail the managing of different points of view. Whether that is coercive in a totalitarian state or democratic in a properly informed population does not matter too much so long as we operate as a team or a unit. Of course, the kind of politics does matter to the individuals who have different reactions according to whether they are coerced or are informed and listened to.

GC: Can one say, though, that the sort of human fulfilment and achievement that we have in mind and to which we aspire as psychoanalysts cannot be achieved under totalitarian rule, however much material production can be increased and perhaps even shared? In fact, my question is broader. Can aspirations and ideas about what fulfils our humanity be specifically linked to "psychoanalytic" perspectives on human life?

RDH: I think we can make the link you suggest. In terms of how one makes political decisions, it is a matter of the fate that personal autonomy suffers. In a totalitarian state, as I suggested in my *Therapy or Coercion* (1997), autonomy of the individual is relinquished under coercion of some kind. Democracies like to think that autonomy survives as a full capacity of the individual. However, the idealisation, and weaponisation of the word "democracy" has rendered us somewhat blind to the obvious failings. On one hand, in a representative democracy it is, interestingly, an autonomous act in the voting station to hand over one's political autonomy to the representatives one votes for. It is one of these social exchanges of parts or our personalities. The key question is whether the handover is coerced or is a decision based on a full and fair understanding of the issues and the representatives one is voting for, or against. The sad failing of democracy is the full and fair process of informing the voters adequately. We are aware of fake news and disinformation, but its roots being in the system of information-for-profit creates a high level of conflict of interest for the informing media. Perhaps we need not go further with this and the impetus for the "rabble-rousing" social media. The issue I think that we have to focus on here is the unconscious exchanges of autonomy and power and the motives for them.

GC: OK, let's return to Marx, then. To begin with, let me refer to your appreciation for his early writing and to your suggestion that the most useful way to look at possible convergences between psychoanalysis and Marx is by thinking together the early Marx and the later Freudian, Melanie Klein. In his early manuscripts, Marx shows great psychological intuition. It might seem like an undue stretch to say that he developed his political economy on those initial foundations made of psychological observations, yet would it be not, nonetheless, reasonable to claim, that no sound social theorising can proceed from a less than sound appreciation of human nature and the working of the human mind? I find these questions compelling because influential political philosophy is grounded in assumptions about human nature that are not observed from the psychoanalytical vertex such as Rousseau's idea of the *bon sauvage* or the assumption of the rational individual and of the social contract, or that mistake aspirations for actual conditions, the sky for the ground on which they walk. If you allow me, I would push this matter a bit further. Do you think Marx's and Klein's anthropologies converge more broadly than so far discussed and in the papers in this part? To stretch this point even further, if Marx's intuition about alienation constituted the ground of his political economy, what perspective on global politics could be developed based on the concept of depersonalisation and the knowledge of the unconscious? Also, what is your own take on these matters around human nature?

RDH: Yes, interesting questions. First, Marx was briefly a neo-Hegelian at first, as was Feuerbach, who Marx took very seriously. All their focus was on Hegel's conception of the nature of man. So Marx was interested initially in the philosophy of mind (as psychology tended to be called 200 years ago). No doubt it was his observations of the grinding poverty of industrial workers—in many cases perhaps worse than the conditions of slavery—as well as is having to flee as a refugee from authoritarian states—that led him to social explanations for the human condition (or conditions in the different classes). Then, would a political economy based on (psychoanalytic) depersonalisation be very different from one based on (social science) alienation? My assumption has been that the developments would have looked much the same (though different terminologies might have emerged). I want to make a small point in relation to your big question. Our preoccupation is the practice of political debate and action. Politics is conducted primarily consciously. The importance of alienation and projective identification is that these are unconscious intrusions into reasonable and sensible debate. It is the hidden pressures of the individual unconscious defending itself against anxiety that promote intransigent positions and ideologies. On the other side, it is the unquestioned social assumptions of class and capital that promote similar intrusions into reasoned debate and action. I do not mention it enough, but the false consciousness that stabilises and even glorifies an inhumane status quo is the social science equivalent of an unconscious interference. It is the subject of György Lukács' treatise on "false consciousness" in 1923—*History and Class Consciousness*. He had written a review of Freud's *Group Psychology* though he did not mention Freud in connection with false consciousness and he attributed the impoverishment and powerlessness of the poor to the social conformity of implicit ideas such as the superiority of the wealthy, which establish the alienation of the poor. Of course, there are other interdisciplinary "convergences" that might be interesting to explore. But the particular interest in understanding the interferences that demand political attention point in two divergent directions—the social pressures of capital accumulation and personal human anxieties. It is the interference of these unspoken influences that destroys (or impedes) full political debate. Both the social alienation and the primitive infantile projective identification are interferences. They are not the whole of political life.

GC: One could say that the social is present in the child's first relations just as much as the psychical of adult individuals contributes to their actions in the social. Perhaps, alienation is passed on at the breast, as it were, informing dynamics of depersonalisation that further entrench alienation in the growing individual. The reproduction of society is not only an immanent process working, as it were, below the awareness and contribution of individuals, it is also invested by the (relatively) conscious decisions made by individuals in responding to their individual and group needs and aspirations. This applies to parenting as well. In this sense, the social and the individual do meet from the word go. Parenting is not only a function of the unique individualities of those involved, but it is culturally and socially informed as well. In other words, the child incorporates social norms and cultural attitudes with its nourishment from birth (with which, eventually, to a greater or smaller extent, it will identify). This is the case even in the absence of any specific form of observable coercion (which seems to be the nature of identification also in large social processes). The content of "free" choices is, in this sense, more interesting, and more puzzling at the same time, than the outcome of deliberate dynamics of oppression. The concept of false consciousness intersects this concern. Equally, one can say that the parents' political attitude, their ability to think, and their attachment to and relation with reality is passed on from very early on.

RDH: Yes, I agree that the infant human receives not just milk from mother, but a range of other less tangible "things" which in their undeveloped state can hardly process for themselves. Much may be of a cultural and social kind. I am reminded of Noreen Giffney's recent book *The Culture-Breast in Psychoanalysis* (2021), which clearly connects the baby's experience at the breast with social and cultural experiences beyond the verbal. Indeed, the currently influential psychoanalytic idea of container-contained is a function to which the infant is introduced immediately they are born. And development consists of the accumulation of ego-functions most of which are not inherently given but derive from interaction with maternal carers. We have to be cautious in recognising the limits of the infant's appreciation of the social as it needs to be interpreted nonverbally via the earliest experiences of the breast, skin, sound, smell, and so on. These are mediated by the individual within him- or herself.

Appearances

RDH: The humanities, including the aesthetic disciplines, investigate the move from what something is to how it appears. So, we have a complicated circularity. If we investigate the making of the appearances (the process of representation), we use the very organ (our mind) that does the making of our appearances to investigate the process of making appearances. More simply put, material science is objective—what appears to be there *is* what is out there; but mental/cultural sciences are subjective. We attempt to see the making of the appearances. So, the *making of appearances* has to be observed in our mind as an appearance of the process of making appearances. This is the complexity of the fabulous (though fallible) ability for self-reflexion. Something of this is debated in my book *Research on the Couch* (2013). Both psychoanalysis and Marxism are theories of the distortions of the process of representing. Both claim that the representations we make are not necessarily good enough. They can be distorted, sometimes badly distorted, and thus a false consciousness.

Lukács' idea was that the attitudes of society are so prevalent and all-embracing that they never get examined and questioned. The elite are simply "there" as a fact of life; and so are the poor. Class is locked into our system of thinking from very early on and is perhaps associated, as you say, with the relationship with the providing breast. In particular, the dominant ideology is formulated by the wealthy bourgeoisie as Marx described, and it implicitly determines the form of cultural, and political norms, beliefs, and institutions. The proletariat accept such ideologies simply because they impregnate every aspect of life. Marx fought for an emerging and more accurate view of the unjust relations, institutions, and practices that existed between the classes.

GC: Could you say a bit more on how "not good enough" perceptions and representations generate false consciousness? This raises two related questions. The first is, how do we define what are distorted as opposed to accurate perceptions of reality? Is the splitting in the act of perception, by the perceiver of the object, the main cause of the distortion? When you refer to distortions as either merely one of perspective or specifically motivated, you highlight the analogous debate on the unconscious as either merely something that is not-conscious or something dynamically made so because of a conflict internal to the mind.

RDH: You raise an important question when asking what a distortion is. A novel is a lie; it never happened. And yet a novel engages some valid appreciation in the reader, and so-called "good" novels could be defined as evoking some truth about human beings, characters, ethical dilemmas, and all sorts of aspects of real life. News media reporting events in the world talk of "stories". It is right to question our words. Is a distortion merely the distortion of perspective, or is it motivated in some way?—a need for certainty when there is none; an urgent denial of something too painful; a powerful urge to deceive or control someone else; a concealed exploitation, and so on. It seems a portmanteau term that needs further definition on each occasion of its use. The question then is, from what process do false appearances arise? It is an important question. Simply, I would suggest there are multiple factors; or two, at least. One obviously is that individuals deceive themselves for all the reasons that psychoanalysts have exposed. To misperceive the world is a powerful means of avoiding painful anxieties and guilt. But the second factor, of course, is the kind of false consciousness that György Lukács described as a collective, collaboration, and thus socially organised misperception. As we have been saying, it is not just the monetary impoverishment that Marx raged against, but in his early work it was the humanitarian impoverishment. Money and capital were the abstract value that depersonalised the worker and his product to become an abstraction, a commodity. This plays on the individual's unconscious defences when they are active for some reason, to become an alienation. How can such a social organisation of the unconscious happen? I deal with this question in my book on *Unconscious Politics* (2024). In brief, the impoverishment itself leads to internal dynamics that arouse anxieties dealt with by projective identification, The risk is that then the projective identification enhances the fear of impoverishment as it weakens the ego and a stabilised vicious circle results. The distortion of alienation results in (and from) both an external and internal impoverishment.

GC: Let me return to something that you mentioned earlier and can be seen now in connection to what you just discussed. The way in which you draw a portrait of positivism and a certain ideological scientism is important. I think that psychoanalysis can contribute to a theory of political action that may take us beyond black box theories (behaviourism) and theories of the rational individual (cognitivism). The idea that what you see is what you get has not only a long tradition but also an illustrious contemporary descendent:

what you see is all there is (WYSIATI), propounded by the economics Nobel Prize winner and behavioural psychologist Daniel Kahneman. This latest version has not replaced the earlier, it has joined it. They set forth an (agnostic) positivist belief in the elusiveness of cultural facts or even a (dogmatic) conception of their irrelevance. They are convinced that in truth nothing beyond what meets the eye (and other senses) exists.

RDH: Yes, Kahneman (2011) and, recently, with Sunstein and Sibony (2021), did his research on economic decisions and how policies emerged from the preceding beliefs and conceptualisations of the researching economists as much as from the validity of the "scientific" methodology. One's pre-conceptions can cloud one's results in even the best science. And ironically it has been contested that Kahneman himself found the results he expected. It is a debate about the way our intellect can act as a noise in the system. Bion himself famously came to the conclusion that we must abolish memory and desire. Behaviourism, despite its support from famous protagonists including Bertrand Russell, cannot avoid a subjectivism creeping in when a subjective instrument of observation is used. And I want to emphasise that in physical science we investigate the reality of the invariant that lies behind our world of appearances. But in the subjective "sciences" we investigate the *process* by which we perceive (and misperceive) that world of appearances. Alienation/projective identification is that distortion in capitalist politics.

GC: I think it is perhaps fitting to end this conversation with one last mention of the core theme of these papers: the relationship between alienation and projective identification. I think that these first two papers describe your work of integrating what could be considered as two large fragments of something that might form a whole and whose (re)integration might be a worthwhile endeavour. Let us then move on to consider some more specific issues related to working together in groups in Part II.

References

Bion, W. R. (1950). Experiences in groups: VI. *Human Relations*, 3: 395–402. Republished in W. R. Bion, *Experiences in Groups and Other Papers* (pp. 115–126). London: Tavistock, 1961.

Bollas, C. (1987). *The Shadow of the Object: Psychoanalysis of the Unthought Known*. New York: Columbia University Press.

Bruner, J. (1990). *Acts of Meaning*. Cambridge, MA: Harvard University Press.

Crichton-Miller, H. (Ed.) (1920). *Functional Disease: An Epitome of War Experience for the Practitioner*. Oxford: Oxford University Press.

Dicks, H. V. (1970). *Fifty Years of the Tavistock Clinic*. London: Tavistock.

Freud, S. (1921c). *Group Psychology and the Analysis of the Ego*. *S. E., 18*: 67–143. London: Hogarth.

Giffney, N. (2021). *The Culture-Breast in Psychoanalysis*. London: Routledge.

Hinshelwood, R. D. (1997). *Therapy or Coercion*. London Karnac.

Hinshelwood, R. D. (2013). *Research on the Couch*. London: Routledge.

Hinshelwood, R. D. (2024). *Unconscious Politics*. London: Karnac.

Hinshelwood, R. D., & Skogstad, W. (Eds.) (2000). *Observing Organisations*. London: Routledge.

Kahneman, D. (2011). *Thinking, Fast and Slow*. New York: Farrar, Straus and Giroux.

Kahneman, D., Sibony, O., & Sunstein, C. R. (2021). *Noise: A Flaw in Human Judgment*. Glasgow: William Collins.

Kim, J. (1982). Psychophysical supervenience as a mind-body theory. *Cognition and Brain Theory, 5*: 129–147.

Klein, M. (1946). Notes on some schizoid mechanisms. *International Journal of Psychoanalysis, 27*: 99–110. Republished in M. Klein, P. Heimann, S. Isaacs & J. Riviere, *Developments in Psycho-Analysis* (pp. 292–320). London: Hogarth, 1952. Republished in *The Writings of Melanie Klein Volume 3*: 1–24. London: Hogarth.

Kuhn, T. (1962). *The Structure of Scientific Revolutions*. Chicago, IL: University of Chicago Press

Le Bon, G. (1895). *Psychologie des foules*. Paris: Alcan. English translation: The Crowd: A Study of the Popular Mind. New Brunswick: Transaction, 1995.

Lukács, G. (1923). History and Class Consciousness. Cambridge, MA: MIT Press, 1971.

Marx, K. (1844 [1975]). The Economic and Philosophical Manuscripts. In: Early Writings (pp. 279–400). London: Penguin.

Menzies Lyth, I. (1979). Staff support systems: Task and anti-task in adolescent institutions. In: R. D. Hinshelwood & N. Manning (Eds.), Therapeutic Communities, Reflections and Progress. London: Routledge.

Mill, J. S. (1861 [1998]). Utilitarianism. Oxford: Oxford University Press.

Neurath, O. (1937). Unity of science and its encyclopedia. In: R. S. Cohen & M. Neurath (Eds.), Philosophical Papers 1913-1946 (pp. 172–182). Dordrecht: Reidel, 1983.

Popper, K. (1963). Conjectures and Refutations. London: Routledge & Kegan Paul.

Suttie I. (1922). Critique of the theory of the "herd instinct". Journal of Mental Science, 68: 245–254.

Suttie I. (1935). Origins of Love and Hate. London: Kegan Paul, Trubner and Trench.

Strachey, J. (1937). Introduction. In: R. Osborn, *Freud and Marx*. London: Gollancz.

Tuckett, D. (2009). Psychoanalysis Comparable and Incomparable. London: Routledge.

Wilson, E. O. (1998). Consilience: The Unity of Knowledge. New York: Vintage.

Wolfenstein, V. (1993). Psychoanalytic-Marxism: Groundwork. London: Free Association.

Part II

Individual psychology with its interpersonal dimensions

The three papers in Part II continue to consider the interaction between individual psychodynamics and social and cultural dynamics and attitudes. The perspective taken in this part is that of the individual. Part II explores various means by which the internal coherence of individuals at the "macro-level" of multiple individuals can emerge from a collection of separate persons with their diverging individuality. Personal experience plays various roles within the social dynamics. The papers attempt to consider how the dynamics of the individual, or the collective, contributes to the "behaviour" of a social group. There would not be group behaviour if there were not individual behaviours, and there would be no group collaboration in thought and action without there being individual thinking that is available for collaboration.

This part starts with the phenomenon of a sequential "flow" of experiences amongst people. Partly this is the result of a defensive use of projection and introjection. This accomplishes a flow of emotional experience comparable to the cognitive flow of ideas and intellectual content between people. It is, however, more than defensive and creates a degree of communal bonding at the emotional level. This uniting flow is exemplified in a working institution in Chapter 3. A similar example is also to be found in Chapter 4, where the social phenomenon, the affect flow, is also illustrated in a session of small-group therapy.

The bonding provided by this interpersonal flow is a contributory dynamic not only to a defensive solidarity against anxieties, but it also contributes to group culture and behaviour and to the overall task. It is important also not to overlook the non-sequential collaborative processes by which a group identifies together around some group ideal, identity, or task, represented by a leading figure or idea. The affect flow contributes to sealing the collaboration.

Chapter 5 gives an account of the culture of a nation mobilised for war. In conventional war the group dynamic is pervaded by guilt and retaliation. However, there are specific features of nuclear war and its finality that push the culture of the group towards mobilising the individuals to the extreme in the paranoid–schizoid position. Crucially they face annihilation, and not their own destructiveness and guilt.

CHAPTER 3

Affect flow

Introduction

In 1988 Mike Rustin and Bob Young of the University of East London and the journal *Free Associations*, respectively, started an annual conference entitled "Psychoanalysis and the public sphere". I gave a paper at the first of these conferences, and it is Chapter 4 in this collection. It was originally published in the collection made by Barry Richards of the papers from the first of these conferences. Chapter 3, however, starts us with a more general discussion of affect flow in the interpersonal network of groups and organisations.

PAPER 3

The individual and the influence of social settings: A psychoanalytic perspective on the interaction of the individual and society*

Psychoanalysis cannot explain social phenomena directly, but the human responses to social, economic, and historical forces can be described. In this paper I want to look at the interaction between the underlying psychology of the unconscious of individuals in groups, and to theorise how that provides a basis upon which social forces may act. Certain aspects of racism and national identity serve as useful illustrations of how the social phenomena interact with the psychology of individuals.

The boundary line between self and the external world bears no relation to reality; the distinction between ego and world is made by spitting out part of the inside, and swallowing in part of the outside (Brown, 1959).

When Freud employed the term "identification" in "Mourning and melancholia" (Freud, 1917e), it was to describe a very odd process. He thought that, in certain situations, an external object would become an object inside the ego. He said this was a characteristic process when ordinary mourning fails. The object that was loved becomes, instead,

* Hinshelwood, R. D. (2005). The individual and the influence of social settings: A psychoanalytic perspective on the interaction of the individual and society. *British Journal of Psychotherapy, 22*: 155–166.

a part of the person who is bereaved. Abraham (1924) described how his own hair went white when his father died. He thought of this as an identification with his lost father. And he located this strange process with the oral impulses, cannibalism. Abraham called it introjection, a term previously introduced by Ferenczi (1909).

There is a proverb: "What you eat is what you are". Freud speaking of the intellectual activity of producing judgements, wrote in his paper on "Negation":

> Expressed in the language of the oldest—the oral—instinctual impulses, the judgement is: "I should like to eat this", or "I should like to spit it out"; and, put more generally: "I should like to take this into myself and to keep that out". That is to say: "It shall be inside me" or "it shall be outside me". As I have shown elsewhere, the original pleasure ego wants to introject into itself everything that is good and to eject from itself everything that is bad. (Freud, 1925h, p. 237)

This all points to a person's extreme interest in what is inside him. Schilder and Wechsler (1935), in an early study, asked children what they thought was inside their bodies:

> The typical answer … was that it contained the food recently eaten … he knows little or nothing about the interior of the body, but he does know what it is to convey food into it—an important libidinal act to the child mind. He pictures even his chest as filled with bread, milk or meat … If he knows anything at all about his muscles and flesh, he believes that they make their appearance under his skin as the direct result of the food he eats. (Schilder & Wechsler, 1935, pp. 358–359)

There is a little rhyme:

> What are little girls made of?
> Sugar and spice and all things nice.
> What are little boys made of?
> Slugs and snails and puppy-dogs' tails.

Such views that children have are not just confined to children.

The physical world inside

This very primitive idea of identity is based on a belief system of what is inside the "ego", and it is experienced very concretely. One might suppose that the ignorant ideas of children cease when we grow up, and the reality-ego comes into play properly. But these odd ideas about our inside are not a simple form of ignorance. Psychoanalytic work finds these phantasies occurring in the adult mind, too. Melanie Klein tried to make this explicit:

> My reason for preferring this term [internal object] to the classic definition, that of "an object installed in the ego" is that the term "inner object" is more specific since it exactly expresses what the child's unconscious, and for that matter the adult's in deep layers, feels about it. In these layers it is not felt to be part of the mind in the sense, as we have learnt to understand it, of the super-ego being the parents' voices inside one's mind. This is the concept we find in the higher strata of the unconscious. In the deeper layers, however, it is felt to be a physical being, or rather a multitude of beings, which with all their activities, friendly and hostile, lodge inside one's body, particularly inside the abdomen, a conception to which physiological processes and sensations of all kinds, in the past and in the present, have contributed. (Quoted in Hinshelwood, 1997b[1])

This may be seen particularly clearly in disturbed patients. Paula Heimann (1942, pp. 8–11) reported the following case in which her patient concretely experienced "things" inside her.

The woman with a devil inside

The patient had begun her psychoanalytic treatment with the experience of being full of devils inside her that demanded her obedience. In unconscious phantasy, the self had taken them in and came to be dominated by these objects felt to be bad. The following

[1] This passage is from the Melanie Klein Archives in the Wellcome Library for the History of Medicine. It was published in an appendix to a previous paper (Hinshelwood, 1997b).

description of a session shows this "mad" internal state actually coming about:[2]

> She began the hour thus: "I am fed up. My mouth is full of ulcers." She then told me a story of what had happened to her car that day. She said: "A fool of a man drove into it. Would you believe it? All the scratches on my car have been made by other people."

We can pick out the passive complaint about damage to her car as a way of representing her persecuted state. But she was also internally scratched (the mouth ulcers were a handy way of expressing that internal state)—a damaged external object (her car) is linked with the sense of something damaged inside.

> She then proceeded to describe in a very emotional way another unpleasant experience she had had that morning. When she was going along in her car, after all her excitement and anger about the man driving into it, another car exceeding the speed limit drove up on her wrong side. "Of course," she said, "it was a woman driver." In front, there was a lorry which gave a sign and turned to the right into a side turning. Immediately after that the woman on her left, without giving any sign, turned to the right also, passing in front of my patient's car, and in order to avoid a collision she herself quickly swerved her own car into the same right-hand turning.

More passivity and helplessness—being pushed into acquiescing to an external object; again, it is like the devils that demanded obedience inside her:

> She was "livid with anger" ... and now took her revenge on the woman by getting in front of her and crawling along at five miles an hour and making it impossible for the woman behind to pass. Presently they came to red lights. The woman pulled up and was now on the same level with my patient, who poked her head out of the window and said: "That was the worst piece of road-hogging I have ever seen. Do you know that by cutting in front of me from the wrong side you forced me to turn to the right so as to avoid a collision, though I wanted to go straight on?"The woman, who had a red beery face, gave a shrug and a laugh and said: "What do

[2] I discussed this case for other purposes elsewhere (Hinshelwood, 1994).

> I care?" My patient was furious and sat trying to think of a most scathing remark. Finally she found it: "On second thoughts," she said, "there is an excuse for you. I can see you are well beyond your prime. You should leave driving to women who are younger and more intelligent than yourself." The woman gasped, but before she could reply the traffic lights changed and my patient drove off. She was very pleased with herself.

This describes a powerfully hostile relationship with an external "bad" object that forced her into a new direction. So far, it seems she has mastered that external object with her triumphant insult. However the consequences of her aggression are considerable and fascinating:

> My patient now drove to her art school and started on a sketch to a given theme … but found that there was something wrong with her drawing, both while she was working on it and when she had finished and hung it up on the wall. She could not find out what it was, and she said to me: "That was the most awful thing about it."

The patient now turns to an awful quality of some internal, though unconscious, interference in her abilities:

> When the artist who criticized the sketches came to hers, he said in surprise: "Good God, what has happened to you? This looks like a drawing from a Victorian family album." My patient now realized what it was she felt to be wrong with it. She said: "It looked like a drawing that had been done 50 years ago."

Something had literally got into her that turned her off from her own apparent intention and diverted her into following a style of someone fifty years ago, that is, a much older woman. The explanation that Heimann offered is that the older woman in the car that had turned her off the road she had wanted to go along, had actually got into her—an introjection of, and then a dominance by, that "bad" object:

> She felt so awful about this that she had to go and have three sherries. Later she noticed the ulcers in her mouth.

The identification with the "beery-faced", drunken woman had become extremely concrete and internal and further expressed in drinking.

The scathing attack that she made on the woman with her mouth was experienced by the patient as a corresponding attack upon part of herself, her own mouth, of which the ulcers were serendipitously noticed evidence for this:

> She had carried out her impulse to hurt the woman and was consciously pleased with her success. But unconsciously—as the woman stood for me and her mother, towards whom she had love impulses as well as hostile ones—she could not bear the injuries she had inflicted on her nor could she remain at a distance from her. She had immediately internalized this mother-figure and she had internalized her in the injured condition for which she felt responsible and guilty, namely as a worn-out, 50-year-old ...

Because the object had been internalised in hatred, she related to herself internally in a hostile way, so that the internal world was dominated by hostility. The patient's sense of who she was had changed. She felt taken over by the alien object, like devils controlling her, and felt a depletion of her own life, of her own direction and intentions. She then performed as if she was that woman fifty years old—the old style of drawing, the alcoholic drinking. Capture by this internalised object replicated the hostile aggressive relationship in which the external object had diverted her and made her helpless. Internally, it disturbed her sense of self and identity by sending her in another direction, the Victorian-style painting.

The manner of internalisation, in hate or in love, has profound implications for the sense of personal identity. Moreover, it also affects the fate of the object inside.[3] These odd beliefs and phantasies occur in the immature mind of the child, and as the action of a very disturbed patient. But are they important for the ordinary identity of all the rest of us? I shall argue that our ordinary identities are just as fragile and fluid, and depend on similar beliefs—unconscious beliefs—about what is inside us, very concretely.

[3] This controlling internalised object typically forms a part of the superego, which commands a certain kind of identity through this alienating form of identification.

Identity as social psychology

A similar form of alienated identity was described by Herbert Marcuse (1955). He also drew attention to an internal object—he used the theory of the superego—and noted that the quality of the contemporary superego in Western society is appropriate to a previous age. Now, in the age of plenty, the Protestant work ethic still drives the Western workforce. A century ago, far more work was necessary, but now it is unnecessary and represents, he says, "surplus repression". We see there is a time-lag, an historical delay, in changing the superego ethic about work. As Freud commented, "a child's super-ego is in fact constructed on the model not of its parents but of its parents' super-ego" (Freud, 1933a, p. 67). Processes of psychological internalisation transmit that Protestant ethic; it is a psychosocial historical process: "The super-ego thus enforces not only the demands of reality but also those of a past reality" (Marcuse, 1955, p. 43).

This anachronistic occurrence is in the descriptions in Michael Sebek's work on the totalitarian object. Years after the collapse of the Soviet system in Eastern Europe, Sebek made simple observations in the Czech Republic: totalitarian compulsions survived, even though the political reality had changed (Sebek, 1998). It is as if people still retained inside themselves a totalitarian figure—one who was more compelling than the present external reality that had come to exist. Such people seemed not to notice the freer political and social climate, and operated as if a harsh political authority still oppressed them. This is an oppressive superego that demands obedience to rules that no longer exist but hang on within individuals. Thus, totalitarian ideologies continue as internal states of mind.

He described an interesting incident to illustrate this obsolete internal society. The scene was the waiting room in a large bureaucratic organisation, in Prague, which resembled the offices of old government departments. It also ran according to old-fashioned rules that reminded one of the past. There was, no longer, a need for people to wait, given modern technology; but the institution seemed to be an end in itself. When one person (this was Michael Sebek himself) suggested a protest to bring the institution up to date, he was shouted down by four others in the waiting room who all claimed that the protester would be harshly dealt with and his contract would be stopped. They asserted that nothing had changed from the socialist state, and even the Austro-Hungarian empire. Suddenly, as he said, "One can observe how a group is evolving from an anonymous crowd" (Sebek, 1998, p. 306).

This is an important observation. In this immediate setting, a number of people suddenly revealed a common internal object; it provided an important social tie between the people. They each related to each other's internal object and aroused an early internalisation. The joint result was an anachronistic object for the group which enforced the (totalitarian) demands of a past reality.

National identity

On occasion it appears many English people behave as if there were still a British Empire, even though it can only be a British Empire in their minds. There is a national identity, internalised more than fifty years ago, as a domineering object with which the person can identify, for instance, the shameful behaviour of British football fans who attack and try to dominate fans from other nationalities. The dominance of England still lives on in their internal world—or rather they identify with a dominant imperialistic object in their internal world. In crowds, a social group is formed by common consent to identify with a single internal object. The loss of Empire has led to the clinging to an internal "imperial" object (our monarch). Then that internal and no longer realistic object is projected back into the external world as the sovereign Britannia that "rules the world". In fact, it rules the internal world.

This contributes a psychological grounding that can be socially exploited. As a consequence, Britain has the utmost difficulty in imagining itself as part of Europe (not the conqueror of Europe) because so many people feel an identification with a compelling idea of Britain, of its power and its Empire. A proper historical distance is difficult to achieve because the idea is present as an internal reality that can be mobilised in the right circumstances.

Illustrative of this anachronistic internal object that is "Britain" and its power are certain aspects of football culture.

The football state of mind

Perhaps the high tide of football hooliganism was at the time of the World Cup in June 1998. The football culture was suffused with a domineering, even murderous, jingoism that infected English fans in Marseilles. Running through the streets, they craved to murder the Tunisians, one team the English had to beat. Many newspaper articles "explained" this hooliganism in one rational way or another. But we read, with surprise, that so many of the hooligans were not previously known to the police, prior to the riots in Marseilles. The surprise is because we expected hooligans to be known villains, recognised by the police, who can pick them out, count and label them. In fact, that view of hooliganism is based in individual psychology—some*one* is a hooligan. It needs a step of the imagination to move to a social point of view and to recognise that a hooligan is not a person but a state of mind. Moreover, it is a state of mind to which even fairly ordinary law-abiding citizens could sign up. They accepted the state of mind in a process that was like a contagion.[4] In this instance, the state of mind was Englishness. Englishness was the hooligan.

Thus, anyone with an English state of mind is at risk of becoming a hooligan when identified with England. But what does it mean to say that Englishness is the hooligan? It frees us from the conventional view of the individual making his autonomous decisions about how to behave. The idea of an unconscious "contagion" infecting the individuals with a particular state of mind could explain the problem we have in understanding persons who are hooligans. People catch a state of mind, they are infected by it. It is not that one is a hooligan in an essential sense. Rather, that identity comes as a bug that can be caught, and which gives a temporary illness. As a *Guardian* leader commented in June of that year: "Violence, racism and xenophobia have still not been eliminated from the English psyche" ("Football's rotten core", *Guardian*, 16 June, 1998, p. 17).

Some notion of being English goes the rounds like a very swift form of flu. Hence, it is difficult to deal with when it is a set of ideas rather

[4] In fact, a long time ago, Le Bon (1895) described crowd behaviour as if there was a rapidly spreading emotional contagion that ran through the people in the crowd, as an infectious epidemic might.

than a set of individuals.[5] It is not innate in the individual as some essence of the group which individuals come to possess—or with which they identify. As Jonathan Friedland, also in the *Guardian*, said, it is a "Nationalism of ideas, not of blood" ("England, our England", *Guardian*, Saturday Review, 20 June, 1998, p. 2).[6]

Identity and the internal world

Nationalism is an identity grounded in a state of feeling. It is not an argument led by reason. Though nationalism may be justified by reasonable appeals—usually appeals to high ideals, but frequently to actual ancestors—those, of course, which have been internalised. Like other states of feeling, nationalism when it becomes intensely felt can lead to irrational and self-denying acts. These emotional states become so easily coordinated across a group or crowd as each person locates another's internal object. Something appears to pass from one to another, like an emotional epidemic.

The idea of an obsolete internal object is a very useful way of linking the internal history of the individual with the external history of his cultural or national group. The descriptions of Sebek and Marcuse offer an important contribution to the psychoanalytic understanding of social and cultural forms. But it is also a statement about how the internal world works, about the personal identity of individuals, which easily distorts identity in social settings.

To understand this linking between the individual mind and the external world of interpersonal and social forces, it is usual to employ the concepts of introjection and projection as described by Freud, Ferenczi, and Abraham, and subsequently elaborated by Klein as

[5] Indeed, probably ethnic identities are themselves ideas about race rather than actual physical features.

[6] Perhaps more recently this kind of compelling identification is worth considering when trying to understand the identification of suicide bombers. What kind of an object are they identified with? It might seem to be an object representing a desperately harmed image of Islam, but detailed work would be needed to define this group identification. The suicide bombers' identification with such an object is not so different, of course, from the more "normal" identification of soldiers going willingly to death in war. This line of thought leads further—to the phenomenon of brainwashing which I tried to examine elsewhere (Hinshelwood, 1997b). It is a line of thinking and investigation that can only be hinted at here, but which might, or should, become an extensive field of study.

projective identification. Projection can be, literally, the removal of parts of the mind of patient and analyst—the removal of their experiences or mental functions. Such parts may reappear as the mind of other persons, or other groups, a process that involves introjection by the "other". Melanie Klein (1946) introduced the term "projective identification" for this particular kind of projective process, which can radically distort the perception of the other person's real personality. Indeed, it not only distorts the perception of the other; that 'other' may introject it, and really change in their behaviour.

Identity and the ideal

If a state of mind behaves like the flu virus then we need to know more about how people catch it. Can we catch a national identity? Identity seems such a personal thing. But we do talk, for instance, of someone being a "chip off the old block"; we mean that he has somehow taken on the characteristics of a parent, some bits of identity transferred from one person to another, from father to son. Alternatively, we could say that he has taken his father's identity, perhaps votes for the same political party, plays golf, tells jokes in the same way as his father, and so on.

Now, when a person joins any group, something of this kind occurs too. Each member of the group holds something in common, something that forms part of his identity—that makes him feel he belongs to the group and the group to him. This something Freud (1921c) called an ego-ideal. In a group, each person accepts the same ideal. It takes up residence as it were inside that person and becomes a part of his identity. One example is the Christian church. All believers have Christ in their hearts. There is a very literal truth about such a statement. Individuals take something in—a set of ideas of what they are like or what they should be like—and together identify with each other's ideal. A group identity is formed from people who all have the same ideal inside them. Moreover, a person moves from group to group—even in the course of a day. With each move, he changes a little the ideal he identifies with: at work, he identifies with the task; then at home, as a father; whilst driving home he identifies as a car-driver; later a lover; and so on.

Identity remains under constant pressure from interpersonal processes which involve projections and introjections between people, and reconstructions of their internal state. We are familiar with the processes that constitute countertransference, and the way certain feelings and states of mind can come to reside in the analyst. In this case, quite severe distortions may occur. Instead of a process of identification with another person's internal objects, an analyst receives a whole chunk of the patient which has taken up residence in the analyst's mind (Hinshelwood, 1997a). Here a radical form of denial of the self has led to parts of the self being split off and projected into another's identity.

In an example used elsewhere to demonstrate this social possession of identity (Hinshelwood, 1989), I illustrated this as a fairly normal process.

Chains of projection

In this observation you will see how some "thing" gets passed around through the interpersonal network. This "something" has psychological "substance" rather than physical substance.

- One morning, Dr A arrived in the hospital building and found that the room she normally used was occupied by Dr B, a new locum. Dr A was annoyed with the newcomer.
- She was unable to interrupt Dr B, who was interviewing a patient, so she tackled the receptionist, Mrs C, blaming her for directing Dr B to the disputed room. Mrs C was affronted and put in a bad humour by this.
- It happened that Dr A's 10-year-old son, D, was away from school that day and she had brought him to the hospital. Mrs C displaced her anger, when Dr A was not present, from the mother to the son. Mrs C told him off for running around and being awkward, but he remained difficult.
- Mrs C then tried to gain support for her criticism of D. She complained to Miss E who was one of the clinical staff in the day hospital and therefore responsible for seeing that the behaviour of patients within the hospital remained orderly.
- However, instead of asserting discipline over D, Miss E attempted to calm the situation by talking to Dr A about her son.
- But this was not welcome. Dr A, unknown to Miss E, was still angry about Dr B and the disputed room. Dr A did not

wish to control D. So Miss E's efforts in this direction came to nothing.

- Miss E tried again. This time she pursued the authority structure by informing Dr F, the consultant with overall responsibility for the hospital. She told him that D had been annoying Mrs C.
- Dr F considered the problem. In his experience, the most troublesome children in the hospital were those who attended the weekly "school group" for children with severe behaviour disturbances. They constituted something of a problem for him. Dr F decided that Mrs C was really annoyed with the children of this "school group". He conveyed his anxieties about controlling these children to the weekly staff meeting of the whole hospital.
- The staff meeting discussed this and became concerned about the impact of children in the hospital as a whole. In particular, there was concern that the adult day patients were disturbed by them. It was known in the past that they were disturbed by the special group of children who were autistic (another group, quite different from the "school group").
- In the end, the staff meeting resolved that Miss G, the psychotherapist in charge of the Autistic Unit, should give a talk to the adult patients about the children in her unit, with the aim of reassuring the adults about their supposed anxiety.

In the network of relationships, an emotional state commenced with Dr A and flowed through a winding course, changing character and interacting with other anxieties, until it ended up as an activity of the institution. A split-off piece of experience comes adrift from one person and is projected as if it were a package, a discrete quantum of experience. In the unconscious minds of the individuals, it can be taken in and given out. A depersonalisation of one individual's experience had occurred. Here there is a constant interchange between people, as some "thing" is passed around. These projective/introjective steps influence the identity of the individuals, their experiences of themselves, and of others. A process takes place to move from the level of interactions between individuals to a different level. Groups of minds come together and, in a collective operation, they convert the process into institutional action.

Change from the personal to the institutional is common; and this illustration shows how something of the person is swept away into the group or institutional activity. Its unconscious character leads to the familiar experience of institutions as impersonal, faceless, and monolithic. People feel depersonalised; that is, their identity feels diminished.

Conclusion

To return to Sebek's example, we can see it as an example of this move from the individual to the collective group action. Together the waiting room became an "evolving group", developing a common attitude. This is the formation of group identity. It is because there were two people in the waiting room that they could then form a group that excludes others (in this case, the protester who had different identifications). It seems to be very important in human social psychology that two or more people with the same identifications support each other's identification with an internal object. Or, perhaps it is more accurate to say, they support each other's projection of that internal object into the external world. Here, Freud's description of these processes is very important. He described two processes:

> In the former, the ego has enriched itself with the properties of the object, it has "introjected" the object into itself, as Ferenczi (1909) expresses it. In the second case it is impoverished, it has surrendered itself to the object, it has substituted the object for its own most important constituent. (Freud, 1921c, p. 113)

He is describing exactly the two processes we have encountered. First, the slavish "bondage" (as he called it (p. 113)) to an internal object; and second, the depletion that results from a constituent of the ego being displaced into the identity of the object.

We can conclude that there are two sides to the phenomenon of personal identity: one is the internal situation with internal objects that may be out-of-date. The other is a social situation in which more than one person together, in a group dynamic, find an external object into which to project similar internal ones.

We are also drawn to the alarming conclusion that our sense of personal identity is radically mobile and fragile, depending uncomfortably on the others around us. This is very different from the usual conception of personal identity, which is considered—at least in Western culture—as unitary, discrete, and indissoluble. Our internal world (identity) and our external world (reality) are under constant reconstruction and change. These conclusions from psychoanalysis are surprising, as the notion of the stand-alone individual has been strongly supported by the individualistic treatment situation which psychoanalysis has adopted. In this sense, psychoanalysis is also surprisingly subversive.

References

Abraham, K. (1924). A short study of the development of the libido, viewed in the light of mental disorders. In: *Selected Papers on Psycho-Analysis* (pp. 418–501). London: Hogarth, 1927. Reprinted London: Karnac, 1979.

Brown, N. O. (1959). *Life Against Death: The Psychoanalytical Meaning of History*. Middletown, CT: Wesleyan University Press.

Ferenczi, S. (1909). Introjection and transference. In: *First Contributions to Psycho-Analysis*. London: Hogarth.

Freud, S. (1917e). Mourning and melancholia. *S. E., 18*. London: Hogarth.

Freud, S. (1921c). *Group Psychology and the Analysis of the Ego*. *S. E., 18*. London: Hogarth.

Freud, S. (1925h). Negation. *S. E., 19*. London: Hogarth.

Freud, S. (1933a). *New Introductory Lectures on Psychoanalysis*. *S. E., 22*. London: Hogarth.

Heimann, P. (1942). A contribution to the problem of sublimation and its relation to processes of internalization. *International Journal of Psychoanalysis, 23*: 8–17. Reprinted in P. Heimann, *About Children and Children-No-Longer* (pp. 26–45). London: Routledge, 1989.

Hinshelwood, R. D. (1989). Social possession of identity. In: B. Richards (Ed.), *Crises of the Self* (pp. 75–83). London: Free Association.

Hinshelwood, R. D. (1994). *Clinical Klein*. London: Free Association.

Hinshelwood, R. D. (1997a). *Therapy or Coercion*. London: Karnac.

Hinshelwood, R. D. (1997b). The elusive concept of "internal objects" and the origins of the Klein group, 1934–1943. *International Journal of Psychoanalysis, 78*: 877–897.

Klein, M. (1946). Notes on some schizoid mechanisms. *International Journal of Psychoanalysis, 27*: 99–110. Reprinted in *The Writings of Melanie Klein, Volume 3* (pp. 1–24). London: Hogarth, 1975.

Le Bon, G. (1895). *Psychologie des foules*. Paris: Alcan. English translation: *The Crowd: A Study of the Popular Mind*. New Brunswick: Transaction, 1995.

Marcuse, H. (1955). *Eros and Civilization*. New York: Beacon Press.

Schilder, P., & Wechsler, D. (1935). What do children know about the interior of their body? *International Journal of Psychoanalysis*, *16*: 355–360.

Sebek, M. (1998). Post-totalitarian personality—old internal objects in a new situation. *Journal of the American Academy of Psychoanalysis*, *26*: 295–306.

CHAPTER 4

Fluid identities

Introduction

During the 1970s and my training at the London Institute of Psychoanalysis, I was impressed by the course on infant observation and Esther Bick's detailed perspective of the *process* of interactions between mother and baby. I recall being on holiday one year in France. Not speaking the language very well, I was thrown back on making observations of the processes of interaction, and the way a bodily expression, readable in any language, was carried forward by someone else's bodily expressed reaction. This set me picking up on observations in the institution I was working in, the Marlborough Day Hospital, in 1976. The result, as mentioned, were the reflections contributed to the first "Psychoanalysis and the public sphere" conference on this process of felt identity circulating interpersonally.

PAPER 4

Social possession of identity*

The psychoanalytic concept of projective identification is a mechanism of intra-psychic defence (Klein, 1946). It is also an element in interpersonal relatedness (Ashbach & Sharmer, 1987). It is therefore one of the bridging concepts that we have between the intra-psychic and the social. There are other bridging concepts between the individual and the social, ones that come from the social sciences; in particular I will deal with "role" (Miller & Rice, 1967; Agazarian & Peters, 1981) and "alienation" (Geyer & Schweitzer, 1981; Meszaros, 1970).

I shall describe a process that consists of a sequence of repeated projective identifications that proceed through a network of relationships (Hinshelwood, 1982 [see also Chapter 3]). It is as though a path can be traced from one person to another; I shall illustrate with material first from a small therapy group and then from a working institution. This process throws light on the difficult and alienating experience of being in large institutions. I shall then examine the general properties of this process and its relationship with the concepts of "role" and "alienation".

---

* Hinshelwood, R. D. (1988). Social possession of identity. Paper given to the "Psychoanalysis and the public sphere" conference; published (1989). Social possession of identity. In: B. Richards (Ed.), *Crises of the Self* (pp. 75–83). London: Free Association.

A small-group example

It is a quite ordinary session of a group with five members and a therapist. At the beginning of the session it had been announced that a new member would be joining the group. After an initial half an hour of discussion about one member's domineering manner of talking, Mrs A became quite angry at what felt to her like criticism. She turned to Mr B, a reticent man, who had been less involved than the others and said "Well, at least I do more than you."

- In this interaction Mrs A was justifying herself and passing on her sense of being criticised to Mr B. The insertion of her own feeling-state into Mr B is a projective identification by Mrs A.
- Mr B looked up rather surprised and awkwardly said that he had been thinking over, since the session last week, what had been said by Mr C who had told Mr B that his silence was a kind of dishonesty because it kept people mystified about what he was thinking and made them uncomfortable. He continued that he thought Mr C was wrong, and that there was nothing wrong with being fairly quiet. It was a question of keeping one's own privacy; one was entitled to do that. Mr C, he complained, was now pestering Mrs A in an equally unkind way. He asked, rhetorically, why could Mr C not stop getting at people.
- Mr B, in turn, was passing on the sense of being in the wrong to Mr C.
- Mr C looked around him rather startled, as he had not really been the only one tackling Mrs A on her intrusiveness. He went a little red in the face and started to justify himself on the grounds that someone in the group had to confront difficult things, but this defensiveness abruptly changed to a more hectoring quality as he began to complain that the therapist did not do these things which were so difficult for the members of the group. The therapist should control things if they went wrong.
- At this point the therapist suddenly felt on the spot and that he was letting the group down. He felt he had to do something to stop the nasty atmosphere that was developing in the group.
- Provoked in this way to do something, he came in quickly to say that Mr C was clearly seeing him (the therapist) as irresponsible.

> He rather clumsily related this to what the group knew about Mr C. Mr C was a rather direct man from an unsophisticated background who had come to treatment because of repeated violent episodes in pubs and finally once at work with a customer. The therapist explained that Mr C felt bad because it played on his feeling that he was a violent man.

I hope it is clear that so far there is an uncomfortable interchange going on in which Mrs A's sense of guilt or blame was transmitted first to Mr B who then tried to put Mr C in the wrong. Mr C in turn made the therapist feel guilty and irresponsible.

The therapist's hasty intervention did not alter the atmosphere significantly as it returned the focus to Mr C. Mrs A made a pun on Mr C's name (Vic) suggesting he had a violent need always to be the victor. There was laughter that relieved some tension for the members of the group, apart from Mr C who erupted with rage in a punitive outburst against the whole group. The smiles faded rapidly as an atmosphere of fear gripped the group, and Mrs D, a depressed woman, began to cry. Her crying seemed to make Mr C feel reproached even more. He seemed to be torn between hitting her and leaving the group. His control was sufficient for him to stand up and turn slowly towards the door. At this point, the therapist intervened more thoughtfully and said that Mr C was needed by the rest of the group to take away from the group everybody's anger and rage at being let down. Mr C remained standing at the door for some ten minutes while the group, in fear, began slowly to pick its way consciously through what had happened. As some of the other members of the group became aware of what Mr C represented for them he was able rather sullenly to return to his place and remain a brooding presence silently reproaching the group.

The whole sequence has five steps. (1) First, Mrs A was put on the spot by the members of the group in order to examine an aspect of her relationship with them, her domineeringness. She began to feel to blame for what she does. (2) She then made the point that she was not as bad as someone like Mr B and thus passed on her sense of being blamed to Mr B. (3) He adeptly managed to pass it on again, this time to Mr C, blaming him for what Mr C had said the week before. (4) Mr C managed to control himself by, in turn, passing on this sense of blame to the therapist. (5) The therapist then tried to make an interpretation but was filled with the blame put into him, and succeeded only in passing the sense of blame back to Mr C. And there it rested for a while, as Mr C acted in such a way as to accrue more blame for his explosive outburst.

I am drawing attention to the way that a *feeling-state*, in this case a sense of blame, is passed on from one member of this group to the next. The process halted when one person, Mr C, came to be established as the blameworthy culprit—a scapegoat.

My thesis is that an essential ingredient of a social network is that bits of experience, affects, emotions, feeling-states, are moved around. These channels of unconscious, non-symbolic communication are separate from, but intertwined with, the verbal and cognitive communication. I will term this aspect of the network, the *affective network*.

An institution's network

The other example[1] is a set of observations from a day hospital. It shows a chain of similar emotional events (projective identifications) taking place in the affective network of an institution.

1. Dr A had advised one of his patients, Mr B, to leave the hospital and return to work, and was thus pushing him to accept that he had failed at his university career.
2. Mr B's symptoms intensified. He believed one of the occupational therapists, Miss C, was in love with him. Delusionally, a failure at university had become a success in love. When Miss C did not admit she was in love with Mr B he became abusive and threatening towards her. It was an intimidating attempt to make Miss C feel a failure—that is, a projective identification of part of his feelings into Miss C.
3. Miss C sought support from a fellow occupational therapist, Mrs D, against the abuse from Mr B. She passed on part of her fear and intimidation to her colleague.
4. Mrs D then tackled Dr A and attacked him for not giving sufficient support to the non-medical clinical staff. Failure and blame had come around full circle to be put back to Dr A.

---

[1] This illustration was used elsewhere to demonstrate general characteristics of affective networks (Hinshelwood, 1982).

5. Dr A then had a further discussion with Mr B about leaving and about his abusiveness towards Miss C.
6. Following this Mr B became aggressive with other patients, throwing a piece of wood across the workshop in one of the occupational therapy sessions.
7. The effect on the patients was a paradoxical one. Mr B's violent event was a very concrete form of projecting his state of mind at the rest of the patients and occupational therapists. He frightened the others and they turned to each other for support. This took the form of another delusion intended to reassure everybody. It was asserted that the hospital was a peaceful and tranquil paradise.
8. The patients' view of the hospital as a soft option, a peaceful, untroubled paradise, had been a recent topic of discussion among the staff; and it seemed to them that consequently patients stayed there too long and became chronic. As a result the staff believed they should challenge the view of the hospital as paradise and introduce a stricter regime.
9. The staff then reacted by increasing their resolve to toughen up the hospital regime and new energy was put into discussing and shaping this new policy.

So, the affective network "contained" the initial traumatising of Mr B by passing on the emotional element or piece of identity (in this instance, Mr B as a failed student) from one person to another. As it flowed through the network it changed—from failure, to aggression, to fear, to delusional peace, and to instituting new policies. It is of considerable interest that the initial quantum of personal experience or identity was eventually disposed of as the energy for a piece of work of the organisation as a whole. It is possible to show that institutional actions are frequently driven by energy derived from the split-off parts of personal experience and personal identity.

The projective life of institutions

There are a number of general properties of affective networks that can be seen in these two illustrations:

1. Individuals use the context of the social network as a means of passing on to others certain feeling-states, elements of identity,

which they wish to disown—a form of psychological defence by projection.

2. Personal affects of the individuals come to be possessed by the social network to form the energy for institutional activity.

And as a result of the above two properties:

1. There is a depersonalisation of the individual's experiences and feelings.
2. The individual becomes deeply fused to the group or institution since the social network, to a degree, is the individual.

The individual becomes raw material for the developing culture, its structure and activity. His unconscious investment in it is based on primitive mechanisms involving splitting. A split piece of experience comes adrift from one member and is projected as if it were a package, a discrete quantum of experience which, in the unconscious minds of the individual members, can be taken in and given out.

The individual actually loses his own experience in the ramifications of the network and with it some of his sense of self or identity. A large institution feels inhuman because individuals literally lose themselves (or parts of themselves) in it.

Because these processes are based on the unconscious mechanisms of individuals, the institution comes to be felt unconsciously as alien, split from the individuals who make it up—"the faceless bureaucracy", "the monolithic organisation", terms we use to convey the way institutions reduce the sense of identity of the individuals. At the same time, the process binds the individual into an identification. from which the individual has great difficulty in extricating himself whole.

Roles and the unconscious

In the field of social science, roles are the collections of functions performed by the individual for the social group. Typically, these roles belong to the institution but are voluntarily adopted by individuals. They can be thought about rationally and altered or adhered to for rational and conscious purposes.

However, it is not necessarily like that, since a role can be felt to be imprisoning or alienating. One reason for the imprisoning experience was shown in the example of the small therapy group arising, at the unconscious level, from projective identification. One individual came to play a specific part for the others. In that case it was a scapegoat, a well-known phenomenon that goes back to biblical times. Its relationship to widely held feelings of guilt in the group was always known too.

The precise means by which this unconscious role for the group was established is the process I have drawn attention to—a quantum of emotion, of a feeling-state or of an identity, was passed around by projective identifications and finally localised in one individual who was subjected to an "enforced introjection"—as Menzies Lyth (Menzies, 1960) called it. Such a process causes the individual a distortion of his identity. Then, greatly enhancing certain aspects of his personality will obliterate others. At the same time, it also distorts the identity of others, depleting them of certain aspects (Hinshelwood, 1982, 1987). This unconscious function of carrying the guilt (or some other emotional aspect of identity) for the other members of a group needs to be carefully distinguished from performance of conscious, rational roles.

We need, at this point, to make some careful distinctions. A role entered into may be congenial or it may be uncongenial. Acceptance of a role may be voluntary but that does not exclude the occurrence of the processes I have discussed, in which the person, in addition to his conscious role, is also unconsciously elected to a position that distorts his own personal identity. A role within an identified institution may acquire specific personality characteristics through the social projective system; Menzies Lyth (Menzies, 1960) showed, for instance, that student nurses were regarded and treated as irresponsible without regard to their actual individual personalities, so much so, in fact, that it worked to the detriment of recruitment to the nursing service.

Also, many roles that are consciously entered into are alienating because of a specific impoverishment due to socio-economic exploitation, for example many work roles, or the role of "mother", for some women. And many, being alienated already, may attract psychological exploitation as well: Black people may not only be correctly identified as different from white people but become stereotyped as "Black people", with anal and faecal connotations that are attributed socially but unconsciously.

The question arises of the relation between the role that is alienating because of socio-economic exploitation, and those that are so because of the psychological exploitation. In my view, alienation in socially exploited roles invariably attracts exploitation for projective purposes as well, giving rise to a state of affairs in which economic exploitation and psychological exploitation go hand in hand.

Carrying a socially projected emotional identity that turns a social role into a highly restricted personality is usually felt as an alienating experience and destructive of personal development. Yet some people will take up such places that will seriously hinder their own identity development; perhaps we all do to some extent. However, it is not always consciously experienced in this way: Turquet (1975) has described the advantages, as well as the threats, of a group-defined identity. Compliance with the unconscious projected identity is, at the level of the individual, akin to "false consciousness" at the class level (Lukács, 1971). The invitation for projective exploitation is clear in the small group example, in which Mr C's emotional role, that the group needed to exploit, was close to one aspect of his personality—into which he was restricted by the group.

Alienation

The depersonalising effect of projective identification at the psychoanalytic level of the individual becomes alienation at the level of the group network (Hinshelwood, 1983), a depersonalisation of the individual actually within the institution which, to an extent, is him. Expropriation of a particle of his own experience comes about through transformations that occur and the individual actually loses some of his experience as it passes away through the ramifications of the network.

In our own culture the affective networks of institutions have come to be remarkably efficient at exploiting individuals' feeling-states and experiences, reifying bits of human beings and estranging them from the human world.

The affective network is an exchange system of human emotions and identity, of reified bits of human beings. In this sense, affective networks parallel the exchange systems of commodities which are also reified bits of human relations. And it is possible that economic exploitation is a concrete precipitate of projective exploitation; that is to say, the projective processes are the special medium by which economic exploitation takes a hold on individuals. Capitalism has learned to accurately reflect and exploit the potential in human beings to alienate and reify qualities and identities. The way the capitalist system aligns the psychological potential for projective identification in groups and commodity fetishism in the economic system is a powerful union. To dismantle such a system requires attention to the psychology of institutions as well as the economics and politics of the capitalist system. The losing of parts of human emotions and identity in the affective network compares with the expropriation of surplus value in the labour of economic production. Both are alienated from the individual to be exploited by the (capitalist) institution. It is likely that both "surplus identity" and surplus value are needed in the oiling of the wheels of capital accumulation.

References

Agazarian, Y., & Peters, R. (1981). *The Visible and Invisible Group*. London: Routledge.

Ashbach, C., & Sharmer, V. (1987). Interactive and group dimensions of Kleinian theory. *Journal of the Melanie Klein Society*, *5*: 43–68.

Geyer, F., & Schweitzer, D. (1981). *Alienation: Problems of Meanings, Theory and Method*. London: Routledge.

Hinshelwood, R. D. (1982). The individual in the social network. In: M. Pines & J. Raphaelson (Eds.), *The Individual and the Group. Volume 1: Theory* (pp. 469–477). New York: Plenum Press.

Hinshelwood, R. D. (1983). Projective identification and Marx's concept of Man. *International Review of Psycho-Analysis*, *10*: 221–226.

Hinshelwood, R. D. (1987). Social dynamics and individual symptoms. *International Journal of Therapeutic Communities*, *8*: 265–272.

Klein, M. (1946). Notes on some schizoid mechanisms. In: *The Writings of Melanie Klein, Volume 2* (pp. 1–24). London: Hogarth.

Lukács, G. (1971). *History and Class Consciousness*. Milton Keynes: Merlin.

Menzies, I. (1960). A case-study in the functioning of social systems as a defence against anxiety: A report on a study of the nursing service of a general hospital. *Human Relations*, *13*(2): 95–121.

Meszaros, I. (1970). *Marx's Theory of Alienation*. Milton Keynes: Merlin.

Miller, E., & Rice, A. K. (1967). *Systems of Organization*. London: Tavistock.

Turquet, P. (1975). Threats to identity in the large group. In: L. Kreeger (Ed.), *The Large Group* (pp. 87–144). London: Constable.

CHAPTER 5

Stability or annihilation

Introduction

During the 1980s there was a re-emergence of concerns about nuclear war and analysts formed, at Hanna Segal's instigation, an action group titled Psychoanalytic Psychotherapists Against Nuclear War. Because of my interest in nuclear disarmament some twenty or more years previously, I contributed a couple of papers on this topic. Because of copyright problems, these are not reproduced here, but some revised reflections on those papers were written for this volume. This paper reflects on the individual undercurrents of a powerful political issue on the deeply buried reactions, anxieties, and defences aroused by the nuclear threat. These personal events in individual minds are collectivised as group dynamics across a nation because of the common originating stimulus in the external political life.

PAPER 5

Psychological defences and nuclear war*

This paper attempts to illustrate how a social occurrence can impact on individuals all together as a group, society, or nation. The concerns we all have about war demonstrates these unifying impacts on individuals generated by a cultural event. The two primary anxieties (according to object relations psychoanalysis) are particularly apparent in the reactions to war. These anxieties take two forms. The first, persecutory anxiety, is about the fear for one's own survival, and the second, depressive anxiety, is a concern about harming, damaging, or the death of others.

War is an example of the way deep-going fears for survival—of self and others—mobilise many individuals, as a group. Indeed, the fate of non-combatant citizens increasingly becomes drawn into the fate of military personnel. And over historical time whole populations share actual or imagined death as a preoccupation for long periods as a reality, and not merely as a deeply unconscious phantasy. Such a situation clearly demonstrates not only the play of political life upon the internal world of an individual, but it plays on the unconscious life of huge numbers of people in a similar way across a whole nation. Collective terror provokes collective

* 2002, unpublished.

psychological defences. It arouses powerful reactions in people including fear, rage, righteousness, and grief, as well as the defences against these basic emotions that then numb the impact of death and fear. This paper focuses on the common element and how these internal states are shared. Crucially there is a qualitative difference between conventional war and nuclear war. The fear of loss in ordinary warfare is exaggerated in nuclear war with the fear of an annihilating destructiveness of everything.

Projective identification is a powerful means of communicating nonverbally and indeed unconsciously. However, it relies on the object, some other person or persons, to accept what is projected; so, a successful projective identification has to be met by an accepting introjection. A baby, before language is learned, relies on this method of communication, although various forms of body language are quickly developed. Nevertheless, this non-symbolised communication occurs all through life. For instance, at its most conscious, the threat of death is dealt with by a visit to a health professional. The anxiety is introjected by a doctor or nurse who then with an attitude of competence advises on what is wrong and the measures to take. But not only bodily problems are dealt with in this way. Anyone can go to a friend with some distress on their mind and, as we say, "share" it. In common speech we have the adage, "a problem shared is a problem halved".

In wartime the general colleaguely comfort of all being together in danger sustains soldiers in the military. It also sustains ordinary citizens as current warfare increasingly involves attacks on non-military persons in cities and towns as well. This sense of fraternity can, however, fail and we will consider an example which distinguishes two kinds of warfare, conventional and nuclear.

Though the projection–introjection process may be forced, either by a powerful projection or an "extractive" introjection, it may also fail. Inevitably, at times a mother, or a carer, fails to respond adequately to a baby's discomfort or fears and this remains a possibility all through adult life as well. One of the more common failures is when the experience is so painful that the potential receiver cannot bear it either and rejects the projection or, we can say, refuses to introject. Then, after a while, projective identification will be abandoned and other, usually less adequate methods of coping, are turned to. This failure of projective identification and of the flow in the affective network will be described in terms of warfare.

War in the heart and on the battlefield

The psychoanalytic literature on war starts with Freud's "Thoughts for the times on war and death" (1915b), written during the First World War. Later, the League of Nations invited a discussion between Einstein and Freud, a correspondence now known as *Why War?*, published in 1933 (Freud, 1933b). Einstein had written to Freud for this reason in 1931: "I offer these suggestions to you, rather than to anyone else in the world, because your sense of reality is less clouded by wishful thinking than is the case with other people" (Einstein to Freud, 29 April, 1931, in Nathan & Norden, 1960, p. 187). He suggested the following to Freud:

> Once … an association of intellectuals—men of real stature—has come into being, it might then make an energetic effort to enlist religious groups in the fight against war. The association would give moral power for action to many personalities whose good intentions are today paralyzed by an attitude of painful resignation. I also believe that such an association of men, who are highly respected for their personal accomplishments, would provide important moral support to those elements in the League of Nations … (Ibid.)

Einstein wrote to Freud again in July, 1932 and Freud replied in a sceptical vein—both letters are contained in his well-known paper (1933b, pp. 203–215). By then, aged seventy-seven, and having been fighting cancer for ten years, he focused largely on "an instinctual inclination" (1915b, p. 284) to aggression. Freud's sophisticated psychology, despite his rather amateurish and imaginative anthropology seemed to walk parallel to Einstein's hopes of superior intellects, which Freud regarded as devoted to the invention of superior weapons. He suggested that an association of intelligent people having an administrative overlordship of all nations could only occur once nations relinquish their own military power.

It seems to be the case that the human species pursues violent competition rather more thoroughly than most animals. On the whole, animals, individual or in groups, compete with a member of their own species, until the opposition turns to flee. Then the fight is abandoned. For humans, however, the fight goes on, and a determined pursuit of the fleeing opponent frequently ends in the actual death of the defeated.

By the time the Einstein–Freud correspondence was published by the League of Nations, Hitler had already taken power in Germany and both Einstein and Freud were to become exiles from his violence. Glover (1933, and expanded 1946) took up in more clinical terms the roles of sadism and masochism which Freud had described in his instinct theory as an underlying, unconscious source of war. Sadomasochism is primary, and the economic and sociopolitical factors act as conscious screens or rationalisations for the release of these impulses. Freud's gloomy picture and the gloomy times in which he wrote it provoked others following the Second World War. Alix Strachey (1957) pointed out that love is personally and privately expressed while aggression is reflected in social phenomena (see also the extensive scope of the edited book by Covington, Williams, Arundale, and Knox (2002)).

Of course, there are other factors, too, and other emotions aroused by the vanquished (see, for instance, Figlio, 2017). Fornari (1975) takes mourning as the model of a process in which society itself creates opportunities or institutions for supporting the individuals with their own methods of coping with guilt and loss; and war is this social process gone wrong. Mourning is a collective, social, group activity, as in funerals. But it is individually aimed, to give assistance with the bereavement and guilt each member of the group is feeling. In developing his theme in this way, Fornari used Jaques' (1955) notion of a social defence system (see below).

Psychoanalytic investigations have a tendency for a biased focus on the internal dynamics and impulsions. Koenigsburg (2009) puts his finger on it with the title of his book, *Nations Have the Right to Kill*. There is a boundary across which we pass when we go from individual morality where murder is potentially a capital offence with a legal death penalty, to the behaviour of large social groups organised as a political state. As Freud mentioned in *Why War?*, justice is, at bottom, violence or the threat of it. The dynamics of groups and crowds differs in some fundamental ways from those of the individual. And it may be this is particularly true as the group gets larger. And to put it another way, the individual in a group is not the person he is when on his own, an observation made long ago by Le Bon (1895) in his study of crowds.

Though Freud took Le Bon into account in his *Group Psychology* (Freud, 1921), he made no distinction between a group of two (such as lovers, or a hypnotist and their subject) and vast organisations like the church or an army. He saw in that spectrum a common dynamic thread, but it has to be recognised that the thread becomes more dominant as the group enlarges. The thread Freud picked out to categorise all groups is the allegiance to an ideal, whether that is a loved one, a group task, a leader, or a national identity. War, even civil war, conforms to the last. Aspiring to a supreme identity characterises the human in their group even more than individually. Or, slightly differently, aspiring to the ideal of a group seems so often to be an aspiration more achievable as a group. And it also entices the individual by offering a sense of omnipotence when he is identified with the group itself. A group after all, is likely to be more powerful than an individual alone. As Le Bon described, being in a group makes the individual a different person as he conforms to the group. That gain for the individual is an identification with the power of the group, where so often a group performs and achieves much more than an individual on his own.

War as a defence against mourning and guilt

Fornari (1975, p. 210) says that war is a state of mind, politically expressed in "a fundamentally psychotic manoeuvre … a paranoid elaboration of mourning". Fornari's claim is an interesting description of a self-sustaining cycle of internal events. If war is the projection of guilt into the other, war then becomes an innocent defence against the evil in the other. Nevertheless, the violence unleashed in the pursuit of innocence enhances the guilt, with a resulting further projection—and so on. Thus, war is a consequence (as well as a cause) of guilt. Central to war is the problem of guilt arising from the liberated sadism, cruelty, and murder. To understand how guilt arises, Fornari used the theory of the depressive position. He looked to Jaques for the idea of a collective "social defence system", to describe how sociopolitical structures and activities, not least armies and war, are evolved by groups and nations to mitigate intolerable anxiety and guilt in the participating individuals.

The communality of humans is enormously enhanced by the fact that people feel guilty when they feel concern or responsibility for others who are suffering or damaged. It comes from a phantastical appreciation of one's own aggressiveness. We have all raged against our loved ones and developed bitterly destructive thoughts towards them, most commonly in infancy. Our children's world has frequent intense feelings of anger and extreme fantasies of destruction. Fairy stories are full of people being turned into toads, killed, eaten, and so on. It is out of the child's nightmare world that the sense of guilt and punishment erupts. Personal development entails a movement beyond, although as adults we may still be very drawn to cyber games of war and killing, horror films, and reading crime thrillers, which all touch on the unconscious and avoid the destructiveness in us. Aggressiveness is originally terrifying and generates great concern for damaged others. It carries a quality of anguish—so much anguish that at first our aggression cannot be tolerated and psychological defences set in. On the surface, children appear quite untroubled by their uninhibited intention to cut off Daddy's head, or to shut Mummy out in the garden and never let her in. It is only in the night when they wake with nightmares that one can see that this carefree aggressiveness has another side to it, a desperate terror hidden by the defences.

This paranoid defence elaborated by Klein, but also by Rosenfeld (1965; see Hinshelwood, 2023) is what Fornari means by the paranoid elaboration of mourning. In war it becomes coordinated socially as an intergroup relation with another group to be fought. Harmony within a group is bought through denial of the aggressiveness of its members and the displaced experience that hostility comes from outside—Freud (1930a) used the term "the narcissism of minor differences".

The social structure of war as a defence

Individuals split off their bad aggressive impulses on either side, attributing them to those of the other side. Thus, their own aggression can be regarded as good since it confronts evil courageously. Symmetrically, the individuals of the other nation split and project bad aggression in a similar "self-defensiveness". However, this is not all. Individuals project good aggression into their own army, and their soldiers introject it as heroic saviours. As their introjections are amassed from the whole nation, they can feel themselves equally massive. The omnipotence and indestructibility quell fear, and feats of great bravery can be nonchalantly performed. This is a system organised socially that supports the individuals' psychological defences. However, at the national level, the eventual consequence of such socially coordinated projections and reprojections back and forth sooner or later risks actual military aggression.

Large group dynamics

As mentioned, the size of the group impacts on the intensity of these paranoid reactions to aggression and guilt. The greater the size of the group, the greater the sense of power and destructiveness. Kreeger (1975), in focusing on large groups, described four main changes as the group gets larger: (1) the defence mechanism; (2) a propensity to form subgroups; (3) power related to size; and (4) the relations with the leadership:

1. First, the larger the group the more there is a resort to the primitive processes of splitting, projection, introjection, and forms of identification typical of the paranoid–schizoid position. Kreeger calls these psychotic mechanisms, and Klein referred to the paranoid defence against guilt.
2. The larger the group and the less people can know of everyone in the group, the more likely it is that subgroups will form. It becomes a relief to reject the group as a whole and to split into smaller groups that are cosier and more homogeneous. All difference and danger can be attributed to the imagined large group, or to another subgroup into which the bad hostility can be projected.
3. The large group gives a sense of size and power which dwarfs the individual. He may feel faced with fear and intimidation; or by introjecting or identifying with it, he feels swollen up into an omnipotence, even to the point of being taken over by that belief (Hinshelwood, 1982).
4. So often the power felt in the group can seem to lie in the leader, and it generates a docile or sullen dependence with leaders felt as swollen "good" or "bad" figures who dominate.

The dynamics of groups of people, the military and citizens, will on the whole manage to collaborate in keeping the flow of affect, the fear of death, reasonably tolerable. However, in the last century that means of coping significantly failed with two world wars.

The special qualities of nuclear war

The threat of nuclear war is different from ordinary war. It is not just the primitive form of anguishing guilt, but something quite radical is added. It is a sense of an irreparable annihilation. Something beyond repair. This sense of annihilation is, like guilt, a bedrock experience, which we have all known in earliest infancy. But it is not just an annihilation of the other, but an attack *by* an annihilating other as well; so, it is the annihilation of oneself as well as all others. No one survives to even be aware of the need to repair. Nuclear weapons are thus the ultimate threat: a destructiveness that can only lead to a resigned despair and apathy and obliteration of everything.

It is true that the idea of omnipotent destruction is not new. The saturation bombing at the end of World War Two, chemical warfare in the First World War, the scourge of medieval epidemics of plague, all touch on this core experience, and for the people of the time they feel irreparable and impossible to survive.

Visiting Hiroshima on one occasion, on 6 August, 2017, I remember the experience of looking out from the viewing platform of a new high-rise block only a few metres from where the atom bomb exploded high in the sky above the city. The carefully preserved ruins of a dome dramatically memorialised the impossible-to-conceive war crime. I learned that some 60,000 ordinary citizens died in seconds or minutes, and much the same number more slowly from the effects of radiation. This was not a strategic bomb it was obliteration—of a city and of a people. Trying to imagine on that quiet, sunny, and not too hot Sunday the event of destruction was impossible to connect with the new-born buildings and streets, bridges, and parks there today. Trying to contrast what had happened then and the tranquil weekend when I was there has remained an occupation my mind has wrestled with since then.

Klein expressed the view that the alternation between the two positions, paranoid–schizoid and depressive, causes, slowly over the course of development, the intensity of anxiety (and the rigidity of the defences) to lessen (see Britton, 1998). So there are degrees of paranoid–schizoid anxiety, and then nuclear war takes us right back to the deepest fear for survival of everything.

Omnipotence and omnipotent destruction

It is something about the scale of the violence that overwhelms. It is the destruction of *everything/everyone*. In cold psychoanalytic terms it is an experience of omnipotence; in this instance, not of being omnipotent but of being a near witness of what omnipotence can do. An American official claimed that if only there were enough shovels, the USA would recover from a nuclear war. The shovels were to be employed digging holes in the ground, covered by disused doors on which a mound of earth a few feet deep is placed. "The dirt really is the thing that protects you from the blast as well as the radiation … You know, dirt is just great stuff" (Scheer, 1982). This is simple denial. I think it is quite understandable if one has been to Hiroshima and stood 200 metres beneath the "hypocentre" in the sky where the bomb exploded. Such denial is quite accessible as a defence against the omnipotence of destruction which we can barely conceive in our minds: "The denial of psychic reality becomes possible only through the feeling of omnipotence—which is characteristic of the infantile mind" (Klein, 1946, p. 102).

In such disastrous internal states, we feel collapsed, destroyed, obliterated in our own mind or in our own identity; going to pieces emotionally in an explosive personal disaster, being stirred by such powerful anger that there is no ability to retain personal civilised control—these are perhaps the impossible-to-verbalise experiences of the earliest moments of life for each of us. The nuclear threat is an actual external version of this phantastical fear which could be lived in reality. A realisation of that momentary and momentous disaster can be visited, over there, in Japan. The fact that reality so nearly replicates this worst of all our phantasies gives the nuclear war threat a special place in human achievements.

We all of us have our methods of coping with our desire for immortality, some with institutionalised religion, some with family descendants, some with physical or academic achievements. But none of these will remain. So, unlike death in ordinary war, we know there will be no one left behind to glorify it and the sacrifice it cost, or to keep us and our achievements in their hearts. While, normally, death is a living event for the survivors, in nuclear war even one's death is obliterated. It is a new kind of war because it brings to the fore this different internal state. Glover (1946), shortly after the Hiroshima and Nagasaki bombs, wrote:

> No doubt the discharge of atomic bombs does not differ in principle from snowballing … Nevertheless the actual and potential destructiveness of the atomic bomb plays straight into the hands of the Unconscious. The most cursory study of dream-life and the phantasies of the insane shows that the ideas of world-destruction are latent in the unconscious mind. (p. 274)

Kovel (1983) tried to capture the experience "the formation of terror out of fear". It is the most basic of the terrors of the earliest moments, the operation of the paranoid–schizoid position at the deepest layers of the personality. As Melanie Klein said:

> [Aggression, at the earliest stages] is felt as fear of annihilation (death) and takes the form of fear of persecution. The fear of the destructive impulse seems to attach itself at once to an object—or rather it is experienced as fear of an uncontrollable overpowering object. (Klein, 1946, p. 100)

When these kinds of phantasies and inner experiences take a hold they amount to a psychotic state, and Klein turned to the Schreber case, describing how

> God and Flechsig also represented parts of Schreber's self. The conflict between Schreber and Flechsig, to which Freud attributed a vital rôle in the World destruction delusion, found expression in the raid by God on the Flechsig souls. In my view this raid represents the annihilation by one part of the self of the other parts—which, as I contend, is a schizoid mechanism. The anxieties and phantasies about inner destruction and ego disintegration bound up with this mechanism are projected on to the external world and underlie the delusions of its destruction. (Klein, 1946, p. 109)

Klein, like Freud, focused on this dream level of the mind and how these deep fears, anxieties, and guilt can be experienced when actual external aggression occurs. However, nuclear weapons and warfare approach that level of destructiveness and annihilation *in reality*. They are not, in fact, delusions or merely fantasies; they are all too real.

In another context, Menzies Lyth described the social and organisational problems when the deeper anxieties become conscious ones. Menzies Lyth described the culture of a nursing service in a general hospital and wrote:

> The objective situation confronting the nurse bears a striking resemblance to the phantasy situations that exist in every individual in the deepest and most primitive levels of the mind. (Menzies, 1960, p. 98)

In this case, the stirring of such deep anxieties led to the nursing practice in that hospital becoming distorted and to a degree dysfunctional. The fear of a nuclear holocaust has stirred entire national populations, way beyond the single hospital in Menzies Lyth's study.

Defences against annihilation

As infants we are almost helpless to protect our own minds (let alone our bodies) against the experience of annihilating threats, and as adults our resources seem to be just as limply inadequate. The denial and dissociation in the public statements made by politicians about the perils of nuclear war impressed Martin Roth (Roth & Blugrass, 1985), who pointed out that the regional governments and civil defence bunkers proposed at that time, even if they survived a war, would never be functional in the midst of the devastation. In truth, they were established and the reality of total annihilation was thereby denied. They are inadequate gestures at civil defence. That official response was not a realistic plan; instead it was psychological protection that disregarded the real impotence in the face of the threat (Richards, 1989). Realistic information on the real danger was withheld as too unnerving for the public. Civil defence was a freedom-from-information act, and merely a civil *psychological* defence. It is a social defence system of an extreme kind against that infantile helplessness which invests the terror.

The nuclear shelter is needed as a *psychic* protection; and we can see it has certain characteristics: (1) one's own sensibility is turned off and we become cold—Adorno (1973) despairingly described his own way of dealing with his survival of the Nazi Holocaust in these terms: "very survival calls for the coldness, the basic principle … without which there could have been no Auschwitz"; (2) there is flippancy, like the American official singing the praises of dirt; and (3) fear is trivialised.

The callous and flippant indifference to the nuclear holocaust aligns us with the perpetrators of Auschwitz. E. P. Thompson, with bitter humour, exposed the official propaganda pamphlet *Protect and Survive* with his own parody *Protest and Survive* (1980), but, collectively, that kind of irony has been all we have had to put between us and our helplessness in the face of groups as large as a nation stockpiling nuclear warheads. The problem has always been to change such numbing defences on a wide social scale and attempt to view the reality. It could almost be described thus:

> [In the extreme autistic states] an almost impenetrable cystic encapsulation of part of the self which cuts the [person] off from the rest of his personality … manifests itself by a thinness or flatness of feeling accompanied by a rather desperate and tenacious clinging to … the sole source of life. (S. Klein, 1980, p. 395)

But that omnipotent destruction is not encapsulated psychically; it is becoming a potential *reality*. The degree of infantile helplessness which nuclear war promises seems almost impossible to face and cannot adequately flow even with those distortions and displacements typical of a group's affective network.

New cultural forms

It appears that as objective reality comes to approximate to the deepest destructive phantasies, new cultural forms appear, based on denial and omnipotence. That reality has come to the fore due to the actual reality of mass exterminations during the two world wars, 1914–1918 and 1939–1945. Affect flow based on projective identification seems to become overloaded. It is interesting to speculate on new cultural expressions that appear to be thrown up and based on denial and omnipotence.

Popular culture, like individual dreaming, may displace underlying stress into aesthetic productions. There has been a considerable production of disaster movies, which encapsulate our terror within cinemas. Although both *King Kong* and *War of the Worlds* were produced prior to the invention of nuclear weapons (*War of the Worlds* was originally a radio drama), they have both been remade frequently since. *Alien* caught the public imagination and has inspired numerous sequelae. There is also the highly rated recent *Don't Look Up*; but there are many more in this booming genre of disaster. Could it be that such popular works attempt to capture *something* of the helplessness, but are safely wrapped up in a capsule (rather than healthily "contained")? Or, at a more intellectual level, is the nihilism of contemporary philosophy, literature, and art a similar manifestation of an implicit or hidden catastrophe?

Of course, the intense war-mongering in so many cyber games did not exist much before thirty years ago. Their popularity now seems a similar engagement with some hidden urge within us. The games do not concern nuclear war and they bring the game down to the manageable intensity of conventional warfare. In fact, it becomes more than manageable. When a game ends in defeat, one merely switches off and starts a new game. In this process, death is something that can be merely switched off. There is a profound denial of real death, and it would appear to be a means of denying the grave seriousness of a real death. Just switching over to a new game is not really an adequate projective identification comparable to communicating with a helping friend. In fact, the reverse; it minimises the seriousness of death as if it can merely be dismissed.

Denial of disaster has gripped many segments of many countries in the recent pandemic. It was perhaps an exaggerated panic, deadly to only some of us (the elderly and infirm) but felt in terms of a global disaster for everyone. Was that dialectical structure of panic vs scepticism a replay of the hidden terror of annihilation that is background to the politics of our age? In other words, was the deeply felt threat suddenly erupting in a different form as the Covid-19 virus. And managing the virus more effectively keeps at bay other fears of total annihilation (stemming partly from the reality of the nuclear bomb). The pharmaceutical companies and the vaccines they produce appear to master something feared to be uncontrollable. At the same time, there is a significant suspicion that something is not quite right and the anti-vax movement may express unconsciously a suspicion that the triumph over Covid-19 is not a real conquering of the omnipotent destructive phantasies provoked by the reality of nuclear weapons. My account here suggests that the displacement of our terror onto the virus has created a suspicion (still largely unconscious) that we need to cope with some other unmanageable threat.

Similarly, has the fear of an unstoppable disaster led to an omnipotence that gives an unrealistic confidence about our seemingly unstoppable exploitation of nature itself? The result of such unthinking omnipotence fosters a confidence in exploitation, and moreover, if it causes harm to the environment, we just have to change course to rescue everything—omnipotently. The foundational attitude that keeps the terror threat at bay is the omnipotent belief that we humans can manage nature as we wish and need. But it is based on a denial that we are a part of nature and within it. The denial is that there is a climate disaster or, if there is, we can simply put it right. This denial and omnipotence is then driven by the suppressed threat of a nuclear holocaust.

Another speculation is whether the sense of helplessness, so provoked in 1945, has led to individuals putting their confidence in accumulating not just millions of dollars, euros, pounds, roubles, yuan, but billions of them. The contemplation of such wealth in an individual could well be a necessary support for the omnipotence needed to survive total disaster—from nuclear warfare or the climate.

Conclusion

I have illustrated anxieties that can be shared in common across the membership of a nation. Fear and guilt are shared around the affective network on the principle of "sharing is halving" in various ways. And the unconscious management of these basic anxieties of fear for survival and concern for others are dealt with by various collectively organised defences that combine denial of seriousness and the assumption of an omnipotent control over threats.

In response to the alarming anxieties felt by all (or most) people, culturally supported mechanisms of defence relegated the experience to the unconscious domains of the individuals' minds. It could then be of interest, even importance, to consider if those anxieties emerged in disguised and distorted forms as cultural manifestations. In particular, have such cultural expressions increased since the destruction of cities and citizens became possible with the saturation bombing and the atomic bombs in 1945?

These thoughts are speculative and aimed at illustrating the collectivisation of individuals' terrors in contemporary civilisation arising from cultural attitudes and event. The aim has been to trace the spread of anxiety as a collective experience that draws people through sharing this infectious distress with each other.

References

Adorno, T. (1973). *Negative Dialectics.* New York: Seabury, 1973.

Britton, R. (1998). *Belief and Imagination: Explorations in Psychoanalysis.* London: Routledge.

Covington, C., Williams, P., Arundale, J., & Knox, J. (Eds.) (2002). *Terrorism and War: Unconscious Dynamics of Political Violence.* London: Karnac.

Figlio, K. (2017). The mentality of conviction: Feeing certain and the search for truth. In: N. Mintchev & R. D. Hinshelwood (Eds.), *The Feeling of Certainty: Towards a Psychosocial Approach* (pp. 11–30. London: Palgrave.

Fornari, F. (1975). *The Psychoanalysis of War.* Bloomington, IN: University of Indiana Press.

Freud, S. (1915b). Thoughts for the times on war and death. *S. E., 14*: 273–300. London: Hogarth.

Freud, S. (1921c). *Group Psychology and the Analysis of the Ego. S. E., 18*: 67–143. London: Hogarth.

Freud, S. (1930a). *Civilization and its Discontents. S. E., 21*: 59–145. London: Hogarth.

Freud, S. (1933b). *Why War? S. E., 22*: 195–216. London: Hogarth.

Glover, E. (1946). *War, Sadism and Pacifism.* Edinburgh: Hugh Paton & Sons.

Hinshelwood, R. D. (1982). The individual in the social network. In: M. Pines & L. Rafaelson (Eds.), *The Individual and the Group.* London: Plenum.

Hinshelwood, R. D. (2023). *Introduction to Herbert Rosenfeld.* London: Routledge.

Jaques, E. (1955). Social systems as a defence against persecutory and depressive anxiety. In: M. Klein, P. Heimann, & R. Money-Kyrle (Eds.), *New Directions in Psychoanalysis* (pp. 478–498). London: Tavistock.

Klein, M. (1946). Notes on some schizoid mechanisms. *International Journal of Psychoanalysis, 27*: 99–110. Republished in M. Klein, P. Heimann, S. Isaacs & J. Riviere, *Developments in Psycho-Analysis* (pp. 292-320). London: Hogarth, 1952; and in *The Writings of Melanie Klein, Volume 3*: (pp. 1–24). London: Hogarth.

Klein, S. (1980). Autistic phenomena in neurotic patients. *International Journal of Psychoanalysis, 61*: 395–402.

Koenigsburg, R. A. (2009). *Nations Have the Right to Kill.* New York: Library of Social Science.

Kovel, J. (1983). *Against the State of Nuclear War.* London: Pan.

Kreeger, L. (Ed.) (1975). *The Large Group.* London: Constable.

Le Bon, G. (1895). *Psychologie des foules.* Paris: Alcan. English translation: *The Crowd: A Study of the Popular Mind.* New Brunswick: Transaction, 1995.

Menzies, I. (1960). A case-study in the functioning of social systems as a defence against anxiety: A report on a study of the nursing service of a general hospital. *Human Relations, 13*(2): 95–121.

Nathan, O, & Norden, H. (Eds.) (1960). The Einstein–Freud correspondence. In: *Einstein on Peace* (pp. 186–203). New York: Schocken Books.

Richards, B. (Ed.) (1989). *Crises of the Self: Further Essays on Psychoanalysis and Politics.* London: Free Association.

Rosenfeld, H. (1965). *Psychotic States.* London: Hogarth.

Roth, M, & Bluglass, R. (Eds.) (1985). *Psychiatry, Human Rights and the Law.* Cambridge: Cambridge University Press.

Scheer, R. (1982). *With Enough Shovels: Reagan, Bush and Nuclear War.* New York: Random House.

Strachey, A. (1957). *The Unconscious Motives of War: a Psycho-Analytical Contribution.* London, Allen & Unwin.

Thompson, E. P. (1980). *Protest and Survive.* London: Campaign for Nuclear Disarmament.

Discussion of Part II

GC: In your 1983 piece (Chapter 1), you wrote "projective identification is the primitive forerunner of all social relations". In the papers collected in this part, you show how multiple projective identifications by individuals create dynamic unconscious matrices in groups and, by extension, to whole societies. The multiplication of unconscious projective identifications and their interactions generate complex figures that may be difficult to make sense of: figures representing unconscious group dynamics, whose consequences at the level of collective action (or inaction) are just as important as they are difficult to study. A theory of force-fields can begin to illustrate the systemic entanglements in mechanical systems, but things become exceedingly complex when consciousness and the unconscious are also factored in, in human groups. In these papers, you show some of these complexities (for instance, how system-wide policy changes are spearheaded by what may seem a trivial incident—one person finding her office occupied) and propose (following Klein, Bion, Jaques, and Menzies Lyth) a theory of groups that dynamically aggregates one-to-one projective identifications. How do you see, through your experiences in groups, therapeutic communities and institutions as well as your research, group dynamics contributing to macro social dynamics and structures?

RDH: It has been my view for a long time that one cannot simply transfer an understanding of individual dynamics to social phenomena, attitudes, and politics. The interpersonal interactions of minds creates a new level of phenomena and of experience. That interpersonal level depends on a direct transfer of experience. We could call it an "evocation", which is different from communicating, the latter being a representation in a cognitive mode. As you may know, I accept Bion's crucial conclusion that he expressed in his late book in 1970:

> The point that demonstrates the divergence most clearly is that the physician is dependent on realization of sensuous experience in contrast with the psycho-analyst whose dependence is on experience that is not sensuous. The physician can see and touch and smell. The realizations with which a psycho-analyst deals cannot be seen or touched; anxiety has no shape or colour, smell or sound. For convenience, I propose to use the term "intuit" as a parallel in the psychoanalyst's domain to the physician's use of "see", "touch", "smell", and "hear". (Bion, 1970, p. 226)

This is really only a restatement of Freud's (1912e) puzzling over unconscious-to-unconscious communication, and Le Bon's (1895) idea of "infection" of states of mind in a group, and especially in an unstructured crowd or mass of people.

Communication, "infection", and projective identification

GC: The communication of minds beyond the manifest content of verbal language is central to these papers and a key contribution of psychoanalysis. Ideas around unconscious communication (the transfer of information, emotions, states of mind) have been explored under the rubric of contagion, infection, evocation, and projective identification (Freud himself and later Hanna Segal mused with the possibility of telepathy too). In a paper that is not collected here ("Communication flow in the matrix") you illustrate the passing of emotions in groups with the game of "tag" played by children all over the world (I indeed used to like it very much, we used to call it "muffa" or "fulmine"). Can you say how these terms or the ideas they carry differ from each other and how the concept of projective identification differs from these? You discuss its centrality in human dynamics throughout your work and in these papers you show how projective identification allows the distribution of emotions and states of mind between individuals in groups and networks. Do you think that your findings (and those of other psychoanalysts) warrant extension to a more generalised theory of human communication? Contemporary behavioural psychology (as we briefly touched on in our previous conversation) admits the importance of internal stimuli in thinking and communication (bodily, like hunger, and emotional like anger, sadness, etc.); wouldn't a consideration of projective identification better explain certain aspects of interpersonal communication and decision-making in affective networks that are not considered by cognitive psychology and by extension by mainstream social and political sciences? I ask this with in mind the strikingly vivid example of the small therapeutic group in "Social possession of identity" (Chapter 4); it seems important to be aware of these processes as we enter any kind of interaction. The disavowal of emotional dynamics deprives individuals and groups of their life and creativity and sometimes, as it was about to happen in your small group example, violence may erupt. In that group, violence was about to erupt as the end result of a chain of projective identifications that transferred blame rather than internalise feelings of disappointment in the therapist but, even more perhaps, of sadness for the loss of the group as it was now that a new member was perhaps imagined as killing the present familiar identity of the group.

RDH: This transfer of some element of one mind into another mind is a key idea in these papers. It is more than merely Freud's conception of the group ideal (Freud, 1921e), as it becomes a part of the experience in a group and not merely a set of aims and goals. It was evident in the example of a flow of some mental "substance" through the network of relations between people (Chapters 3 and 4). In that instance, what flowed between the individuals was converted by each person depending on their personalities, their roles, and the immediate circumstances at the moment of flow. Depending on these socially contextual factors the individual personalities establish intentions together as well as jointly arranged relations with other groups and interruptions and obstructions to the activities. These various emotive influences drive cognitive activity to plan or provide defensive rationalisations for the group behaviour. The notion of projective identification has been a very helpful model for this interactive flow at the individual level.

I agree it is a profoundly important general characteristic of all communication. There are, as suggested in Part I, various forms of projective identification including the semi-conscious process of empathy, and we have seen that it is implicated in both social and individualistic causes. It also indicates the way group membership can lead to experience alienation from oneself. I indicated through the quote from Bion above, the quality of intuition and a direct evocation of a feeling as opposed to a naming of it. It may be an extension of the psychologists' conception of nonverbal communication, but it is not a sign language, it has a direct impact, like a snarl, baring the teeth to instil fear. Moreover, it also includes *unconscious* experiences bypassing conscious meaning.

However, projective identification in itself is not enough of an explanation. As I have just indicated, the individual's role in the network, the immediate stresses and social pressures, as well as the reasonably agreed task of the group are joint or social factors operating as well as the specific personality characteristics of the individuals. In other words, projective identification operates in the context of many varied social factors, transient or permanent. My observations were made in the openness of a therapeutic community and therapy groups, but something similar must surely apply in the more emotionally closed systems of larger organisations and institutions. It is through a continuing back and forth re-iteration of these influences—personalities and social intentions—that a culture emerges in the group.

GC: In these papers you show how affective networks, embedded in and extending across, organisations and institutions, give social groupings the ability to enforce the exploitation of individuals' emotions and parts of their personality by commodifying them. Something quite striking is that social media seems to be able to commodify, capitalise, and exploit individual emotions, ambitions, expectations while individuals produce content for free that are monetised by corporations the size of which is mind-boggling.

RDH: Yes, it may have implications for the depersonalising that goes on with the communications on social media. And I like your hypothesis that its commodification (and depersonalisation), implicit in the affective journey through a smartphone app, may be associated with the exchange and accumulation of the abstract value that money represents. Money is no longer a measure of the relative value of objects that have important qualitative functions; instead it has become a quantitative system of abstract value, without personal relevance. It is a bit complex, and I think it may require much more extended discussion elsewhere (see Hinshelwood, 2024).

For a greater appreciation of these cultural (and often hidden) aspects of organisations, I would say I lean heavily on the group relations approach of the Tavistock Institute from its inception in 1948, and the developing idea of the system-psychodynamic concept that embraces field theory, systems theory, and unconscious psychodynamics (for instance, Long, 2013; Armstrong & Rustin, 2014).

GC: In Chapter 3, you report the case of a patient full of demons (an experience often resonating in common parlance when referring to this or that person's internal demons). You show how the mind takes in external objects and relations to make them parts of itself. The predominance of feelings of hate or love changes the nature of the object introjected and the identity of the person. You write "as the object had been internalised in hatred, she related to herself internally in a hostile way, so that the internal world was dominated by hostility". You add that such powerful, "odd", phantasies tend to belong to children and very disturbed individuals, but also that "our ordinary identities are just as fragile and fluid and depend on similar beliefs—unconscious beliefs—about what is inside us, very concretely". The circulation of feelings and representations in groups, and their potential creativity, relies on this fluidity but so does the exacerbation of hostility and destruction. I find this illustration striking and convincing. You later show, through more group experiences and individual clinical cases, other aspects of the fluidity of identity and we'll return to that later, but now I would like to ask you a more general question. How much can we rely (and what is the best way to do this) on the clinical experience in the consulting room (in both individual psychoanalysis and group settings) to understand group dynamics in society at large and vice versa?

RDH: A good question!—but it is important that the analyst is not a remote professional object, but remains a sentient being with a mind much as the analysand's. It is a group of two, and the exchanges go on just the same. In my view, the exchanges have to be seen as interpersonal—between persons. I tend to resist the description of a group as if it were the "group" that operates its own psychodynamics or has its own unconscious. It is the personal exchanges that in psychoanalysis have come to be called transference and countertransference and that come together and aggregate as the group dynamics. Those abstract terms, transference and countertransference, characterise the exchange of experiences between the two in a psychoanalysis, and between the many in groups and society. In Bion's description of containing, he exploited the fact that these exchanges go on in a very alive way. He described how a mother successfully comforting her baby would have "taken into her, and thus experienced" (Bion, 1959, p. 313) the babies own distress. She has to *take it into her*. That exchange is the nature of our work.

Regarding the quality of projective identification, I think it must be the communicative kind because the massive or evacuative kind based on fragmenting splits will leave the group incapacitated. In the group example, the group members did nearly evacuate the distress by sending Mr C as far as the door out of the room. The first paper considers Freud's (1925h) analogy of bodily spitting or swallowing of mental experiences. It seems to parallel closely the work of Abraham (1924) on introjection and projection so that one wonders how much Abraham had been a (temporary) influence on Freud at that moment.

There is a constant interchange every day as we have moments with this person or that person. Despite a consistency in the sense of self, there is a pervading "change of weather", as it were, that we live through and which challenges to a greater or lesser degree a stable sense of self. These challenges from outside may not always be a challenge, of course, and in the process of development one seeks a partner who will help to conform and stabilise one's own self. What this points to is a focus on a personal sense of identity, as experienced from inside. However, that "inside-ness" includes the beginnings of commonality with other(s).

That paper on identity (Chapter 4) addresses the way in which individuals form their identity in collaboration through the constant exchange of projections (of experiences and defence). It contrasts with the hypothesis that people come together through having a common anxiety, which can be managed in common with socially organised common defences. This is explored in Chapter 5 in terms of the highly emotional states of an army and a nation at war with a pervasive rage and fear common to all. Such social defence systems were described by Jaques (1955) and Menzies Lyth (Menzies, 1960). Chapter 5 argued that there are two main anxieties—about personal survival and about guilt.

Thus, individuals cohere by sharing one or other of these basic anxieties and group attitudes and practices to evade the conscious experience of the anxiety. In war, an enemy is identified as guilty of something bad—even evil, as President Bush described the attack on New York on September 11, 2001. Retaliatory killing has an effect unconsciously to provoke more guilt and then that has to be assigned to others. We can add two that the more recent attempt, in 2023, of the Israeli army to exterminate the "evil" of Hamas.

There are two alternatives to these coordinated emotional attitudes—either the communicative flow in the affective network or a common anxiety affecting everyone in the social context (plus socially organised defences). They are not necessarily exclusive and may combine in a multi-factor system. However, they do imply a fluidity of personal identity and maybe therefore restrict the meaning of the word, "individual", even though our experience of having an identity may feel very stable and consistent.

GC: As you show, in the relation between the individual and the collective, social environment, you sketch a theory of organisations that resonates with internal states of mind. You write of totalitarianism, of football and hooligans' states of mind, of imperial and of protestant configurations and the list could continue. Equally, psychoanalysts (starting with Freud himself) have used political and group imagery to discuss psychic configurations. Rosenfeld for instance described the mafia-like gang deadening the internal world of certain individuals. Can you say more about these correspondences between internal and group organisation in relation to their development and possible "treatment"?

RDH: I do think there is what could be called a correspondence between internal and group. But I do dislike talking of a group having an "unconscious". Really it is individuals only that have an unconscious, though they may pool their unconscious minds in the fluid way I think I have observed. A "group unconscious" is a shorthand for talking of the collectivisation in these networks and sequences of fluidity. We really should not fudge the collectivisation and gloss over its mysteries. So, I would maintain the differences between individual and social worlds. There may be analogies between them, but analogies are not equations. The internal mafia gang is an analogy and develops inside someone's personality from very different reasons from the actual mafia gang in Southern Italy. We need a language that translates from one world to the other and does not equate them. I am postulating that the language that uses "projective identification", "affect flow", "fluidity of the personality/ego", and so on might help.

Community and "democracy"

GC: What you write on the difficulty to relate individual behaviour with group processes and with even larger societal dynamics is fascinating. This research is particularly interesting as it follows on from, and develops, the concerns of the two papers in Part I. What I find striking is the apparent contrast between, on the one hand, your detailed account of some of the phenomena of group formation and the influence of groups on individual identity and behaviour and, on the other, your statement that "psychoanalysis cannot explain social phenomena directly". You seem to negate the possibility of psychoanalytical insight into social phenomena. However, the aspect of this statement that may be more revealing is the term "directly". Psychoanalysis as the study of unconscious dynamics works, necessarily indirectly. It can apprehend the conflicts storming in the psyche's depth by observing their effects on human behaviour. I would like you to say something more about this.

RDH: Yes, you are right, I want to be careful about saying that psychoanalysts can simply understand the unconscious effects in society and politics. We have a special instrument for understanding the unconscious, that is the psychoanalytic setting. That cannot be used for understanding society. However, we are not completely defeated by the unconscious *outside* that setting. And Freud wrote his book on *The Psychopathology of Everyday Life*. I am sure it is not as reliable as an investigation within the psychoanalytic setting. However, something is possible, just as Freud could begin an understanding of his own dreams without the benefit of an analytic setting. There is a necessary reliance on the logic of inference. And we do not have the benefit of mathematics, which physicists do when making inferences about our material universe. Nevertheless, inference can be an effective tool in psychoanalysis, just as in the material sciences. We do have a responding analysand to confirm or disconfirm our inferences.

But, I also had in mind the fact that truly social phenomena do exist that cannot be reduced to the psychology of the unconscious—or of the conscious. Economics is an example. The pursuit of individual ends financially leads to an overall set of trends not intended by any one individual; conceived by Adam Smith as the notion of the invisible hand: "[H]e intends only his own gain, and he is in this, as in many other cases, led by an invisible hand to promote an end which was no part of his intention" (Smith, 1776 [2007, p. 349]). The individual's economic gain, he suggested, is an unwitting gain to the whole economy. As Smith says, there are many other cases apart from the financial/economic one, and the assumptive, intentional culture is another. For instance, the unconscious or hardly conscious circulation of affects does not intend the effects it has. There is a sphere of social phenomena (such as economics, but many other disciplines) which is independent of the intentionality of our individual desires or the defences against the anxieties they cause.

It is important that psychoanalysis does not intrude on these more social phenomena and attempts to be a "theory of everything" in the humanities. As in a psychoanalytic treatment, we restrict ourselves to the fantastical distortions of the transference (and the countertransference), so in considering social groups we should restrict ourselves to the distortions which do not prove amenable to conscious solutions in political and other settings. Specifically, in the politics of a group, some problems remain resistant to conscious strategies. We might take the troubling occurrence of populism which keeps cropping up in the politics of many "democracies". The difficulty of understanding the eruption of this phenomenon and restoring democracy to rationality points directly, it seems to me, to the occurrence of some collective dynamics of the *unconscious* disturbing large numbers of people in unison in many nations without there being effective conscious insight or intention.

Dimensions of group dynamics

GC: I found it interesting to consider, in relation to the first two papers in this part, the dynamics that lead a group to form out of an anonymous crowd. It is the effect of the size of the group on the individual. You write that, "the size of the group impacts on the intensity of these paranoid reactions to aggression and guilt". In a way, it seems as though the effect of groups on individuals depends on their anonymity vs institutionalisation and on the size from small to big. Are these the axes mapping the force/power of influence of groups on individuals? Is there a force/power going in the opposite direction, from the individual/s to the group (both in its transformation from anonymous crowd into a group and with respect to the group's increased institutionalisation)? Otherwise put, what is the weight of individuals in primary and secondary groups (according to Freud) and in small, medium, large, or very large groups? My question wishes to better understand whether you think that as degrees of magnitude shift, so do dynamics and ways to make sense of them.

RDH: Yes, it is an important issue when considering how a group comes to operate as a coherent entity. These issues were considered by Freud (1921c), but also Wilfred Bion (1948) and Elliott Jaques (1955), which I can briefly run through. First, Freud understood that identifying with a group is closely connected with a person's own identity. He described how a person can be absorbed into another person, and he exemplified with the hypnotic trance and the way the subject gives over his autonomy to the hypnotist; and Freud associated the hypnotic trance with falling in love and the enormous enhancement of the loved one as the lover shrinks in his own estimation. In a group, people do something similar. They invest much of themselves in the group's ideal, its task. In the army they may sacrifice themselves entirely.

And the larger the group the smaller the individual. As Turquet (1975) described it, this is a "threat to identity". Only identifying with the group allows the individual to feel large enough in himself to contribute to the group. But he thereby tends to lose his own sense of self. More than this, the anonymity of most of the group in those larger than twenty or thirty, reduces many others to impersonal entities. In those larger groups or crowds, it becomes impossible to know everyone personally, or to be known personally by everyone. There is a pressure towards a depersonalisation. One can only be known by rather disembodied vocal announcements that are given a voice conforming to the unconscious demands of the others.

Bion's (1962) brief reference to Aristotle saying man is a political animal means he has to manage his affairs amongst those of other persons. The word "political" comes from the ancient Greek word for a city, or more precisely for the city walls. It makes me consider that the boundary around the group is also a crucial element. So, it may be that we should consider boundary issues. This may gain in importance as the group increases in size, and if the level of anxiety is high. The process of transmission between individuals or parts of their egos (as Freud described in hypnosis and falling in love) must have a considerable impact on the sense of a boundary to oneself.

Unstructured groups (or primary groups) without consciously assigned roles or purpose can easily form a mob in which individuals rush with each other towards very destructive disorganised behaviour and panic. There may be a wild kind of excitement and sense of freedom as if there are no longer moral or other restraints or limits. The boundary gets lost more or less completely for the moment. As the individual's identity becomes closer to the group identity, the sense of a bounded self depends to an increasing extent on the boundary of the group. This disorganised state can be overcome by membership being restricted to persons adopting the task of the group, such as a church or a football team or a business committee. There is also a coherence if the group is based on intimacy, such as family or other intimate emotional relationships.

The group dimensions of boundary, coherence, anonymity, size do not apply to individuals. If they are important (I agree that they are) they point to the fact that a group psychology cannot be collapsed into the psychology of the individual. Those dimensions are the dimensions of institutionalisation which may take the person away from the individual.

GC: Allow me to interrupt you here for a moment. What you just said is very important and I would like you to say a bit more about how institutionalisation in groups comes about as a result of hidden anxieties and what that says about different processes of institutionalisation and their outcomes. With reference to social movements such as the peace movement (CND) which you supported for a time, and others that I have worked with, institutionalisation is often regarded as the opposite of spontaneity and as the process that kills the group's creativity and eventually leads to its demise. What are your thoughts on these matters?

RDH: An institutionalised group distributes a set of fixed uncreative performances of roles defined consciously and prosaically as job specifications and matching skill requirements. But there are also unconscious influences and distortions according to the anxieties and conflicts that arise from doing the task or upholding the ideal, together with the existential anxieties about one's personality as the group becomes bigger. An institution usually has a specific task and exists for the task rather than for the persons. With effective leadership, the different people have different skills and characteristics in a division of labour to meet the task. This can be consciously ordered. I think of a team of builders, bricklayers, carpenters, electricians, and so on. This is a consciously creative form of instituting a distribution of skills around the group. But also the characteristics of unconscious dynamics, insofar as the anxieties are shared in common, create a rigid system of unhelpful identities (such as the old psychiatric institutions). This institutionalisation comes, I suggest, like rigid ideologies, from the unconscious pressure to deal with hidden anxieties—or more precisely to deal with anxieties by keeping them hidden. In the old mental health institutions, what had to remain hidden was the inherent fear of insanity. Or in the stress of general nursing the anxiety of caring for deathly conditions, as Menzies Lyth (Menzies, 1960) researched.

GC: With reference again to social movements of one kind or another, I wonder whether you have reflected on some of the internal dynamics of the psychoanalytic movement in over a century of existence in light of your study of groups and institutions. I am particularly interested in the interaction between theoretical and political controversies and some of the conflicts and mediations that we have observed both in the UK and in the global IPA. One further and closely related question: are psychoanalysts, in your opinion, making the best use of group theories to negotiate their institutional (unconscious) dynamics and development?

RDH: Oh, yes, this is a painful one, isn't it? Psychoanalytic institutions are not immune from interference by anxiety-driven ideologies (I mention them briefly in our discussion of Part I papers. It is even true of group therapy organisations who really should know better, shouldn't they? I did once consider the possible group dynamics, based on hidden anxieties, between the early groups in Vienna and Zurich (Hinshelwood, 2018). It is heartening to me that at the time of writing, the International Psychoanalytical Association is considering adding a fourth part to the standard three-part Eitingon requirements for psychoanalytic training—the fourth part being an experiential group to explore unconscious *group* dynamics. But it should be an important question to consider why psychoanalysts so readily get into quarrelsome controversies with each other. It so often seems a professional disagreement and yet there is no proper engagement in debate. Usually, it is merely a repeated statement of one-sided opinions. It was aptly expressed thus:

> Controversy is the growing-point from which development springs but it must be a genuine confrontation and not an impotent beating of the air by opponents whose differences of view never meet. (Bion, 1970, p. 211)

If people are unwilling to meet each other in debate, then there are unconscious forces pushing them apart; and that implies anxieties not faced and probably not tolerable. I would suggest there are powerful emotional problems in practising as psychoanalysts. It is a very difficult form of practice, exploring areas in patients (and often in themselves) concealed in the unconscious. Certainty in our profession is very difficult to achieve. Uncertainty in the face of the desperation of patients coming for help is a painful conflict. I suspect that one defence is to cling to one's set of theories as more like an unquestionable ideology to protect against uncertainty. Interpretations are made according to our theories first of all, and only secondly measured against the patient's confirming or disconfirming responses. There are other anxieties too, not least the fear of patient's whose unconscious mind is set violently against help and intrusion. And so on.

It is really important that analysts should consider the unconscious anxiety–defence structures within the group of two. And a training with an element of a group relations approach would be one step towards that kind of reflection.

GC: Your analysis of some of the predicaments of anti-war protest movements resonates very closely with my interests and experiences. It would be particularly interesting for me to hear your thoughts on the vicissitudes of the anti-war movement around the invasion of Iraq, the environmental movements and its recent incarnations in Extinction Rebellion and Fridays For Future, and the #MeToo and #BlackLivesMatter movements.

RDH: Again, I am not sure I have very much to say on this. But these are important protest actions. My main concern is the tendency, it seems to me, to simplify the issues. There has been a longstanding move within medicine to attempt to treat causes rather than symptoms. With single issue politics my interest would be to pick out whether it is a symptom of some unconscious anxiety that is an underlying cause, or if it is a symptomatic expression of a cause yet to be revealed. This is not a popular point of view. I could argue that current race relations, in the West at least, are strongly influenced by the systematic trading of slaves in the past. The value of a human being as a commodity valued in terms of money is an utterly depersonalising form of commodification. That process was then simply transferred to the employment of industrial labour. Though there are, of course, differences, the depersonalisation seems to me to be consistent. Indeed, we use the term "wage-slaves". The evaluating of human worth in terms of money could therefore be a much more basic "cause" than simply a conscious prejudice to be removed by condemning it. Indeed, that very cause might be implicated in a number of other political issues. It is an underlying process of depersonalisation that is at the route of industrial relations, gender prejudices, religious intolerance, and so on. Such a hypothesis might need some formal research. But until that can be undertaken, I would feel more convinced than simply an array of separate single-issue politics which seem more like symptoms. Underlying the depersonalisation of other humans, there are some specific anxieties, not least the need to abolish guilt by making certain others not worthy of consideration. In fact, this question is dealt with in more detail elsewhere (Hinshelwood, 2024).

The new forms of annihilation

GC: Can you say something about whether, and how, the study of groups you conducted, and more broadly the psychoanalytic approach to large groups, can help elucidate societal dynamics, even global dynamics, leading to geopolitical confrontations and war? Can such escalations be observed and countered before they explode? In other words, with *Why War?* in mind, what are your thoughts on the matters discussed almost a century ago by Einstein and Freud?

RDH: I am not sure that the letters between Einstein and Freud are particularly helpful. Einstein did not understand the unconscious Freud discovered, and proclaimed politics to be the responsibility of the rational even if he consigned them to a restricted class. Freud was sceptical and saw irrationality in everyone. So far as I could see, their points of view never met. However, I do commend the League of Nations making an attempt to mobilise the best brains to stop wars. I would prefer it if our current United Nations were to intervene more creatively. If ever I were asked (!), I would write a letter stating that the UN should ban all private armies of any nation on earth. All militaries should be ceded to the UN itself and under its sole command, and only used for rogue states or civil wars within states. All armaments should be similarly under UN control and banned from unnecessary production. This is, of course, a *conscious* reality-based solution to a problem, and it won't happen. It would create a powerful *unconscious* threat and existential anxiety of the paranoid–schizoid kind that would beset all of us and our most insecure leaders.

GC: In the paper "Psychological defences and nuclear war", you write that war is both a consequence and a cause of guilt. Earlier you illustrated this with reference to 9/11. There is perhaps something particularly disturbing about the connection between the thought of war today and nuclear annihilation, as you discuss in your paper. It has fallen from reality for a time, but it has instead returned forcefully recently after the Russian invasion of Ukraine.

RDH: Well, nuclear war is something altogether different. It threatens to destroy everyone. Even the memory of everyone. But you are right, I do think there is a self-sustaining cycle of guilt in the aggression of war, ordinary war. That guilt at killing gives rise to a fear of a retaliatory threat and the need then for defensive forces to protect us, often in a pre-emptive attacking mode. This further aggression leads to a righteous belligerence as aggression becomes a defence against the guilt of military aggression. And the more powerful the army, the more potential unconscious guilt and so the more entrenched the unconscious cycle becomes. This may be one reason (an unconscious one) that made the British Empire convert from a trading empire to a military one—sometime in the mid-nineteenth century. And maybe a similar conversion of the preceding Spanish Empire. It looks a very convincing (to me) change that has occurred in the US Empire around the middle of the twentieth century. There may be a retreat from the depressive guilt of the exploitation of poorer nations through trade towards a paranoid–schizoid fear of annihilation.

However, nuclear war is different. It is not just soldiers on active service, today the back-home population is no longer secure—it has been forced into the front line. Everyone is in the front line of potential extermination. Good sense and vulnerability are essential attributes for political thinking on this. And, so far, that has operated in the years since the atomic bombs in 1945. However, more recently, as international competition—in trade, first, and then military capability—has increased, and the international cooperative spirit of collaboration (in the form of the UN or the EU) has dwindled, the risks to the entire human species has escalated. Indeed, more than this, the emphasis on trading the earth's resources has brought into play a second string to this annihilation theme. The environmental crisis of the progressively disrupted climate and weather conditions, plus a humankind-promoted mass extinction of other biological species and their ecological habitats, threatens human annihilation as well. The latter is not so vivid a danger as the imagining of an insane national leader with a finger on the nuclear button. So, the swaggering omnipotent defence against the terror of annihilation can take the form of an omnipotent competition in trading. That trade has then been supercharged by a revision in the way we see the value of money itself; in neoliberalism, money is not just the oil that facilitates trading, money is itself traded. This has somehow disarmed the reality of the environmental peril so that guilt and survival anxieties are hidden only to provoke another turn of the cycle of guilt and denial—ultimately another possible self-sustaining cycle. Well, you have got me onto some of my own political wonderings and imaginings, which is not the purpose here. I am intending to put forward the more psychoanalytic hypothesis that the unconscious dynamics of terror interfere with the best conscious reasoning (as exemplified in my rant just now).

GC: This is a rousing call and one that we had better heed, not only for civic engagement and political commitment but, in so doing, to look beyond symptoms and address our action to the underlying circumstances. You also show us that when we are unable to do this, to take in the broader picture and we let ourselves be fully taken by the symptoms, we may be doing this to protect ourselves from feelings that we are unaware of and that we unconsciously fear we might not be able to bear and that therefore we fear might make us lose our mind. However, you also show the risk of this protective behaviour. You tell us that if we only aim to protect ourselves from our most disturbing anxieties, we end up preventing ourselves from living fulfilling lives together on this planet, but we might also prevent this possibility for future generations too. The link between individual decisions and social phenomena (present and future) is discussed in the papers collected in the next part from the perspective of the individual who struggles with, and often is unable to resist, the encroachment of collective ideologies and other expressions of anti-thinking.

References

Abraham, K. (1924). Short study of the development of the libido. In: *Selected Papers on Psychoanalysis* (pp. 418–501). 1927. London: Hogarth.

Armstrong, D., & Rustin, M. (2014). *Social Defences Against Anxiety: Explorations in a Paradigm*. London: Karnac.

Bion, W. R. (1948). Experiences in groups: I. *Human Relations, 1*: 314–320. Republished in W. R. Bion, *Experiences in Groups and Other Papers* (pp. 29–40). London: Tavistock, 1961. Republished in *The Complete Works of W. R. Bion, Volume IV* (pp. 121–130). London: Karnac, 2014.

Bion, W. R. (1962). *Learning from Experience*. London: Tavistock.

Bion, W. R. (1959). Attacks on linking. *International Journal of Psychoanalysis, 40:* 308–315. Reprinted in W. R. Bion, *Second Thoughts* (pp. 138–152). London: Heinemann, 1967. In: *The Complete Works of W. R. Bion, Volume IV* (pp. 247–265). London: Karnac, 2014.

Bion, W. R. (1961). *Experiences in Groups and Other Papers*. London: Tavistock. Republished in *The Complete Works of W. R. Bion, Volume IV* (pp. 158–169). London: Karnac, 2014.

Bion, W. R. (1970). *Attention and Interpretation*. London: Tavistock. In *The Complete Works of W. R. Bion, Volume VI* (pp. 211–347). London: Karnac, 2014

Freud, S. (1912e). Recommendations to physicians practising psycho-analysis. *S. E., 12*: 109–120. London: Hogarth.

Freud, S. (1925h). Negation. *S. E., 19*: 233–240. London: Hogarth.

Freud, S. (1921c). Group psychology and the analysis of the ego. *S. E., 18*. London: Hogarth.

Hinshelwood, R. D. (2018). Symbolic equation and symbolic representation: An appraisal of the Hanna Segal's work. *British Journal of Psychotherapy, 34*: 342–357.

Hinshelwood, R. D. (2024). *Unconscious Politics*. London: Karnac.

Jaques, E. (1955). Social systems as a defence against persecutory and depressive anxiety. In: M. Klein, P. Heimann & R. Money-Kyrle (Eds.), *New Directions in Psychoanalysis* (pp. 478–498. London: Tavistock.

Le Bon, G. (1895). *Psychologie des foules*. Paris: Alcan. English translation: *The Crowd: A Study of the Popular Mind.* New Brunswick: Transaction, 1995.

Long, S. (Ed.) (2013). *Socioanalytic Methods: Discovering the Hidden in Organisations and Social Systems*. London: Karnac.

Menzies, I. (1960). A case-study in the functioning of social systems as a defence against anxiety: A report on a study of the nursing service of a general hospital. *Human Relations, 13*(2): 95–121.

Smith, A. (1776). A*n Enquiry into the Nature and Causes of the Wealth of Nations.* Oxford: Oxford University Press, 2007.

Turquet, P. (1975). *Threats to Identity in the Large Group.* In: L. Kreeger (Ed.), *The Large Group* (pp. 87–144). London: Constable, 1975.

Part III

The sociopolitical penetrated by the mental

In the previous part, we considered some reflections on the kind of individual psychological processes that become collectivised in groups and nations. In Part III, the attempt will be to understand some of the processes by which the collectivisation may occur. Whilst Part II has emphasised the importance of emotions that can infect individual minds, we start here (Chapter 6) with the imposition of ideas by a group ideology. Ideas can be facilitative or obstructive, and the determinants of the category an idea belongs to may only be fully discernible by understanding its unconscious effect as well as it conscious meaning.

Chapter 7 attempts to explore some of this collectivised process in terms of the need to avoid intolerable experience, and how this works out as racism and its relative evaluations. And Chapter 8 highlights again the importance of representation in creating a world of cultural assumptions, based on symbols and their formation. Moreover, symbols organise and collectivise forethought, political loyalties but alternatively the avoidance of "experimental action". This last paper shows how the foundations of ideas are in processes of symbolisation and representation in the mind. But those of ideologies are in defensive or yet unformed processes producing what here is referred to as "symbolic equations", following Hanna Segal and Melanie Klein's seminal formulations on symbol-formation.

CHAPTER 6

Tracking down ideology

Introduction

In the 2000s it was possible to look back on the rabid neoliberalism of the 1980s with some degree of reflective criticism. The ideology that expressed the view "there is no such thing as society" led government in the UK (and the USA) to attend only to economics and the trickle-down theory. This prompts us to take an interest in the nature of ideology itself. This was provoked by the destruction of the World Trade Center Towers at the beginning of the new millennium. They were an emblem of the USA trading empire, and of the emergent economic ideology. Their destruction in 2001 was indicative of the new cold war between the USA and the Middle East, and letter the resumption of the cold war with Russia. This paper, and the next (Chapter 7) provoked my psychoanalytic contribution to understanding ideology. The rigidity and refusal of debate that marks an ideology is shown to have remarkable resemblance to the failure of proper representations with a relapse into identifying an idea and an ideal akin to symbolic equation as described by Segal (1950, 1957) and in Chapter 8.

PAPER 6

Ideology and identity: A psychoanalytic investigation of a social phenomenon*

This paper uses psychoanalytic thinking to understand the way individuals come to be in a social group that develops an ideology. Le Bon was one of the earliest to consider destructive groups and the distortion of individuality within crowds and mobs, and his work influenced Freud's views on the group ideal. Destructive groups are contrasted with constructive ones that can achieve creative and work-oriented functioning. Destructive groups have various characteristics, one of which is the place that ideas have in the group and in the minds of the members. When ideas become overvalued and thus an ideology, the relation between the individual and the ideas changes. On one hand, in ordinary constructive work and groups, the idea is an abstract notion useable in aspirations and achievements. On the other hand, in ideological and destructive groups, the individual is equated with the idea, which becomes an end in itself. This movement involves the pressure of social forces upon forms of

* Hinshelwood, R. D. (2009). Ideology and identity: A psychoanalytic investigation of a social phenomenon. *Psychoanalysis, Culture and Society, 14*: 131–148.
This paper was published (2007) in an earlier and rather different version in French, as "Idéologie et identité: une étude psychanalytique d'un phénomène social", in the *Revue Française de Psychanalyse, 71*: 1027–1045.

individual distress that affects their sense of themselves. It is possible to understand the excitement in primitive destructive groups, their unreality and the erosion of individuality as coming from the equation of self with the ideal.

Introduction

The evidence of the twentieth century is that ideology plays a fundamental role in the channelling of the destructive power of mankind. The millions upon millions of lives sacrificed in the course of recent history for the sake of a belief in an idea, whether the idea is Christian, Muslim, socialist, fascist, and so on, suggests mankind would indeed be better off without ideas at all (see also Hinshelwood, 1997). How did ideas get human civilisation into such a state?

A specific phenomenon of groups is that the higher functions of the individual seem the most vulnerable to being lost or perverted. The result is that each of us is at the mercy of emotional pressures (Hinshelwood, 2023), and unrealistic and insightless modes of behaving result. Le Bon (1895) gave the formative account of how the crowd brings out the worst in people, and the person in a group is no longer properly himself.[1] Gangs of yobs and hooligans, lynch mobs, and so on exemplify how the individual is reduced to behaviour, and an identity, much less sophisticated than that of which he is potentially capable as an individual. This puzzled and troubled many early social psychologists including Freud (1921c), who was impressed with Le Bon, as were McDougall (1920), Trotter (1916), and politicians from the nineteenth century onwards.

However, groups are not always destructive. Even in groups, individuals do sometimes give their best. The nature of our species is to be the “Homo” with “sapiens”, that is, with wisdom. And ideas shared in a group can be highly creative. Many of the greatest achievements of mankind arise from group activity—a research team, a football side,

[1] Ever since the revolutionary experiments following the American and French revolutions in the eighteenth century sent shock waves through the ruling elite in the rest of Europe, there has been a preoccupation with how to manage society in a rational way. Conservative elements have worried about crowd behaviour, and especially how to control it and prevent revolutions (see Nye, 1975; Moscovici, 1985).

a group of painters such as the Cubists, relaxed after-dinner wit, and so on. Constructive groups bring out the best and most enduring results. It appears that the mix of ideas and group life can be as explosive as gunpowder or as creative as genius (Hinshelwood, 1998). The greatest and the worst emerge from groups.[2] There is more here than can be left to the intuition of politicians.

The duality of groups

The evident divergence in the characteristics of constructive and destructive groups correlates with certain characteristic features in the psychology of individuals in the different groups. Managing this duality of groups appears to be vital to the very survival of mankind. But to deal with the variable mix of ideas and groups, we first need to understand them. Can psychoanalysis, as an individual psychology, say anything relevant about this social phenomenon?[3] Can it say how destructive groups differ from constructive ones? This paper will use psychoanalytic concepts to explore the fate of the individual in an ideological group.

The constructive group

A work group "is necessarily concerned with reality" (Bion, 1961, p. 127); it has met "for a specific task" (p. 98); and, "[i]n work-group activity time is intrinsic" (p. 172). Bion picked out these three functions: reality, task, and time. However, in addition, to achieving its purpose, there is some division of labour among the members of the group. This entails that the members retain some realistic individuality, and that they accept a role commensurate with their identity. Therefore, the work group has certain specific features:

---

[2] This distinction is vividly indicated in Bion's division between the work group and the "basic assumption" groups. Bion explicitly connected the "work group" with McDougall's (1920) "organised" group, which contrasts with psychologically primitive groups where quasi-instinctual processes dominate. Later, Bion (1952) explored the possibility of reinterpreting these instinctual group processes in terms of very early anxieties of the infant, which are stirred in the process of becoming a member of a group. Nitsun (1996) called the negative state, the "anti-group".

[3] Freud comes close to giving a priority to the social dimension: "individual psychology … is at the same time social psychology as well" (Freud, 1921c, p. 69).

- respect for reality
- an agreed task
- time
- individuality of the members.

The destructive group

In the contrasting destructive groups, time has no place; nor do development and learning take place; nor is there a place for the discovery of reality; nor allegiance to an explicit task. These groups appear to have no task, or an implicit, deviant anti-task, to be mindless and to tend towards amorality. In addition, individuality succumbs to a mass urge that spreads like a "contagion" to each member; the group therefore is characterised by being:

- disorganised
- thoughtless of consequences
- amoral
- spreading a contagion of emotion
- prey to a loss of individuality (homogenisation).

In addition, we will address the hypothesis that the destructive group is the home of an ideology. Ideas will then occupy different positions in the psychology of the individuals in the two different groups. In effect, ideas are used in constructive groups in the realistic service of the primary task, whereas in the destructive group, ideas become the primary task. Therefore, an ideology (as the primary task) has the function of promoting the devotion to, and survival of, the ideas held by the group. This paper is dedicated to exploring the possible nature of an ideology.

What is ideology?

There are various ways of understanding what an ideology is, and its role in the formation and the survival of a group. It is not perhaps contentious to say that a group of any kind embodies a set of shared ideas, assumptions, and attitudes.

Ideas as a marker of group boundaries

Indeed the ideas, attitudes, and beliefs of the group are formative of its membership and boundary. Kernberg takes a rather broad notion of ideology when he says:

> [Ideology] refers to a system of beliefs that a group, a mass, or a society share concerning the origin and functions of their common social life and the cultural and ethical demands and expectations they hold for society. (Kernberg, 1998, p. 277)

Kernberg claims that all systems of beliefs and ideas count as an ideology. However, any definition as broad as this can hardly be accurate, since shared ideas serve to define constructive groups as well as destructive ones. For instance, the members of a football team share the common idea that it is good to score goals and win a match. It defines who is in the group and who is outside the group.[4] However, the simple function of the idea as a marker of the group is quite different from the more distinctive function of an ideology (such as the Christian promotion of the idea that Jesus rose from the dead, or the Marxist–Leninist idea that a state-run economy is the route to Utopia).[5]

The boundary function is more than the cognitive and semantic functions of an idea; the idea plays a part in the intergroup dynamics between this group and others. Mannheim similarly described these markers as performing a specific function within the relationship of one group to another: "The term [ideology] denotes that we are sceptical of the ideas and representations advanced by our opponents" (Mannheim, 1936, p. 49). The central place of ideas in defining a group not only expresses the group's boundaries, but also a particular

[4] There is a coherent view that it is not ideas which determine the inclusion in, and boundaries of, a group, but that like many other primates and mammals, there is a primitive, and instinctual herd-like quality which brings people together, see, for instance, Trotter's (1916) influential *Instincts of the Herd in War and Peace*. Bion, in his earlier writing on groups (excluding his "Review" (1952)), followed this tradition. While I do not want to exclude this possibility or other reasons for association together, this paper is concerned with sophisticated groups, in working organisations and in political societies. Indeed, Bion's work on the innate valency to form groups still described the phenomenon as manifesting itself in shared ideas and assumptions—the basic assumption groups.

[5] I do not claim this as scholarly historiography, but merely illustrative of the kinds of dynamic processes that a psychoanalytic approach might expose.

emotional attitude to another group—scepticism. Implicitly, there is a value judgement about the home group in comparison with the other group, whose ideas are viewed with that scepticism. This definition points to estimations of comparative value between groups. This is different from the idea of a football team that it should win a match; in that instance the idea gives value to the ability of the team members and not to the group's idea as such. Of course, a football team, or at least its fans, have been known to develop their group identification into such an extreme value judgement of other teams that they have actually fought, and harmed, and occasionally killed, the fans of opposing teams. The idea has moved from a means of assessing ability to an extreme value judgement of another group. In that instance, an ideology has taken the place of the primary task.

That altered relation of the idea to the task delivers an intense motivating value to the idea, and this distinguishes the destructive group from the constructive one. In the destructive group, the individuals validate the beliefs and ideas of the group by simply being members, and other matters of reality and reason are ignored. Knowledge can therefore have a culturally determined truth for group membership. Mannheim (1936) developed this observation as a sociology of knowledge. What people know—or think they know—is constrained and moulded by their membership in groups, not by the reality or utility of the knowledge or the capacity for curiosity. Reflective thought and ordinary ethical conduct are amputated. Mannheim tried to disentangle the problem of a truth somewhere behind the socially constructed forms of knowledge. Despite an ideology being socially constructed, that knowledge is felt to be self-evidently true. This implies that a process in the individual is encouraged and sustained by membership in a group.

False consciousness

The most pertinent political discussion of ideology as an intergroup dynamic is that of György Lukács (1971, originally published in German, 1923), which I shall take as a paradigm. His notion of "false consciousness" was worked out in a Marxist context. It is a set of beliefs and assumptions adopted by a particular group of people, which gives rise to their way of seeing themselves and others; but from another point of view, it is a false way of seeing things. For instance, the working class misperceive their place in society because of the dominance of another class; this false ideological consciousness results from the economic dominance by the class that owns the means of production. As Craib (1994) confirmed:

> [Ideology] is a systematically distorted set of beliefs that can be seen in two ways. One is that it is a set of beliefs produced out of the immediate experience of people. … [At the same time] it hides a deeper social reality. A simple example would be the way in which an industrial worker might have some idea of what a fair day's pay for a fair day's work might involve and would be happy if he or she were getting that wage. Marx's argument was that even a "fair" wage hid an exploitation that we cannot see, but could only discover through an economic analysis of the way in which capitalism worked. (Craib, 1994, p. 132)

The false consciousness is the workers' estimate of a "fair wage", which may not be fair but exploitation. Any misguided falsity comes about as a pressure from intergroup relations and influences, notably interclass relations. Misperceiving a whole group of "other" people is a recognisable phenomenon, a stereotyping. One group or class adopts a misconception of themselves, and of other groups, and it becomes embedded as a part of the consciousness of the members. It does not feel false; it becomes a "natural" way of seeing things. There are, therefore, two levels: one a true state of affairs that is concealed, while, at another level, there is a more obtrusive, false (and exploiting) representation, which is believed to be true. However, one could equally say that this falseness of consciousness occurs in gender relations, or race relations;[6] or in religious and political convictions. The processes of false consciousness are integral to the dynamics of intergroup prejudices in general.

The narcissism of groups

The conviction of the truth, especially a value judgement, can be a product of group forces, especially those forces between groups. Under these conditions, one's own ideas are unquestioned and free from the

[6] Many would say that these are not different; rather the exploitation in gender and race relations is also due to a hidden economic dominance—of men, of white people, and so on.

scepticism to which other groups and their ideas are subjected. The ideas of one's home group can become extreme, the holders excited by their revelation and by their own identification with these unquestionable truths. Such an ideological group exists in contrast to its "other"; that is, another group held in sceptical suspicion. That group of "others" is then a necessary evil, the common enemy that unites a group. As Freud remarked about groups of neighbours who are adjacent to each other:

> The same thing happens when men come together in larger units. Every time two families become connected by a marriage, each of them thinks itself superior to or of better birth than the other. Of two neighbouring towns each is the other's most jealous rival; every little canton looks down upon the others with contempt. Closely related races keep one another at arm's length; the South German cannot endure the North German, the Englishman casts every kind of aspersion upon the Scot, the Spaniard despises the Portuguese. (Freud, 1921c, p. 101)

This is the phenomenon that Freud later called "the narcissism of minor differences" (Freud, 1930a, p. 114). Clearly, it is not just restricted to classes or nations, but underlies many intergroup prejudices, including race and gender; it would include the whole phenomenon of scapegoating, and the expulsion of individuals who are considered socially deviant. What then are the conditions that drive ideas to become ideologies?

Psychoanalytic relevance

Psychoanalysis investigates a different kind of false knowledge. Remarkably, the psychoanalytic understanding of the individual and his psychological quirks, such as a neurosis, reveals a structure similar to false consciousness in groups. A set of beliefs, attitudes, and assumptions is adopted falsely, and the true state of affairs cannot be perceived. For instance, a neurotic person may believe that spiders are evil and dangerous, and act on that belief. This belief is driven by unconscious forces, for example, a repressed terror arising from phantasies of the Oedipus complex, with retaliation threatened by a powerful parent. So, in the neurotic functioning of the mind, certain mental contents are hidden by a substituted (preferred) conscious awareness: spiders are lethal. A spider is a substitute for a predatory mother, for example. That knowledge is quite false; spiders are not deadly, at least in this country. Nor is anyone's mother, however formidable, an actual spider in reality. This view is nevertheless rigidly held and distorts behaviour and life. Such a neurosis immobilises thought and learning (about spiders, in this instance). So, neurosis purveys a false "truth", and, like neurosis, a group's false consciousness is rigidly sustained as true even though false from another perspective. An individual's false truth is called a neurosis; the group's is an ideology.

Self-deception: Social or individual

Given the similarity, it seems likely that the two forms of false consciousness interact. In other words, an individual in a destructive group (committed to an ideology) is in a mental state that resembles a neurosis. The capacity for the individual mind to harbour a false neurotic belief seems likely to be the method by which a false social belief (an ideology) may take hold of the minds of the individual members of a group.

However, an ideological group cannot simply be a collection of individuals who merely happen to suffer a similar neurotic repression with identical unconscious processes. There must be more than a serendipitous coming together of such people. Something must coordinate them. The obvious candidate for this extra coordinating factor are the *social* forces. A stable ideological structure is likely to come about when both the social forces and unconscious fantasies are in play together. We can take it that for a stable ideological structure to persist the two forces must coincide. Any interactive relationship exists between the two originating forces and that relationship is likely to be intricate.[7] The social pressure to adopt a false consciousness must act upon an intra-psychic pressure to repress or abolish certain realities.

---

[7] Social attitudes, assumptions, and myths have some similarities with individual unconscious phantasies, and are unfortunately sometimes confused with each other. Freud insisted the Oedipus complex was ubiquitous and the motivation for all social institutions (Freud, 1912–13), as well as individual personalities. Róheim (1950), for one, assiduously applied this psychoanalytic calculus to the mythologies of actual tribal cultures. For various attempts to solve this psychological–political interaction, see Parker and Spiers (1996), which includes Hinshelwood (1996 [Chapter 2]).

We assume, therefore, that social forces act upon the potentialities of the deep psychology of the individuals. Thus, social phenomena are determined from multiple origins, individual and group processes, interacting together. Whereas a neurotic is alone with his spider phobia and is estranged from society, the ideologue finds a second realm to enter, in which he can share his deception with willing others.[8]

To illustrate how the intricate relationship between individual and social processes might look, let us consider the following speculative example.

Germany in 1934

The social forces in Germany after the First World War included the punitive reparation demanded, leading to the catastrophic economic collapse. The impact of those events on individual German citizens is generally presumed to have laid the grounds for extremist ideologies—communist or national socialism. The preceding imperial ideology, expressed in German unification and expansionism during the nineteenth century, had collapsed due to the war. So, not only was Germany, nationally, in ruins and loaded with a crushing burden of reparation, individually a person identified with the nation could be said to have had a ruined and crushed ego. Germany had become a nation of collapsed egos, as it were. There was therefore a common state of mind among those identified with Germany. In this instance, in the 1930s, ideological mental functioning on a group scale consisted of adopting the notion of German racial supremacy, which seemingly motivated a large proportion of people who identified themselves as German and who had suffered the indignities of defeat. Then, under the draw of Nazism, they could acquire an explicit sense of value again. The restoration of the idea of German supremacy served a purpose in the depths of the individual psyche—to save the identity of the individual egos. That rescuing idea was shared by individuals and became a marker of those identified with the nation, as did the extreme value judgements against

[8] This sharing may extend to colleagues, who are then frequently estranged from some other group, and form their own sects, esoteric schools, and cabals. Psychoanalytic schools, for all their beneficial work for patients, also cling to certain ideas that can have damaging ideology-like effects and the groups can exhibit behaviour as sects do.

extraneous groups.[9] The idea is that rescued identity can be characterised as an ideology. And then extraneous groups—Jews (despite their German citizenship), Slavs, Gypsies, homosexuals, the insane and the genetically defective—could be identified as suspect pollutants in the German nation. Ultimately, they had to be exterminated in pursuit of racial supremacy to eradicate the recent collapse into ruin.

This idea, with its intense value judgements, inspirited the members of a whole society,[10] the majority of whom were rendered incapable of thinking through and evaluating realistically and ethically the notion of German supremacy. The unthinking unreality is striking; Jews were condemned for their supposed bid for world domination whilst ignoring the parallel Nazi drive for world domination. This selective inattention demonstrates the power of ideas to abolish thinking and the reality principle. It gains its power from the intensity of the collective individual distress. This pressure of common distress enabled the social forces to institute a good-group/bad-group dynamic, which cannot be subject to real thought.

Despite the rather sweeping generalisations of this historiography, the features of the example above approximate the characteristics of the destructive group; the example shows (a) a disorganised group (ruined German society), (b) the amorality (the erosion of the human values towards "others"), (c) contagious emotions (superiority over other ethnic groups), (d) the degradation of rational and realistic thought (for instance, the inconsistencies over who is dominating), and (e) the homogenisation of German individuality (pursued through the elimination of corrupting and alien groups). All these features are organised around the single core idea of German supremacy. This idea achieved an overarching status that dominated an entire national group whose purpose became promotion of the idea itself. The idea became the primary task of that group for more than

[9] Similarly, one could make the case that in September 2001, when the Twin Towers collapsed after the al-Qaeda attack, the majority of US egos also collapsed with the towers, leaving them open to the persuasion of a leader who could promise their re-inflation through military conquest, based, in turn, on belligerent intergroup relations. This remained somewhat precarious because of the failure of the military adventure in Iraq and then spawned the MAGA (Make America Great Again) movement as the decade moved on.

[10] In fact, only 42 per cent of the population voted for the National Socialists in 1933, but it was nevertheless the group with the largest vote.

a decade. Defeat, inferiority, and a sense of contamination provided the individual level of motivation, which the sociopolitical factors could then coordinate. The precise psychological and emotional state of the individuals was the necessary condition upon which the social forces played; this state primed a whole society to identify again with German supremacy, creating a compelling social reality.

Once freed from reality testing, the idea was an overarching philosophy to be defended for its own sake. The end result of this psychosocial process is an enormously overvalued idea, out of touch with reality, and with an ethical quality based on intense narcissistic value judgements.

The overvalued idea and the selected fact

In this attempted illustration of an ideology, the idea was welded to an intense valuation of the group itself, rather than being valued for its contribution to a realistic achievement of the group. It became overvalued because its function was to achieve stability in the members' identity, rather than in the external reality of the group. Although ideas with this status are ideological, they have been studied in most psychoanalytic detail in the clinical session. The most relevant study for present purposes is that by Britton and Steiner (1994).[11] Analysts come under pressure in the treatment session to produce ideas in the form of an interpretation; this pressure is intense for various reasons, and it can lead analysts to foreclose on their thinking, and thus jeopardise their awareness of the reality of the patient. The analyst may then clutch at an interpretation that has arrived in his mind with little reality. This is a false consciousness in the psychoanalytic sense:

> [T]he integration [of the overvalued idea] is spurious and results from the facts being forced to fit an hypothesis or theory which the analyst needs for defensive purposes … an overvalued idea is more likely to be sought when uncertainty cannot adequately be contained. (Britton & Steiner, 1994, p. 1070)

Clinging to an idea avoids painful states of mind, as we saw in the example of the Nazi idea that swept to success in the conditions following the First World War.

[11] I leave aside Therese Benedek's (1936) original use of the term "overvalued idea".

The selected fact

Britton and Steiner's work is of further interest because they contrasted the overvalued idea with an alternative mental functioning which attempts to remain modestly in touch with reality. This is the notion of the "selected fact".

They picked up this idea from Bion (1962), who, in turn, had been struck by the work of the French scientist, Henri Poincaré:

> If a new result is to have any value, it must unite elements long since known, but till then scattered and seemingly foreign to each other, and suddenly introduce order where the appearance of disorder reigned. Then it enables us to see at a glance each of these elements in the place it occupies in the whole. Not only is the new fact valuable on its own account, but it alone gives a value to the old facts it unites. (Poincaré, 1908, p. 30)

The selected fact is a "sudden precipitating intuition" (Bion, 1967, p. 127), a gathering together of facts, memories, and experiences into a synthetic intuition. It represents a creative moment that binds reality into discovered knowledge, and is the hallmark of a process of work. Matters of validity and reality are highly involved in this particular scientific creative process.

Here there is a distinction made in the way an analyst adopts ideas. The individual analyst's mind has a very different relationship with the selected fact, compared with the way that he entertains the overvalued idea. It is necessary now to look further at the different relationships a mind has with these two kinds of ideas.

Belonging and equation

The two kinds of ideas correlate with the two divergent kinds of groups. In one state of mind, ideas belong to the individual and he can use them in an instrumental manner for work and other purposes. In turn, when he uses these ideas he "belongs" to a group with others to whom, similarly, the ideas belong. On the other hand, there is the ideological state of mind in which the person becomes the idea; he is "equated" with it. The ideological group is not only defined by the idea, but so is the individual, and the group pursues the idea for its own sake, because so much hangs on it for the individual and his sense of personal identity and worth. Thus, ideas can contribute to an individual's personal identity in these two alternative forms; the idea either belongs to him or he is equated with it. These "places" an idea can occupy can now be explored with Freud's notions of the ego-ideal and the group ideal in mind.

The group ideal and the primary task

The ego-ideal is a set of standards and aspirations inside the person against which he measures his behaviour and accomplishments. A carpenter who is making a set of window frames, for instance, has in his mind a set of skills, standards, and a specific plan, which go to make up his aspiration to make the windows. Similarly, the constructive group has aspirations to achieve its ends. In this sense the group has an ideal, like the individual; Freud called it the group ideal. The group's ideal can also be called the primary task.[12]

The primary task of a group working on a building site, for instance, is to build a house. In the minds of the individuals, the group's ideal is, as it were, the built house; the team members aspire to achieve that result. Achieving that task may involve a number of secondary tasks; for instance, the carpenter has specific skills that have to be fitted in with those of the plumber and the electrician, and a differentiated matrix of individuals who, nevertheless, all share the idea of how the building is thus formed. In this kind of working group, the group ideal (the built house) does not take over the ego-ideals of the members (their specific individual skills) and eradicate them. This last condition, the individuality of the members, persists, in contrast to the destructive group where, an individual's own ego-ideal relates in a very different way to the group ideal. The analogy would be the football fans turned violent: in that form, the team of builders would persist for its own sake to establish a pre-eminent and narcissistic superiority and would not persist for the sake of the building. Thus, the relations between the person (ego), his ego-ideal, and the group ideal are different in the two kinds of groups.

---

[12] I take the term "primary task" from the concepts of the group relations model. A group has a boundary, and it also has a central focus, like a cell with its membrane and its nucleus. The primary task is the means by which the group and its members coordinate their thinking about reality.

Freud (1921c) described a variance in the relations with the ideal. He showed how a particular aspect of someone's mind can be removed, amputated as it were, and replaced by another person. The aspect of the mind that can be amputated is the ego-ideal. One example he used was the hypnotist who could effectively replicate certain functions of the subject in a trance. This gave Freud the idea that such an amputation with a substitute psychic prosthesis could occur in groups as well. Although Freud was at that point discussing the role of the leader as comparable to the hypnotist, he also acknowledged the possibility of a leading idea being "substituted for a leader" (Freud, 1921c, p. 95). In other words, an idea could function, like a hypnotist, as the substitute prosthesis.

Relations with the ego-ideal

The ego, or the person, relates to the ego-ideal as its aspiration and he may feel pain or satisfaction, according to whether he lives up to his aspirations. However, another possible relation may exist between the ego and the ego-ideal. Normally, the ego (as-I-am) is separate from the ego-ideal (as-I-should-like-to be). If the separation is lost, then the individual experiences an excited, although unreal conviction about himself; he believes he has become precisely as he would like to be (his ego-ideal). Freud wrote, "There is always a feeling of triumph when something in the ego coincides with the ego-ideal" (1921c, p. 131). This is Freud's account of the state of mania in the individual. However, in the group, Freud suggested that the separation between ego and ego-ideal may be particularly hard to sustain; in that case, the ego will coincide with the group ideal. While in the individual the equation of the ego with the ego-ideal is the state of mania, in a group it creates a much more familiar excited state, and Freud pointed out that societies may provide special (and bounded) opportunities through sanctioned festivals and Saturnalia to experience that excitement, when the self is felt to be ideal.[13]

When a person gives up his ego in favour of the group ideal, he becomes at one with all the group members, and so their individuality

[13] Originally, a "triumph" was a public ceremony celebrating an overwhelming military victory by a general of the Roman Empire.

inevitably diminishes (homogenisation). The compensation for such a loss is, of course, the intense feeling of excitement, triumph, and superior value compared with other groups. With this loss of individuality, the members are homogenised to a greater or lesser extent while inestimably valued. Individual identity is therefore built upon two different kinds of relations with the group and its ideal. The individual may either belong to the group (and its ideal belongs to him) or he may be equated with the group and its ideal, with the ensuing triumph. When the group ideal ceases to be an aspiration, and there is a concrete identification between the ideal and the leader and the members, this process resembles the way psychotic minds sink into a form of concrete symbol-formation (as described by Segal, 1957 [and see Chapter 8]).

Leadership

The qualities and the role of the leader are likely to be affected by the culture in the two different groups, and by their relation to the ideal. In Freud's view, a leader can be either a leading idea or a leading person. The relation may be one of representation—the leader represents the ideal. Alternatively, as in his analogy with the hypnotist, the leader may substitute for the ideal. These alternative relations appear to correspond to the leadership role in each of the differing groups.

The constructive group leader

In a work group, a leader represents the leading idea, as the builder who leads his team will represent the plan of the house to be built. He will lead his team to the achievement of that aspiration. This relationship of leader to the group ideal in the constructive group is distinctive and quite complex. He inspires a respect for reality, for the task, for its achievements, while respecting the specific individual talents of the members. In the group working on a building site, the builder himself will have an idea of the construction they are working towards as well as realistic methods for achieving it. He needs to have a clear idea of the individuality of his team—the carpenter, the plumber, the electrician, each of whom has the specific skills of his trade. The builder's idea of the building is their common group ideal, but it is not an ideology, since the group ideal is to achieve the construction in reality and is not aimed at a narcissistic superiority of the group itself. Each person retains something of his own ego-ideal—his trade as a plumber or a carpenter; at the same time, they all aim towards the builder's ideal. There is a clear differentiation of the individual member within the whole shared ideal; the power of triumph together with the loss of reality do not occur. The leader therefore needs to bear in mind the primary task (their group ideal), reality, and time and also the individuality of the members and their skills.

The ideological group leader

In the destructive group, however, leadership appears simpler in its structure, while requiring more specific gifts for its execution. In the destructive group, a leading idea is an overvalued one; it is a group ideal to which the leader must have some specific relation. As Chasseguet-Smirgel (1976) claims, "No absolute leader is without an 'ideology'. He is, in fact, the intermediary who negotiates between the people and the ideological illusion" (Chasseguet-Smirgel, 1976, p. 362). In such a group, the leader is identified with the group ideal; and thus he *is* the group ideal. Leaders of Roman triumphs embodied the ideal that the populace itself wished to embody—an ideal of courage and empire. A leader not only represents the idea/ideology, he *is* the idea. If the member has identified with the leader, he may also become triumphantly equated with the idea. Thus, members achieve a reflected glory in the superior status of the ideal leader whom they then devote themselves to preserving. In 1933, with Hitler's hectoring orations, he suddenly became the ideal of the German nation. Literally thousands of people at the Nuremberg Rally could suddenly adopt the collective ego-ideal, which was both Hitler and the Nazi ideal with which Hitler was identified.[14] Hitler's idea of German supremacy and George Bush's "axis

[14] Leni Riefenstahl's film, *Triumph of the Will* (1935), filmed at the 1934 Nuremberg Rally of the Nazi party, was an extraordinary evocation of the truly triumphal union of leader with the populace and with German ideals. Sixteen psycho-biographies of leaders, such as the study of Woodrow Wilson attributed to Freud and Bullitt (1967), naively derive Wilson's leadership and policies merely from the subject's own personality development. See also Abse's (1989) execrable psychologising of Margaret Thatcher's monetarism on the basis of her upbringing in a grocer's shop. The social forces that bring the leader to the fore are often too difficult for biographers.

of evil" are examples. The ideas of Pan-German greatness in Nazism and of historical materialism in Soviet communism, were ideas identified with the actual existing group; Hitler was Nazism, and Lenin was literally "Leninism". The illusion captivates the group, since members identify with the leader and believe they also embody the ideal that he is. Thus, the leader has a particular relation with the idea; he identifies with the ideal and enables the group members also to identify with that ideal through him. There is a complex, three-way process of equation or identification: the ideal; the leader; and the members.

Conclusion

All groups have a system of beliefs and ideas, that define its members; a group is the collection of people who share such ideas, and the group boundary lies between those who do and those who do not share them. The shared ideas are therefore markers of who is in and who is out of the group. However, ideas do this in two ways that currently are both thought of as identifying. On one hand, the idea belongs to the individual who belongs to the group of people giving value to the idea; on the other hand, the individuals in a group *become* the idea in a concrete form. The latter is a kind of equation, which I claim is the ideological relation with ideas.

Psychoanalytically speaking, these shared ideas reach deeper than conscious levels and in one or another way contribute to the individuals' identity. The shared mental life of groups is a borderland phenomenon between the deeply personal and the broadly social. Socially, the survival of the ideological idea is paramount and substitutes for reality as a motivating principle, because individuals seek relief from a collective existential distress.

It has proved possible to use psychoanalytic concepts to build up a picture of the characteristics of a group under the sway of an ideology:

- an overvalued idea that gives a psychological protection by distinguishing one group, "us", as unrealistically superior to another, "them", in some way;
- a collective sharing of that idea across the group, to become the group ideal;

- an identification with that ideal, so that the individual becomes equated with the shared ideal;
- a narcissistic valuation of superiority compared with other groups;
- a leader who equates himself with the ideal of the group and who mediates the process by which the members then equate themselves with the ideal as well; and
- homogenisation of the individuals whose identity is the group ideal.

Common ideals and values are shared in the constructive group; however, this gives a group ideal that is aspired to and "belongs" to the group, as opposed to equating with the ideal. It has been possible to distinguish features of constructive and destructive groups on this basis. There is an intricate interaction between the culture of each type of group, the psychology of the individuals within each group, and the unconscious processes of the leadership role. This complex interaction is vulnerable to social forces that play upon the identity of the group members. Their experience of their identity is affected by what happens to the group as a part of the social whole.

It has been possible to show, therefore, how an ideology in a group takes hold of deeply felt experiences about self and identity, and, in turn, how inclement forces that cause distress at the level of personal identity push the individual towards a particular kind of identification with the group ideal. This becomes a cycle in perpetual motion, leading to unfortunately stable states in group culture and ideas as ideologies.

The unfortunate complexity of these interactions between personal identity and group ideology means that steps to be taken to mitigate the development of destructive groups will be similarly intricate and urgently need to be investigated so that we avoid another century like the twentieth century. One of the central difficulties in finding strategies for this kind of political–psychological intervention is that it conflicts with the prevailing perception of what an individual person is. The picture described here implies that we as individuals have a strikingly fluid experience of our own personal identity and individuality. This perception of the person is not easily reconciled with the overt and conscious understanding of individuality in contemporary Western culture, where individuality is currently seen as discrete and separate, and durably consistent over time. This is where psychoanalytic understanding of unconscious experience could be revealing and telling.

The difference between a constructive group and a destructive one lies in the quality of the relationship with the idea/ideology, and the part that relationship plays in stabilising the sense of personal identity. The difference between an ideological leader and a mature reality-based work-group leader does not lie primarily in their personalities; it is in the intensity of the social forces playing upon the psychology and the personal identity of the group of individuals. To be sure, the ideological leader and the work-group leader will have recognisably different kinds of personality, but the different personalities come to the fore under the different conditions brought about by specific social forces.

With the modern technology of destruction, we need to know much more about the unreasoning ideological attitudes that grow up so rapidly in groups and cohere around overvalued ideas. There is no simple psychological or sociological explanation that distinguishes ideology from the most creative aspects of group life. We need a complex deep explanation of processes in individuals and their unconscious minds acting as a fertile soil in which social forces plant themselves.

References

Abse, L. (1989). *Margaret, Daughter of Beatrice: A Politician's Psycho-Biography of Margaret Thatcher*. London: Jonathan Cape.

Benedek, T. (1936). Dominant ideas and their relation to morbid cravings. *International Journal of Psychoanalysis*, *17*: 40–56.

Bion, W. R. (1952). Group dynamics: A re-view. *International Journal of Psychoanalysis*, *33*: 235–247.

Bion, W. R. (1961). *Experiences in Groups*. London: Tavistock.

Bion, W. R. (1962). *Learning from Experience*. London: Tavistock.

Bion, W. R. (1967). *Second Thoughts*. London: Heinemann.

Britton, R., & Steiner, J. (1994). Interpretation: Selected fact or overvalued idea? *International Journal of Psychoanalysis*, *75*: 1069–1078.

Chasseguet-Smirgel, J. (1976). Some thoughts on the ego ideal: A contribution to the study of the "illness of ideality". *Psychoanalytic Quarterly*, *45*: 345–373.

Craib, I. (1994). *Classical Social Theory*. Oxford: Oxford University Press.

Freud, S. (1912–13). *Totem and Taboo*. *S. E.*, *13*: 1–161. London: Hogarth.

Freud, S. (1921c). *Group Psychology and the Analysis of the Ego. S. E., 18*: 67–143. London: Hogarth.

Freud, S. (1930a). *Civilization and Its Discontents. S. E., 21*: 64–145. London: Hogarth.

Freud, S., & Bullitt, W. (1967). *Thomas Woodrow Wilson: A Psychological Study.* London: Weidenfeld & Nicolson.

Hinshelwood, R. D. (1996). Convergences with psychoanalysis. In: I. Parker & R. Spiers (Eds.), *Psychology and Society* (pp. 93–104). London: Pluto Press.

Hinshelwood, R. D. (1997). I have an idea. In: D. Kennard & N. Small (Eds.), *Living Together* (pp. 126–144). London: Quartet.

Hinshelwood, R. D. (1998). Groups, paranoia, enquiry. In: J. Berke, S. Pierides, A. Sabbadini & S. Schneider (Eds.), *Even Paranoids Have Enemies*. London: Routledge.

Hinshelwood, R. D. (2023). *The Mystery of Emotions*. London: Phoenix/Karnac.

Kernberg, O. (1998). *Ideology, Conflict and Leadership in Groups and Organisations*. New Haven, CT: Yale University Press.

Le Bon, G. (1895). *Psychologie des foules*. Paris: Alcan. English translation: *The Crowd: A Study of the Popular Mind.* New Brunswick: Transaction, 1995.

Lukács, G. (1971). *History and Class Consciousness*. Manchester, UK: Merlin.

Mannheim, K. (1936). *Ideology and Utopia*. London: Routledge & Kegan Paul.

McDougall, W. (1920). *The Group Mind*. Cambridge: Cambridge University Press.

Moscovici, S. (1985). *The Age of the Crowd*. Cambridge: Cambridge University Press.

Nitsun, M. (1996). *The Anti-Group*. London: Routledge.

Nye, R. (1975). *The Origins of Crowd Psychology*. London: Sage.

Parker, I., & Spiers, R. (Eds.) (1996). *Psychology and Society*. London: Pluto.

Poincaré, H. (1908). *Science and Method*. London: Nelson.

Róheim, G. (1950). *Psychoanalysis and Anthropology: Culture, Personality and the Unconscious*. New York: International Universities Press.

Segal, H. (1950). Some aspects of the analysis of a schizophrenic. *International Journal of Psychoanalysis, 31*: 268–278. Republished in *The Works of Hanna Segal*. London: Free Association, 1981; and in E. Bott Spillius (Ed.), *Melanie Klein Today, Volume 1*. London: Routledge, 1988.

Segal, H. (1957). Notes on symbol formation. *International Journal of Psychoanalysis, 38*: 391–397. Republished in *The Works of Hanna Segal*. London: Free Association, 1981; and in E. Bott Spillius (Ed.), *Melanie Klein Today, Volume 1*. London: Routledge, 1988.

Trotter, W. (1916). *Instincts of the Herd in War and Peace*. London: Unwin.

CHAPTER 7

Socially stabilising identity

Introduction

The preceding chapter reflected on the general nature of ideology and this paper in the present chapter describes in greater detail one particular instance: racial prejudice, how social attitudes fix onto individual structures of unconscious anxiety-and-defence. There is clinical material, from individual analyses to indicate this link-up between social prejudice and intolerable experience within individuals. The external culture brings the individuals into shared collaboration united by an ideology.

PAPER 7

Intolerance and the intolerable: The case of racism*

I take racism to be a typical example of a social phenomenon of intolerance and prejudice. It is also a state of the mind of an individual. This paper will explore the relation between intolerant attitudes such as racism on one hand, and, on the other, states of mind that are felt to be intolerable. As racist attitudes impact on the individual, what exactly in the individual do they impact upon? And how in turn do they recreate social groups characterised by that species of intolerance? I shall present clinical material to demonstrate the existence of a connection between these two phenomena—intolerance and the intolerable. Two forms of this identification—a rigid permanent form and a more flexible form—are identified from two psychoanalytic cases briefly described.

How do external prejudices within the social group impact on the internal state of mind of the individual? And how do they become stabilised within the individuals to support the social prejudices of a group? My starting point will be Freud's theory of the superego and especially the ego-ideal, which he placed at the centre of his social psychology (Freud, 1921c). I shall draw on the recent understanding of the intolerable "ego-destructive super-ego" (Bion, 1959; O'Shaughnessy,

* Hinshelwood, R. D. (2007). Intolerance and the intolerable: The case of racism. *Psychoanalysis, Culture and Society, 12*: 1–20.

1999: Britton, 2003). And then I shall turn to clinical material to show that intolerable states of mind can contribute to social intolerance, which in turn can impact on intolerable states of mind.

Social psychology and the ego-ideal

When Freud turned his attention to social psychology (Freud, 1921c), he specifically concluded that individual psychology must first of all give pre-eminence to relations with others—in effect giving precedence to social psychology.

> In the individual's mental life someone else is invariably involved, as a model, as an object, as a helper, as an opponent; and so from the very first individual psychology, in this extended but entirely justifiable sense of the word, is at the same time social psychology as well. (Freud, 1921c, p. 69)

The basis of this account is the interactive processes between the individual and his social group, which give rise to an internal structure he called the ego-ideal. This was separate from the ego, arising as a "grade in the ego" (Freud, 1921c, pp. 129–133) by which the ego-ideal stands over and is separate from the ego. The idea originated in Freud's development of Havelock Ellis' idea of narcissism (Freud, 1914c). Just before the First World War, Freud was impelled by his work with Jung to look at psychosis. And his "analysis" of the Schreber case led to a study of the narcissistic self-involvement of paranoid patients. However, he became interested in how the libido could be withdrawn; interest in, and attention to someone external, comes to be re-invested in the self. The ensuing extreme interest in the self leads to the creation of an image of the self as especially favourable and lovable.[1] It replaces some loved object in the external world. This idea of the specially lovable aspect of the self was transformed in his later paper on mourning and melancholia (Freud, 1917e).

[1] Here Freud (1914c, p 101) calls it the "ego-ideal". As Mancia and Meltzer (1981) note, there is no general agreement on the use of the terms ego-ideal, ideal ego, and superego. In the present paper, the most general conception is adhered to: the narcissistic withdrawal of the libido results in a remnant of the object cathexis within the ego, which remains somewhat detached as a separate ego-ideal, and an ideal notion of what the ego should be. Finer distinctions are not necessary for the argument of this paper.

In the pathological state of melancholia the self again becomes the object of love, although it becomes the focus of hate as well.

In 1921, this separated-off aspect of the ego had become a concept of considerable interest to Freud. It represented the internalised remnants of actual relations with external persons—the ego is "a precipitate of abandoned object cathexes" (Freud, 1923b, p 29). These relations with external objects remain as significant others within the person's mind, and the individual can then identify himself with them as the basis for social roles.[2] For example, visiting my grandchildren entails resuming a long standing set of attitudes I associate with an ideal parent, originally derived from my own parents' way of relating to children. I may then go to give a lecture to my students and draw then on figures that I retain from my own teachers at university, or further back to my schoolteachers. Then, in my practice as an analyst, I will draw on internalised versions of my own analyst and supervisors. These figures seem to exist inside me as a set of alternatives at any one time. I might think of them as different garments hanging in the cupboard, which may be brought out and worn for particular occasions. Often in ideal form, they imply standards and attitudes against which I can measure myself in whatever relationship I take up socially.

The ego-ideal is thus very fluid. Each variant is an aspect of the internal world, with which the ego may identify, changing as required by being replaced with other variants. These precipitates of past object cathexes remain susceptible to both continuing interaction with, and considerable modification by, the external world of other people. Freud worked this concept hard. The ego-ideal can be replaced by an object taken in from the actual social world. Freud's illustration is a Christian congregation, in which the individuals we say have Christ "in their heart". This indicates a process in which the figure of Christ is taken into the intra-psychic world (an introjection), which then functions as an internal inspiration rather than an external compulsion. Freud also described falling in love as a similar process, in which a person sets up the loved one as the focus of an abject devotion and allegiance. The person thereby becomes depleted in himself as his loved one absorbs more and more of his interest.

[2] This notion of active internal objects was greatly extended of course by Melanie Klein (1935, 1940; Hinshelwood, 1997).

Freud compared this abject allegiance to the hypnotist. A person going into a hypnotic trance can be said to be establishing a new ego-ideal—the hypnotist takes over as the ideal to whom the person gives allegiance. For the duration of the trance, the hypnotist becomes the dominating influence over the subject's mind. Then, as the person comes out of the trance, the *status quo ante* is restored.[3]

The group ideal

Freud was not only interested in the replacement of a person's ego-ideal. He also saw this phenomenon as the basis of group life. It is not just a way for people to acquire a repertoire of social roles; it is also the very basis of group solidarity. The individuals in a group appear to converge or coalesce in the sense that they adopt the same ego-ideal; then it becomes a group ideal. The group is united, as it were ,in its common allegiance to the same ideal. In the example of the Christian congregation, the individual feels bonded with all the others by the same common ideal, Christ, which they have each installed in their hearts.

The ego-ideal becomes, as it were, a condition of entry into a group. The sense of being part of a group comes from the acceptance of the ego-ideal promoted by the group. Being common to all the members of the group it is then a group ideal. The various ways in which the group ideal may be related to by the individuals, and the role of leadership in that, is not a topic to pursue here (but see Chapter 7).

Intolerable states of mind

The ego-ideal—more properly, plural, "ego-ideals"—have the characteristics of others. They are ideals to which we compare ourselves. This comparison is the superego function, which Freud described later in his structural model (1923b). Basing itself on the standards of the ego-ideal of the moment (and of the group), the superego can function extremely harshly. Freud (1930a, p. 130n)

[3] There are varied processes by which the ego-ideal is replaced by some internal object, by some newly internalised object, or by some external object. I shall not pursue this phenomenology of ego-ideal replacements—although Jaques (1955) says something of introjective and projective processes.

commented on the work of Melanie Klein who described the extreme internal persecution effected by internal objects, of which one was the moral super-ego. As O'Shaughnessy (1999) pointed out, late in her life Melanie Klein (Klein, 1958) described a very harsh and intractable root to the superego. Bion stressed this: "[A]n object which when installed in the patient, exercises the function of a severe and ego-destructive superego" (Bion, 1959, p. 314).

The idea of an "ego-destructive super-ego" derives from the primary self-destructiveness of the death instinct. Freud himself (1930a) acknowledged human "aggressive instincts" as having particular relevance in arousing superego guilt.

Internal self-directed violence may not be suicide explicitly, but rather attacks upon the ego's good relations, upon love and upon the need to survive (Riesenberg-Malcolm, 1999). As it is self-directed, that destructiveness is a negative narcissism, as Rosenfeld (1959, 1971) called it, and the ego has to organise itself to struggle with this internal anger. Characteristically, the ego splits itself along the natural fault line between good feelings (and impulses) and bad ones. That splitting creates an internal conflict—not just between wishes, but also between parts of the self. In this way a "negative self" separates off as the instincts defuse (see also Meltzer, 1968; Steiner, 1993; Williams, 1998). The negative self then relates to the "good" aspects of the self in an omnipotent way, dominating the more life-enhancing aspects of the person. The negative aspects are experienced as alien, an ego-dystonic ego! This compares with Freud's notion of a "grade" in the ego that forms the superego (Freud, 1923b),[4] but it is extremely harsh, dangerous, and intolerable.

Negative narcissism is a pathology of destructiveness, creating an omnipotent hegemony of inhuman attitudes, beliefs, and actions embodied in the pathological organisation. The good object is hated even when the ego is actually feeding and satisfying and being good. It is a hatred of the object simply because the object wants the baby to live—and by extension, it is equally a hatred of that life-affirming part of the baby, which wants and does engage with the object when

[4] Conceptualising the "grade" in the ego in this way as a defusion of the instincts differs from Freud, where the "grade in the ego" results from a self-observing agency in the mind derived from his theory of a libidinal narcissism (Freud, 1914c). In this paper, I explore the more virulent "negative narcissism" as the source of intolerant states of mind.

in need (Segal, 1993; Riesenberg-Malcolm, 1999). Such a retreat avoids the pains of life, and the achievements and maturation of overcoming them. The negative narcissistic part of the ego can be experienced as an alien object within. Impelled by the death instinct, it debases needs and dependency that are at the root of both persecutory and depressive anxieties. This internal structure is intolerable because it is intolerant of human values and humane attitudes.

In addition, this object that repudiates the life-giving aspects of the self, objects, and relations, can provide a protection from ordinary frustration when the good object is sought because of its goodness, but not found. Thus, the pathological organisation both satisfies the negativity and is also a defence against the pain of love.[5] In Steiner's (1993) terms, this is a retreat from both paranoid–schizoid and depressive anxieties. The result is a brutalised internal world that often feels dead and at the mercy of the alien internal object that demands the devaluation of external objects and relations, and of all human values, which might be represented by good internal objects. This pathological object, an abnormal superego, made of "anti-matter", as it were, is a creature of the death instinct, not the heir of the libidinal Oedipus complex. The aggression towards the self is particularly apparent when loving and dependent relations with another valued object are recognised. Those relations become intolerable, because the attitudes demanded by the internal intolerant object have consumed the self.

In this description, an intolerable internal object does not arise from oedipal primary figures or their substitutes that form standards and attitudes. The harshness of the superego develops in a different way. To the extent that the ego organises itself on the basis of a negative

[5] Kernberg (1994), in his review of Steiner's book, stressed the defensive nature of the pathological organisation, an alliance or conglomerate of primitive, extremely cruel, corrupt, and tyrannical objects dominating the patient's infantile, dependent self, as a destructive force that apparently promises the patient a protection against the vicissitudes of the pain and terror of unconscious conflicts, but, in fact, perpetuates a self-destructive reality that paralyses the patient within a particular level or type of pathology (Kernberg, 1994, p 160).

Steiner is also clear that this part of the ego's organisation is an instinct derivative; it is a derivative of the death instinct, which is idealised. Pathological organisations are complex in that they have a defensive aspect as well as gratifying primary negative impulses. O'Shaughnessy (1981) called them "defensive organizations", and the aim is to organise the ego in such a way as to create some degree of separation between one's good self and a bad part, however inadequate that separation.

narcissism—a pathological organisation—the superego will exert an intolerable ego-destructive force. As a result, social intolerance has as its counterpart and psychological basis the intolerable states of mind arising from a negative narcissistic pathological organisation.

The hypothesis is that the pathological organisation is an internal potentiality for socially intolerant attitudes, such as racism. Those social attitudes of racism—an ego-ideal of cultural "whiteness" shall we say—come to have an affinity with an internal object that is intolerant of human values, such as need, dependency, gratitude, honesty, and concern, which are replaced by superior, dominating, cruel ,and dishonestly unreal attitudes. Thus, an internal intolerant object may acquire a "content" of social attitudes. I hypothesise that these brutalising internal psychic relations of the pathological organisation can become hooks within the individual on which external prejudicial relations are hung.

In the following clinical material, I shall show two forms of that coming together of the external attitudes with an intolerant internal object.

Clinical material

A superior, denigrating aspect of Miss A had the omnipotent narcissistic character of a pathological organisation. In the right circumstances, after a specific external occurrence, the pathological organisation suddenly became invested in racist attitudes.

Case A

Miss A struggled between the pull towards, and her push against, an omnipotent narcissistic object relationship. This was exemplified at one point in the analysis by an external occurrence with a member of a terrorist organisation fighting a racist war. Her internal world, as evidenced by the transference situation, acquired a racist character.

She was in her early thirties, brought up in Britain by émigré Middle Eastern parents. She strongly identified with her parents' culture while also admiring her father's pro-English intellectual interests. She had a good education and a professional training, although she did not practice in her profession. She was in conflict over her cultural identity as a woman, caught between her parents' traditional view on one hand, and her professional standing on the other.

In the first phase of the analysis, I heard a good deal about her English boyfriend, described as a somewhat ineffectual man. There was some fairly overt scorn of him; for instance, she could bully him into her way of thinking. She also complained of having to look after his things in their flat. The impression was of some annoyance at his helplessness and vulnerability, indicating her debasing attitude towards vulnerability and any need for help. Her characterisation of him brought to mind a grubby little schoolboy which enabled her to feel a superior, "motherly" figure taking care of his washing and clothes, and so on. This was suggestive of an omnipotent attitude undermining in a destructive way any recognition of her respect for, and emotional dependence, on him. In another mode at other times, she conveyed a different axis of superiority and vulnerability. She showed a respect for him as an experienced academic scholar in the department she worked in, and where she had met him. She herself found the rigours that academic life demanded of her research very hard, and felt far from superior, and she struggled to cope. Either she felt superior in a denigrating and destructive way, or she felt inadequate.

In the analysis, she sustained a somewhat similar pattern of superiority in the transference to me and towards the process of the analysis. Her responses to my interpretations were frequently to tidy them up, giving a summary that was more articulate than mine. Often, she gave no other response to what I said, leaving me feeling a bit ineffectual. When I tackled that reaction, she became anxious. For instance:

> Once she gave some material about losing her way and then she had become afraid of being late. I interpreted a problem of identity, as if she was not sure if she was coming to see an analyst or a father. She quite cleverly understood me to be referring to getting lost in her ambiguous feelings about whether she wanted a sexual partner or a paternalistic security. I had meant something like this, though she put it more clearly. She did not give any further associations. I felt a little uncomfortable about my muddled efforts, and remarked that she wanted to make sense of my interpretations, as sometimes she felt I did not express myself very effectively.
>
> She became tense on the couch, and after a moment said: No, she understood what I said and was just repeating it so she could think about it. In fact, I did not at all have the impression she had thought about it. On this occasion, I pursued this by saying I thought she wanted to

> reassure me because she felt I might be sensitive to her opinion. It seemed to make her a bit cross that I had not accepted her reassurance. There was a rather tense silence.

In this little sequence she had seen me, I believe, as a bit ineffectual, which in the countertransference I did feel. At the same time, she wished to conceal that element of denigration, because she felt it as destructive of me. She then attempted to restore my peace of mind by her own efforts. I often described this to myself as "grovelling", but it was clearly a complex transference situation, which took a long time to sort out. The "grovelling" had a component in it that was overtly acquiescing towards me. She claimed a respect for my interpretation, yet it had a hollow ring, and I wondered how much she really thought about what I had said. There appeared nevertheless to be a positive attitude to me and my efforts, yet, on reflection, there was an unspoken sense not just of my weakness and need for help, but of her rather haughty acceptance of my neediness, leading to a compensating debasement of herself. So it was that the apparent helpfulness, acquiescence, and reassuring had made me think of the word "grovelling". It was made up of a genuine wish, on one hand, to put me in good and tidy order, and on the other hand, a superior attitude to me because of my neediness, which avoided thought and led her to want to conceal that haughtiness. The complexity here was difficult, both the struggle to rise above her own neediness by making me the needy one, and a struggle against that superior self, which led to trying to restore me, but in a way that confirmed me as the needy one in need of restoration. The capacity genuinely to have good feelings seemed to have been taken over by a subtle system that denigrated and reduced me. Thus, I was becoming acquainted with an object characterised by being ineffectual, vulnerable, and in need of care.

A rather omnipotent and denigratory object faced and complemented the weak and dependent one. The complexity of this deepened when coupled with the apparent social requirements of a woman from her culture, where she occupied a lowly position in relation to men. It was as if she could nevertheless sustain a hidden belief in being the instrument of a man's elevation. It would make sense simply as a cultural expectation of women in a lowly position, a position that she was also reacting against, turning the relationship around at times. This cultural pattern of gender roles was hardly psychoanalytic, though stereotyped gender relations in a non-European culture often came to the fore in her thoughts, and I often found myself interested and commenting on them. I began to be aware that the configuration in the transference resembled other situations, notably relations with her boyfriend. I could begin to suspect that this was not really a cultural pattern (or not only a cultural pattern). It was something to do with her own omnipotence and its camouflage.

I did not proceed very far with these speculations, which came rather slowly to my attention as I got my bearings in this transference–countertransference dynamic. My progress was interrupted by the key occurrence, which makes this case telling for the purpose of this paper. After about a year, the same complex dominance struggle was represented, but about a different issue. It was not about cultural gender relations, but racial ones.

> She came to one session rather shocked. She was uncomfortable on the couch, and though she was silent for a while, her movements were conspicuous. She was clearly disturbed by something, and I wondered what had happened. She told me in her articulate way that, the previous evening, she had been approached by a member of a radical group involved in violent action in the Middle East. She was embarrassed that this contact was a highly attractive middle-aged man, who clearly evoked sexual interest in Miss A. He invited her to become his mistress—or rather one of his mistresses. She was shocked at how tempted she was to give in to this dangerous man. She seemed to disapprove of his unrestrained and unashamed sexuality whilst also being captivated by it. I found myself also surprised by a number of things, not altogether coherent: that she was so close to terrorism; that such a man with a mission should be so lecherous and dishonourable (as he seemed at that moment); that she seemed to be drawn to follow such a brutal, violent lead; and not least, at a loss to know what I could do interpretively to make this into a therapeutic occurrence.
>
> My first thought was of her English boyfriend and the cultural choice with which she was confronted. In my own perplexity, this was what I took up, because the gender problem was a well-worked theme in the analysis, and gave me, I suppose, a handhold to lock onto, as I found myself concerned about this seductive approach that had clearly affected her so much. I made a comment to the effect that she was again trying to

> grapple with the experience of being an Arab woman, almost a possession; and that she had hesitated to tell me, because of the illicitly sexual quality, but also because she was nonplussed and didn't want to present herself to me as at a loss.
>
> She was quiet and seemingly thoughtful, but I felt that it was not a very powerful intervention in comparison with the overwhelming impact the man had had on her. I felt doubtful she would consider this line of thought on gender, when she had such excited turmoil in her mind over this man's offer. In fact, she continued with some details of his approach to her, implying some sense that she was devalued by the view of her as a female possession rather than a person.
>
> Because this was an articulate and well-worn response to my well-worn interpretation, I tried a new tack—focusing on her turmoil. I then said that I thought this encounter had caused such a turmoil in her mind that it was a bombshell, so that she was unable to collect her thoughts together again properly, but she was intrigued and fascinated by a man who could have this effect on her.
>
> She did seem a little more thoughtful after that, saying "Mm, I don't know. It's a fantasy. He's a typical Arab." Now, she had difficulty in recovering her articulateness, but she seemed to acknowledge that I was at least trying to understand the problem he had faced her with.
>
> Curiously, the next day she said nothing spontaneously about this occurrence, and it was almost as if it really had been a transient fantasy. But a day later, she told me that she had declined his offer.

Clearly, it is understandable that she might have been excited by a libidinal situation of this kind. However, it occurred in the context of her internal landscape of omnipotence and debasement. It raised the question whether the bombshell that had gone off in her mind was in fact merely an overwhelming sexual urge. Alternatively, the terrorist omnipotence of her own mind could have been suddenly overwhelming, provoked by the encounter with this actual terrorist—giving rise to an internally (as well as an externally) experienced struggle with terrorism. It gave a new twist to the regular occurrence of her focus on my ineffectual quality. Was the real bomb the one in the analysis that blew up my confidence?

> By declining his offer, she appeared to be settling the struggle. However, as it transpired, in phantasy he became a very prevalent figure for some

> time. His importance was not in terms of gender, as I had taken up. What began to emerge instead was anxiety over racial identity that we had not previously encountered. She had not previously shown very much interest in race differences, which she now began to express in terms of the attitudes this man represented. A significant change overtook her. She had presented this powerful moment as a potential seduction—to become a mistress of this man; but gradually a full racist influence became apparent.
>
> Shortly after this, she told me she was concerned about her appearance. She was an attractive woman, but it troubled her that she was noticeably Arab. She knew there was no particular cosmetic "treatment" to change her skin colour or her features—or even if she would have it if available. There was a sort of self-mocking quality to this, as if ashamed of a thought she did not quite know what to do with. She told me she had never thought about herself in that way. I said that although on the surface it is unlikely that she had not thought of being Arab, she was trying to tell me there was something new about the way she was thinking of it now. She responded by saying she had wondered, given my profession, and my name, whether I was Jewish. When she said this, I felt some alarm, not so much that she was mistaking my actual identity (which I am used to) but that suddenly there might grow up an alienation or hostility between us, which might be unmanageable. It was a transitory moment of alarm. When I put it into words, that there could be an unmanageable conflict between us if she had to recognise that we belonged to two separate races vying for supremacy, she remained quiet. Later, she said with some bitterness that her boyfriend had once called her "dark".

I think I may have underestimated at the time my own sense of alarm. We had done a good deal of work on her capacity to undermine respect for her boyfriend, and to some extent her undermining of me, and I had some understanding of how she dealt with this. I connected her "terrorism" with this implicit form of damage. However, this new moment was on a different scale. It set going alarm—not merely a feeling of being ineffectual and needy. There was an explosive bomb set to go off between us. She might have been as frightened as I was. The reference to something unmanageable (though perhaps it was technically correct to address) may have served to bring us together in fearfulness to counteract a deep gulf that might have exploded between us—me Jewish, and her Arab.

The sessions during the ensuing period were characterised by quietness, perhaps thoughtfulness, less anxious than previously, but more withdrawn. She became troubled by her concerns that her boyfriend was English; at the same time, she was unable of course to tell him of the encounter she had had with her terrorist. She felt the Englishness in him devalued her and in turn she retaliated with her superior thoughts of her imaginary "affair". Once again, her working through was in terms of her boyfriend. It may really have been that her fear of my "Jewish" retaliation led to distancing in this way: an attempt at a terrorist disengaging.

However, the encounter had confronted her with a need and a vulnerability arising from the sexual need. Underlying a sexual entanglement, she was in a struggle with her omnipotence and vulnerability. Her anxieties led to a stormy period in the relationship with her boyfriend as well. In the analysis, the moments when she felt superior to me and debased by me became increasingly clear to see, and the sense of a race friction between us gradually lessened.

Although she had rejected the man—as an external object—something quite radical had happened, and the episode had created a new internal situation for her. Whatever the sexual gratification the man had offered, he had also offered her a new racist consciousness. It seemed this was a moment of similar transformation in the analysis. If for a year there had been a degree of deadness about the contact between us, typically as we attempted to talk of her cultural conflicts, there was suddenly a new moment that felt more alive, heralded by alarm. Behind the cultural conflict, there was a determined, and perhaps unmanageable, conflict between herself and me, a Middle East war in the consulting room. She could be seduced, as it were, into a quiescent discussion of gender problems, but it deadened the lively engagement with me on the other level, where she sorted out her omnipotence.

This patient's thoughtfulness allowed working through, over time, with a relatively good outcome. It was possible to approach the omnipotent terrorist as a part of herself. This "racist" phase of her analysis was in a way more straightforward, because it showed up more starkly how the terrorist in her, by whom she had so nearly been taken over, was some counterpart to a vulnerable, needy self. It was also more straightforward because we could directly address the complexity of who was needy and who was providing for the neediness, and how this might evolve in a more alternating way. Through this, the dominance and terrorism could be felt more in the analytic situation, and slowly she could identify with the violence and with her antagonism towards help, need, and life. She did become curious, often still anxious to restore me, but slowly she could see the value of, and her dependence on, my help for understanding this. As a result, she began to feel more relaxed in her analysis. Eventually (after four years by now), an incremental step in her appreciation of her boyfriend occurred—he had nice fair hair!—and over a period she tried with some difficulty to acknowledge how hard it must have been for him to tolerate her.

In this case, Miss A needed to sort out the difference between having a particular racial identity and the exciting power of a racist terrorism. Her external encounter with a racist person occasioned the internalisation of troubling prejudicial attitudes into an internal world where the intolerance naturally adhered to the available omnipotent internal object. This "internal racist", constructed from both the ego-destructive object together with racist social attitudes, was driven within her by omnipotent rejection of her own vulnerability. This occurred in a woman whose relations with the internal object were labile, so that she sometimes appeared as debased and weak, sometimes as omnipotent, and sometimes as denying her omnipotence with a servile "grovelling" attitude.

So, Miss A illustrates how external social attitudes can be swiftly internalised into an existing omnipotent worrying narcissism, to create a racist internal object. The rejection of the external racist took a couple of days, but the rejection of the internal state of racist intolerance took a matter of years, and depended on analytic help. I claim that the tenaciousness of the internal racist came about because there existed an internal "hook" characterised by intolerance, as previously described. Prior to its racist politicisation, the intolerance in her was observable as a clinical feature of her transference as well as in her relations with her boyfriend.[6]

It is serendipitous that studying this patient revealed something of the social phenomenon of racism. It demonstrated how fluid

[6] In terms of a psychoanalytic treatment, the social character of her attitudes was less important than the intolerant nature of the pathological organisation. However, in some circumstances, for instance when patient and analyst are from different races, then the actual social "content" of the pathological organisation may become relevant and highly useful defensively for the patient (Tan, 1993).

the ego-ideal is. An encounter one evening evoked a sudden and potentially overpowering internalisation of social intolerance. Given her potentiality for intolerance, it took years to dispel this internal object. Other people do not suffer such a dramatic internalisation. They seem to live with racist attitudes on a permanent basis. A state of racial prejudice inhabits their world without modification, although concealed to a greater or lesser extent. From a social point of view, we might think of the latter as "carriers" of a racist culture. This applies to the next patient, Mrs B.

Case B

Mrs B was a middle-aged woman from South America. Her identity was sufficiently European for her to have married a successful English diplomat, and to have settled in England to bring up a family for more than a decade. However, she had inherited and still owned a substantial farm in her country of origin. She had to oversee the professional manager of her land, and to do so from this distance caused some difficulties. Her possessions had to be looked after by an intermediary, an expert whom she employed, but who seemed to maintain an independent point of view. The notion of distance was significant in her analysis. This pointed to transference manifestations; her response to interpretations was cool, as if she really was surveying my efforts from a distance. For instance:

> She gave some material in which she described a fish on a fishmonger's cold slab; it looked at the world with an appraising eye. I interpreted her own cool appraisal of the world, including the world inside her, which she had invited me to look at with her. She responded, after a moment, with a good-humoured comment about lying on the couch like a cold slab, and then her view that English people thought that South Americans, like herself, were usually rather hot-blooded. There was an implication that she was somehow different and therefore wrong to be a cold-blooded South American. But, quickly she seemed to indicate that I as an Englishman must be contradicting myself by interpreting her as cold-blooded when I knew she was South American. I was not sure which of these fleeting impressions was correct. I wondered how I would find out, and on the basis of past experience I thought I probably would not. So, on this occasion, I waited without saying anything further. My experience of such moments was that she was already getting on in

> her mind with something else, and would ignore me if I remained quiet in my uncertainty. In effect, she left the interpretation, and I did as well. The moment became distant and rapidly lost intensity.

This kind of "dead fish" quality to the analysis was frequent. In fact, anything in her mind beyond her surface associations seemed remote from real investigation and understanding, and from any encounter with it or between us.

> To manage this distant land in South America, she adopted an imperious attitude to the manager, and I frequently felt a tone of that in her analysis. Her attitude could be as haughty to me as if I were an analytic manager, employed by her. Her manner had the characteristic that she talked of what she wanted, and moved on as she wished.
>
> For instance, she talked of the frustration she felt towards her husband who spent so much time in his job, leaving her to feel idle and not entertained. Whilst I formulated some thoughts about how she felt frustrated by my concentration on the analysis, she moved on as if, merely having mentioned the frustration, it was already dealt with. She then talked of her unruly son away at boarding school, who constantly needed things sent to him. Further thoughts involved her giving a dinner party, etc.

She was not curious about such a punctuated stream of thoughts, which I could have taken to reveal unconscious themes. Rather the thoughts were left as a trail, for me to follow and enjoy as crumbs from the table. I gradually became accustomed to her lack of interest in the content of the thoughts, and began to notice the process.

> On one occasion in response to this sort of sequence, I described some fragmented quality to her thinking and said it made it difficult to serve up well-cooked food for me in the way she provides for her house guests. She told me, slightly stiffly, that I seemed slow to follow her today—but she spoke it calmly as if indifferent to whether I did follow her or not.

My role, to manage her psychic affairs for her, consisted of following her thoughts around in the ways she determined. If I said anything arresting, she dealt with it in an intelligent, formal way before moving on in her own direction. Reports of her attempts to control the manager in South America repeated a version of what I so often felt. These reports conveyed a haughty, imperious attitude. She attempted to control him with various communications and visits from time to time to check what he was doing. The impression she gave was that she conducted a busy and superior interference, while he did his best to please her. This reflected the experience of the analysis, where she relied on me to manage her possessions, that is, mental states and internal objects, but to do so according to her requirements.

Like my previous patient, Mrs B could also be described as under the dominance of a superior part of herself, an omnipotent narcissistic self that perverted her relations with those valuable experts (farm manager, psychoanalyst) whom she needed to depend on, as experts. She retreated from her dependency on experts behind a haughty manner, and such feelings of need were carefully excluded from her actual transactions and communications.

> In one session, she told me of her serious suspicions: "He didn't seem to listen. You know, he phones me every other Monday. It's too much sometimes," she added woefully. "I'm here, I tell him what I want done, and I have no idea if he takes any notice." She sounded perplexed, as if her authority were beyond question. "He's there, he's one of them—mixed, a mulatto, you know. So, I expect the usual respect. I do. Sometimes I tell him. I don't know if he understands." Again she seemed perplexed that he might be calling into question the whole social fabric. She believed she instructed him on the best method to develop the land (though in practice, she actually knew far less than he). She continued by insisting, "It's my land, and it is my country." She conveyed a sense of arbitrary power.
>
> I had believed for a moment that she was implying, unconsciously, that I did not satisfactorily respond to her demands in whatever way she determined, and whatever my better judgement. This dealt with the risk of her dependence coming to the fore. So as always, I could not be quite sure if I was truly being asked to listen to the dependent and vulnerable self, or whether I really did have to restrict myself to accord her the imperial authority she expected. I was very familiar with the sense that I was not quite sure to whom I was speaking—the dependent needy self or the autocrat. I also had the enduring conviction that I would not find out; it left me once more in the passive accepting role of powerless indecision.
>
> However, in that material I was struck by her mention of his colour—a mulatto. I had not until then been aware of this. Her frustration at his

> insubordination seemed self-evident to her when she was telling me. So, I recognised a feeling in me of wanting to remonstrate with her about her denigratory attitudes. I realised suddenly that she probably did not think of her remarks as denigratory, and for all I knew of race relations in her country, it was perfectly acceptable. Anyway my job was different. It was not for me to respond to her racism as such. I had to think about that protest in me—clearly, I identified with the manager who was subjected to her attitudes that were now explicitly racist.
>
> I said I thought she looked down on me, too, as the person who was supposed to look after the distant aspects of her experience, and I listed some of the problems she had come to analysis with—now rather distant in our memories. I said I thought she took a view of me rather as she did of the Black man managing her estate, and that she regarded me as a servile assistant she directed, rather than as a guide for her own exploration.
>
> "Hmm," she said, "you do seem a bit like him." And she gave a short laugh as if owning up to something she felt a little bad about. She added that she was not really racist but that she did think of people like that as natural servants. Momentarily, she seemed to feel a little awkward about her own racism. It was an unusual moment when she could think in a concerned way about herself, her conflicts, and her relationships. However, it seemed somewhat feeble. "I suppose we all have quirks"; now she conveyed it did not really matter to her anyway.
>
> Then she told me, with a rising anger, of something he had done, over which she had not had control. It resulted in some mildly damaging consequence for her. It was a small moment, but it entailed a recognition of her own problems, her need for help and her dependence on him, and it sent her quickly back into a rage about his insubordination.

So wedded were her racist attitudes to her imperiousness that I think previously she must have thought that her racial differences were so natural to her, and therefore so obvious to me, another white person, she hardly need acknowledge them. Moreover, my reference now to something so trivial was evidence of my insubordination.

> I put to her in an explicit way. "You saw my previous interpretation as my refusal to accept your control of my views. Then it made you feel disadvantaged by it, and particularly you felt suddenly small and dependent on me." She was silent, and apparently silently furious. She did not speak for the rest of the session. The next day she told me two things.

> First, rarely for her, she had had a dream, though she did not tell me the dream. And second, she was thinking about finishing her analysis.

In this material, there was a lot of evidence of her superior attitudes; a racist component of it emerged almost by accident, and demonstrated how unquestionably equated her superiority and her racism were. However, a brief moment emerged and disappeared in rage when she struggled, weakly, against these domineering and debasing attitudes towards another race. She struggled with this so much less successfully than Miss A. In the end, the analysis was not a success.

> In the last session, she presented me at the end with a book. Its title was *The Book of Heroic Failures*. She laughed very pointedly, indicating the failure of our efforts and her haughty and amused indifference to that outcome. However, there was some hint in her smile, which suggested a rueful regret—and even a comradely regret—at our failure.

I was left afterwards with a prolonged sense that some part of her that might have valued her opportunity had existed but was dominated by her resilient haughtiness. I had never found a useful way to that part of her. Instead, Mrs B maintained a haughty attitude to those who helped her. Importantly, that attitude was strongly linked to racial differences, racial superiority and inferiority. Her dominant haughtiness seemed designed to keep the dependent side of herself a dead fish. Racism was aligned in the most natural seeming way with social attitudes, which she must have acquired while young. There seemed in this case to be a much more enduring welding of social attitudes to a haughty, omnipotent side of her against which she could struggle only weakly. It was not simply that her racism was the source of her haughty superiority; in fact, rather the opposite: her haughtiness was very evident and emerged in an obvious manner in the analysis. It could be shown there, I think, to be derived from her vigilant repudiation of weakness and her dependence on my help. She managed and controlled my help completely. The racism was not the cause. It was an add-on feature, perhaps because it was easily available in her culture.

A reaction to her own entrenched attitudes did still exist, although feebly and transiently. In the last but one piece of material, she did move away towards a more reflective questioning of the racist attitudes that seemed forever unquestioned. However, any small collaborative moment with me was fleeting. Neither she nor I could sustain it. She returned to her entrenched, unthought prejudice, and retreated from her more vulnerable and dependent experiences. The outcome of her struggle seemed a long-settled defeat for her more vulnerable but more human self.

Conclusion

I have presented both these cases to illustrate how a domineering side of the personality was linked with socially racist attitudes. I present these as illustration of, and indeed (in these cases) as evidence of, the way that something internally intolerable meets social attitudes of intolerance, mutually enhancing each. So, social attitudes are not simply internalised and installed like a piece of computer software. There is a receptive "hook" on which such attitudes can be hung. It is a "hook" that contributes anti-human brutality and the poison of intolerance.

At the same time, we could say, certain social prejudices give a particular focus and content to already existing intolerant anti-human attitudes. Thus, a racist society would provide the wherewithal for an individual's harsh internal object to be clothed in a racist intolerance. The internal hook can attract the garments of racist attitudes.[7] In one case, the analysis showed this formative process in action; and in the other case there was a more extended occupation by a racist internal object that had taken up apparently permanent residence.

In both patients, there was some transient movement back and forth between an intolerable sense of helplessness and the domineering attitudes of intolerance. However, the two patients made this movement in an importantly different way. I presented Miss A to show a moment in which a racist structure erupted within her mind. An internal structure became suffused or infected with an internalised figure embodying external social attitudes—those of racial terror. A fluid oscillation

[7] Other prejudicial "garments" can also be stored in the psychic cupboard as intolerant attitudes to be taken out and worn on appropriate occasions. For instance, totalitarian attitudes can be inhabited by this harsh internal object (see Sebek, 1998); various anti-feminist, classist, or religious sets of attitudes could also adorn the intolerant internal object with specific social prejudices. So various sets of social attitudes, the wherewithal of the ego-ideal, can be kept, and worn as it were, or thrown off for a while.

between a self-destructive denigration and a denigration of her external loved object suddenly threatened to harden into a racist intolerance. And specifically this potential change was sparked by a particular kind of intolerant person, who could seductively enter her. This potential new ego-ideal, carried in a person from a racist group, offered a stability organised around intolerance. An internal, intolerant object within her personality could absorb some socially meaningful content—a group ideal. If her receptive internal situation absorbed the external social phenomenon, she was offered a group solidarity with people aligned with the same set of racist attitudes (group ideal).

In the event, Miss A was able to disconnect and to move away from the racist attitudes. With the help of analysis, Miss A could disengage from the new racist preoccupations of her intolerant internal object.

For Mrs B, instead, the link between her internal intolerant object and social attitudes of intolerance was a permanent one. It was so longstanding and so implicit she never needed to mention it explicitly. The investment of her personality in socially accepted complacent attitudes made her struggles against the omnipotent, narcissistic part of her personality so weak that it defeated analysis. Mrs B's racist attitudes were habitual and thus she was somewhat different from Miss A, who could adopt them or put them down. Mrs B's case is important psychoanalytically when we consider the possibilities for therapeutic change; but it is also important socially in considering the possibilities for social change.

From a social point of view, it seems useful on the whole to think of racist attitudes as potential. They can be donned at moments when there is a suitable social context. Football fans suddenly assume xenophobic aggression in the midst of a mob. This fluid situation fits the notion of "contagion", which Freud (1921c) adopted from Le Bon (1895). Group members are particularly prone to pick up the emotionality of others and that emotion flies around like a contagion. For group attitudes to suddenly flare up in this way suggests some potentiality exists in a latent form in individuals, awaiting realisation in some social situation. Thus, Miss A may be more applicable as a model of this liability of the intolerant omnipotent attitudes, awaiting social clothing.

For Miss A, an internal condition met a group with racial differences. That group included individuals with a more permanent internal racial object, ones such as Mrs B had. Miss A may represent something like the racial potentiality of most of us. In this way, we could understand how it is that quite ordinary people can be drawn into the prejudices of racism (for instance, almost overnight the entire population of Germany, after 1933, became murderously racist). Mrs B exemplifies certain rarer individuals who act perhaps as "carriers" of social intolerance of one form or another, and can infect others.

If it is the case that racism is a convergence between a social intolerance and an internal intolerant object, we have to turn to the psychoanalytic method to investigate at least one pole of the phenomenon. A social science point of view is not sufficient. Of course, psychoanalysis is not sufficient either; psychoanalysts can say little about the social conditions that make racism a prevalent social intolerance. However, psychoanalysts may have the clue to how such intolerance can suddenly spark up and break out on a wide scale. We are all prone to states of mind which feel intolerable, and so we can all be rescued from such states by group dynamics that substitute intolerance.

Acknowledgements

The author thanks Sally Weintrobe for her meticulous reading and comments on my paper, which hopefully have made it more accessible to the reader. The author is also grateful to the peer reviewers for stimulating me to restructure, and I hope make the theoretical part of the paper, more clear.

References

Bion, W. R. (1959). Attacks on linking. *International Journal of Psychoanalysis, 40*: 308–315. Republished in *Second Thoughts*. New York: Jason Aronson, 1967.

Britton, R. (2003). *Sex, Death, and the Superego*. London: Karnac.

Freud, S. (1914c). On narcissism: An introduction. *S. E., 14*. London: Hogarth.

Freud, S. (1917e). Mourning and melancholia. *S. E., 14*. London: Hogarth.

Freud, S. (1921c). *Group Psychology and the Analysis of the Ego*. *S. E., 18*: 67–143. London: Hogarth.

Freud, S. (1923b). *The Ego and the Id*. *S. E., 19*. London: Hogarth.

Freud, S. (1930a). *Civilization and its Discontents*. *S. E., 21*. London: Hogarth.

Hinshelwood, R. D. (1997). The elusive concept of "internal objects" and the origins of the Klein group, 1934–1943. *International Journal of Psychoanalysis, 78*: 877–897.

Jaques, E. (1955). Social systems as a defence against persecutory and depressive anxiety. In: M. Klein, P. Heimann & R. Money-Kyrle (Eds.), *New Directions in Psychoanalysis* (pp. 478–498). London: Tavistock.

Kernberg, O. (1994). Psychic retreats: Pathological organizations in psychotic, neurotic, and borderline patients. *International Journal of Psychoanalysis, 75*: 159–162.

Klein, M. (1935). A contribution to the psychogenesis of manic-depressive states. In: *The Writings of Melanie Klein, Volume 1*. London: Hogarth.

Klein, M. (1940). Mourning and its relation to manic-depressive states. *International Journal of Psychoanalysis, 21*: 125–153. In: *The Writings of Melanie Klein, Volume 2*. London: Hogarth.

Klein, M. (1958). On the development of mental functioning. In: *The Writings of Melanie Klein, Volume 3*. London: Hogarth.

Le Bon, G. (1895). *Psychologie des foules*. Paris: Alcan. English translation: *The Crowd: A Study of the Popular Mind*. New Brunswick: Transaction, 1995.

Mancia, M., & Meltzer, D. (1981). Ego ideal functions and the psychoanalytical process. *International Journal of Psychoanalysis, 62*: 243–249.

Meltzer, D. (1968). Terror, persecution, dread. *International Journal of Psychoanalysis, 49*: 396–400. Republished in *Sexual States of Mind*. Perth: Clunie, 1973.

O'Shaughnessy, E. (1981). A clinical study of a defensive organization. *International Journal of Psychoanalysis, 62*: 259–269.

O'Shaughnessy, E. (1999). Relating to the super-ego. *International Journal of Psychoanalysis, 80*: 861–897.

Riesenberg-Malcolm, R. (1999). *On Bearing Unbearable States of Mind*. London: Routledge.

Rosenfeld, H. (1959). An investigation into the psycho-analytic theory of depression. *International Journal of Psychoanalysis, 40*: 105–129.

Rosenfeld, H. (1971). A clinical approach to the psychoanalytic theory of the life and death instincts: An investigation into the aggressive aspects of narcissism. *International Journal of Psychoanalysis, 52*: 169–178.

Sebek, M. (1998). Post-totalitarian personality: Old internal objects in a new situation. *The Journal of the American Academy of Psychoanalysis, 26*: 295.

Segal, H. (1993). The clinical usefulness of the concept of the death instinct. *International Journal of Psychoanalysis, 74*: 55–61.

Steiner, J. (1993). *Psychic Retreats*. London: Routledge.

Tan, R. (1993). Racism and similarity: Paranoid-schizoid structures. *British Journal of Psychotherapy, 10*: 33–43.

Williams, A. H. (1998). *Cruelty, Violence and Murder*. London: Karnac.

CHAPTER 8

Belonging and identifying

Introduction

The problem with rigidly identifying with an ideology with the result that we fail at normal representation is dealt with in more general terms in this paper. It is done through an examination of the work of Hanna Segal who first exposed the phenomenon of symbol equation. Ideas no longer "belong" to an individual, the individual *is* the idea. It becomes an integral part of his/her identity which leads to an existential crisis if the idea is doubted or questioned. This is a theoretical paper that attempts a detailed examination of this identification with ideas underlying ideologies and attempts to take a little further the generalisations of Chapter 6.

PAPER 8

The function of symbol-formation: Pinning down the ego function*

Evolution has blessed the human being with the capacity to represent. That has resulted in the success of human civilisation based on symbols, and systems of symbols like language. In a previous paper (Hinshelwood, 2018), I gave a description of Hanna Segal's (1957) view of symbol-formation, and how her theory developed (Segal, 1978, 1998, 2007). This has led to a complex theory, that started with Klein's case of Dick, the concrete thinking found in psychotic states of mind, and the eventual importance of the various forms of splitting and projective identification.

Most central to Segal's argument, and that of most psychoanalysts, is to learn from what goes wrong. If we go back to Freud's theory of dreams, the role of repression and the abnormal forms of symbols and symbol-formation teach us about normal forms. Is there something "abnormal" about the very fact of symbol-formation, even in the most creative uses of symbols? Coleridge described the process of poetic appreciation in this way: "to procure for these shadows of imagination that willing suspension of disbelief for the moment, which constitutes poetic faith" (Coleridge, 1817 [1997, p. 365]). By this, he is said to mean that though

---

* Hinshelwood, R. D. (2020). The function of symbol-formation: Pinning down the ego function. *British Journal of Psychotherapy*, *36*: 32–44.

we use verbal symbols, those symbols are not the real original that we are trying to represent. There is a willingness to live in a world that is not a world of reality. Our representations are a world of shadows not really there. The real world is glanced at as if projected on the wall of Plato's cave.

This quality of a mirage was expressed most succinctly by Ferdinand de Saussure a long time ago. Saussure (1916) founded modern linguistics and structuralism by picturing a symbol as:

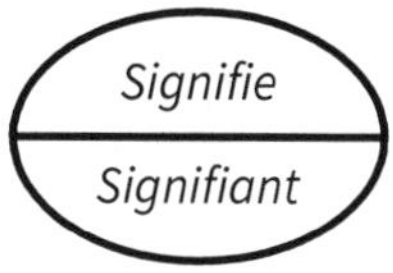

One part, pictured underneath, is the thing symbolised, and the upper is the thing that symbolises it. There is a potential space between the two. The simple diagram indicates that symbolisation functions as if the signifier (the symbol, above) *is* the signified (the thing symbolised, below). The psychoanalytic conception of symbols may differ from the normal symbols that Coleridge was describing. Freud's dream symbols aimed to repress some awareness and meaning, while the normal view of symbols is to express meanings. Both kinds of symbol have in common the same structure: a bipartite one. They both differ from the third occurrence addressed here, the symbolic equation, where the awareness of the reality of the symbol is lost. There is not a bipartite structure. The dividing line that we find in Saussure's diagram is missing. It is not that awareness of the difference between signifier and signified is suspended (symbol proper); the difference has gone (symbolic equation).

The two parts of Saussure's diagram (the signifier and the signified) may have some similarity, but that is not necessary for symbol-formation to be effective. When I make the sounds with my mouth which emerge as "c–a–t", it is not the cat itself which is lying there on our sofa. Nevertheless, the sounds carried across the air alert my wife to the cat on the sofa, and she looks at it. The word and the object are as if one—or at least as united, as Saussure's little diagram above demonstrates. The line in his diagram both unites and separates. Thus, we can conceptualise normal symbols. They are at the heart of creativity and yet they do not respect reality fully and can only give some superficial resemblance as a map does of the full landscape. The creativity of representation is at the heart of the human capacity to form our civilisation, knowledge and technology.

Freud (1911b) characterised the reality principle as the key to the origins and mature development of the ego and the personality. And as Coleridge says, the poetic imagination violates that principle. And yet it is not a complete violation. We retain in our minds the realistic knowledge that a symbol is just a symbol and not the reality itself which we are representing. When we come out of a performance in the theatre of *Titus Andronicus* we are in some state of shock at the blood and tragedy. We feel, as Aristotle once described it, full of fear and pity. And yet we also know that it was only actors representing the violence, and it was not the real thing. Our ability to recognise the reality can be suspended for a while without being lost and we can remain very emotional.

The reality has moved into the background. That move is like riding a bicycle; it becomes second nature. We know what we are doing, but we forget reality and do not have to bother to think about what we know. Magritte captured this kind of double-vision with his well-known painting, *La trahaison des images* (*The treachery of images*), which consisted of the image of a tobacco pipe under which he had written in words, "Ceci n'est pas une pipe" ("This is not a pipe"). Actually, he was quite right: it is not a pipe, it is canvas and oil paints. But it is as if the painting is real.

This has been called the "paradox of fiction" (Paskow, 2004; Konrad & Petraschka, 2018) in a persisting philosophical debate (Tullmann & Buckwalter, 2014). Fiction is not a lie—artistic representation does not deceive—writing fiction deals with a different kind of truth, one that relies on a process of "evocation" (Bion, 1967). We might call this function of symbol-formation the "as-if" function, because it allows us to treat a fiction as if it were real. This duplicity and double-dealing involved in the representation of something is a ubiquitous property of human mentation, and the secret of our success (Deacon 1997; Burling, 2005).

The capacity to balance reality and an as-if unreality is not such an odd idea. We have noted Magritte's visual representation of it, and Coleridge's "suspension of disbelief". We do not believe the actor on stage is actually the character he portrays. But we willingly suspend that ordinary respect for reality in such a way that fictional reality is functional and it effectively arouses emotional states and conflicts as much as our real material life. This has led to a philosophical interest; according to Holland (1979), even Shakespeare was intrigued by this paradox in *A Midsummer Night's Dream*.

Segal's theory of symbolic equation

Segal attempted to isolate the detailed means by which a mind can achieve symbolic representation. She investigated patients in psychiatric care, notably Edward in her first paper "Some aspects of the analysis of a schizophrenic" (Segal, 1950) who showed abnormal symbol-formation. That initial paper reported her work in order to show that knowledge of the schizoid mechanisms, as described by Melanie Klein (1946), allows psychoanalysis to provide the explanatory theory for the symptoms found in psychotic states. It has been of great service for many psychoanalysts in studying and clinically working with difficult cases where patients function in psychotic and borderline psychotic ways. However, it also does the useful job of bringing the unconscious symbolisation processes of dreams and symptoms in line with the ordinary use of the term "symbol" in linguistics and other disciplines.

In the "concrete thinking" of disturbed mental states, patients lose the capacity to form symbols proper, or to use them as representations, and therefore fail to sustain a reasoned train of thought. Segal showed that the capacity to suspend perception of actual reality is lost. Instead, with symbolic equation, reality is lost.

We can refer to my previous paper (Hinshelwood, 2018) on the investigations Segal made in "Notes on symbol formation" (Segal, 1957) and later publications (1978, 1998, 2007). There she achieved a number of things. First, the abnormality is found in the formative process of symbols. Then, she took a step on from Freud's explanation of psychosis as, more simply, a disturbance of the reality principle (Freud, 1911a, 1911b). Segal unpacked the problems of reality, in a different way using the mid-twentieth century understanding of schizoid mechanisms, especially projective identification. The specific disruption of reality was the confusion of self with external reality. The separating line in Saussure's diagram had been erased.

So the loss of a clear boundary between self and other, she claimed, translated into this other confusion of identity, the confusion between a symbol and the thing symbolised:

> [D]isturbances in differentiation between ego and object lead to disturbances in differentiation between the symbol and the object symbolized and therefore to concrete thinking characteristic of psychoses. (Segal, 1957, p. 393)

Segal vividly conveyed this with two examples of violinists. First, a schizophrenic patient who, playing a violin, experienced it as actually masturbating his genitals; and in contrast, a non-psychotic person experienced playing the violin as a sublimation of masturbation, giving added pleasure when playing music together with a young woman. The disturbance of the ego–object differentiation results in what she called a "symbolic equation". When the symbol is experienced as actually being the thing it symbolises, the concrete thinking observed by psychiatrists results. In this way she could demonstrate the strong explanatory power of the concept of projective identification.

So, in the course of developing her explanatory model, Segal brought the psychoanalytic view of symbols (Jones, 1916) into line with the more usual view of symbols in general in human culture and consciousness by showing Saussure's bipartite structure applies to both normal symbols and psychoanalytic symbols:

> [T]here are very great advantages in extending the [psychoanalytic] definition … Jones' concept [of a symbol] excludes most of what is called "symbol" in other sciences and in everyday language. (Segal, 1957, p. 392)

Later, she believed her theory had some limitations and she added to her theory in a follow-up paper (Segal, 1978). That subsequent paper developed her theory by connecting symbolic equation to container–contained theory (as developed by Bion, 1962b, 1970), or at least to the failure of a containing relationship. This attended to some of the limitations:

1. Verbal symbols seemed to take second place in the classic paper in 1957, even though they are such a dominant mode of symbolisation;

2. In the course of time it became clear that the problems of symbol-formation also occur with people who are not psychotic. Such non-psychotic conditions may manifest as severe personality disorders, but in spite of concrete symbolisation they maintain a good enough recognition of the reality.

She argued that these limitations in her theory could be dealt with by using the new knowledge about projective identification: "[I]t is an oversimplified view to think that projective identification per se leads to concretization" (Segal, 1978, p. 317). She turned then to Bion's (1959) postulate of a communicative (or "normal") form of projective identification at the core of the container-contained relationship. This was distinct from the original separation-denying form apparent in the psychoses. "Normal" projective identification is the basis for the container-contained relationship, here most succinctly described by Bion:

> When the patient strove to rid himself of fears of death which were felt to be too powerful for his personality to contain he split off his fears and put them into me, the idea apparently being that if they were allowed to repose there long enough they would undergo modification by my psyche and could then be safely reintrojected. (Bion, 1959, p. 312)

However, Segal now elaborated her modification of the theory of symbol-formation by stating that problems of symbolisation are due to the occasions when it fails:

> [A] great deal can go wrong in the projection. The relation between the container and the contained may be felt as mutually destructive or mutually emptying, as well as being mutually creative. (Segal, 1978, p. 317)

It is not the place to consider in detail any further the limitations as well as the criticisms seen by others as these are fully indicated in my previous paper (Hinshelwood, 2018). It is sufficient to indicate that over the fifty years or more of the development of Segal's thought, the understanding of splitting and of projective identification has developed, and various forms of both have now been recognised. Whilst there is a great interest in projective identification, there has been less interest in the nature and types of splitting.

And the neglect is even greater when we try to consider abnormal forms of splitting and which specific ego-function is being split off.

Nevertheless, one of the big (major outstanding) problems is that a psychotic form of splitting with projective identification denies separation, and results in symbolic equation. But the non-psychotic form of splitting—associated with "normal" projective identification—aims for a functional relationship between subject and object, and that does not show how non-psychotic people can develop disturbances of symbol-formation. One solution was Freud's description in his paper on fetishism (Freud, 1927e).

Freud's account of fetishism had opened up a debate on splitting of the ego. The fetishist deals with the fear of castration in two separate ways: a woman is evidence of the fact that castration happens. So, the fetishist first denies the reality of castration, and second he accepts the reality but represses it, with the substitution of a conscious fetish as a substitute penis. Both denial and repression operate in parallel in parts of the personality that are split from each other without communicating. Interestingly, Freud had also observed this kind of non-integration of parts of the personality in psychosis:

> [O]ne learns from patients after their recovery [following psychosis] that at the time in some corner of their mind (as they put it) there was a normal person hidden, who, like a detached spectator, watched the hubbub of illness go past him. (Freud, 1940a, p. 202)

The part of the personality that operates in a psychotic way can come to dominate, for the time being, the non-psychotic, reality-based part of the personality. By establishing in this way the possibility of psychotic functioning in non-psychotic persons, Segal could argue that such people still have the propensity for pathological projective identification, at least in one part of their mind, and therefore for concrete symbol-formation. So, the upshot was an increasing complexity to Segal's model.

Splitting and the willing suspension

The fetishist can both accept reality and also deny it simultaneously. His disturbance is that both defences create a psychological disorder—based on denial and on repression. Or rather he depends on both repression and denial in different parts of his personality, which are by necessity split apart. Now, let us suppose that these strategies might not be defensive and pathological resulting in non-communication. Then we would get a curious convergence. With this hypothetical comparison with fetishism, we would have, first, the denial that is only a suspension of the reality principle, and second, the acceptance of the reality principle is not therefore repressed. With a suspension and no repression, then we would have an interesting new situation in which both acceptance and rejection co-exist; although in the case of symbol-formation it is not relegated from consciousness. Now, this more integrated co-existence of a suspension of reality and an acceptance indicates a pattern just as we find in symbolism—an acceptance of the reality that the symbol is not the thing symbolised, and at the same time a rejection of the reality, so that we proceed as if it really is the thing symbolised. This would be different from the non-communication of the psychotic state or of fetishism, where the two attitudes to reality, accepting and rejecting, are not in communication. There is no non-communication (nor lack of ego integration) and no defensiveness in the as-if function, so there is no psychological disorder; just an anomalous double relation with reality. The reality that the symbol is not the thing symbolised is both accepted and at the same time it is rejected—the "violin" is not in reality the penis, yet the violin stands in as a sublimated representation as-if it were the real penis. And Magritte's pipe is just as we know it in reality, whilst also we know it to be *only* a representation.

The human mind appears to possess some capacity to bring together these two contradictory perceptions of reality. It enables us to enter a new reality, the reality of cultural representations (that is, the world of external representations), as well as the perceptual (or internal) representations. This capacity to represent depends on imagining one thing being another, without also losing the capacity to know that the representation is not reality. Thus we can postulate:

- We may call this function a key ego-function;
- We can know reality and suspend our knowing at the same time;
- Certain problems occur with this as-if ego-function;
- It is distorted in the fetishist due to a defensiveness;

- It is split off in psychosis to create concrete symbolic equations due to a defensiveness comparable with, though not identical with, that of the fetishist.

When not distorted or split off it is a function that is elaborated and magnified to the nth degree to give a cultural influence on all aspects of human life. The ability to live in a cultural reality depends on the as-if function.

So now we can argue, the function of symbol-formation requires a splitting of the personality somewhat similar to the one accomplished by the fetishist:

- A denial of a reality, the symbol is as if the thing symbolised; a high-heeled shoe is a penis;
- And at the same time an acceptance of reality—the symbol is not actually the thing symbolised, and the shoe can be known to be just a shoe.

However, the fetishist fails to keep both of these together in his mind. So he loses integration. In the psychotic state, the part of the personality that operates the psychotic mechanisms destroys the ego-function and eliminates it due to a hatred of reality in general. When, however, symbol-formation functions normally, the as-if function allows reality and non-reality to co-exist, and there is a non-destructive cooperation between the parts of the personality.

Representation and the reality principle

This as-if function becomes automatic and unthought, like riding a bicycle. But of course the world of aesthetics is more than riding a bicycle. It is beyond the material world of things and physical actions. Human beings have created a new immaterial world, as Caper (1999) called it. Of course, we do sometimes make mistakes and think of our representations as realities. Witches who stuck pins in dolls as a magical way of influencing reality conflated the dolls with the persons they wished to curse. There is a large industry that creates celebrities for popular consumption by those of us who think we actually know those people and their seemingly larger-than-life nature. But for psychoanalytic psychotherapy, the interesting case is the psychotic belief in the reality of representations. One example we shall return to later is Segal's psychotic patient Edward (Segal, 1950), who not only thought the hospital he was in was like a prison, he thought it was a prison. Much of the work with Edward was to help to restore his capacity for a willing suspension of the disbelief in his characterisation of the hospital as a prison. His capacity to know that the hospital was not a prison was suspended—and in the psychotic state perhaps we could say it was not willingly suspended, but compelled by the psychotic defences to believe the representation was truly a prison. In such conditions it was not possible to keep in the back of his mind the disbelief that his representation was not reality.

However, to further this description of the details of these mechanisms it is worth going back to Freud's original description of the reality principle which came out of his work with Schreber's psychotic memoirs (Freud, 1911c). In "Formulation on the two principles of mental functioning" (2011b, pp. 220–221), he lists:

1. a heightened importance of the sense-organs directed towards the external world;
2. the consciousness attached to those sense organs;
3. consciousness comprehends sensory qualities in addition to the qualities of pleasure and unpleasure;
4. a special function that periodically searches the external world—the function of attention—meeting the sense-impressions half-way;
5. a system of notation to lay down the results of this periodical activity which we call memory;
6. repression, which excluded unpleasure;
7. an impartial passing of judgement whether a given idea was true or false (i.e. in agreement with reality or not);
8. a new function allotted to motor discharge, no longer merely a means of unburdening the mental apparatus of stimuli, but now employed in the alteration of reality; thus converted into action;
9. a restraint upon motor discharge (upon action), by means of thinking, and the presentation of ideas; and
10. thought, to tolerate the increased tension of stimuli while discharge was postponed, an experimental kind of acting.

These ten functions are a comprehensive list, and we can consider which of them are willingly "suspended" for the purposes of representation. Those most applicable to the suspension of disbelief are numbers 4, 5, and 7: the functions of attention, a system of notation we call memory, and judgement of an idea as true or false. In terms of Saussure's diagram above: (i) attention is directed towards the upper level; (ii) judgement of whether the representation is a true reality or a false reflection is willingly, or unwillingly, disabled; and then once that has been achieved (iii) the content of the upper level is developed into a systematic notation.

There is a further function that allows the reality principle to be modified, but not in the interests of the more satisfying pleasure principle, but quite differently, it is to allow a system of representations, including the notation that Freud conceived of. Instead of simply disqualifying these three functions, numbers 4, 5, and 7, in normal symbolisation they continue—in a kind of latent form, available to resume when necessary. In contrast, in a psychotic state, hatred of reality disables the three functions completely. So the function we need to add to Freud's is a modification of number 7, judgement, which enables this willing suspension and which in turn allows representation to be a reality. I have referred to it as the "as-if" function. It diverges from the subsequent functions, 8–10.

Alpha function

Segal's turn to container–contained in 1978 is significant as it implied, though she did not go into it, the essay written by Bion (1962b) on alpha function. Bion's work, and in particular his reflections on Freud's reality principle, was clear from his work with psychotics who dismantle those functions (Bion, 1957). Bion's postulate was an alpha function that took off from function 1, perception, together with attention, function 4. Perception produces raw sensory data, and the mind works on this to produce a meaningful experience that is then laid down as a notation (function 5). In fact, Bion developed a complex notation he called the "Grid", which he linked with function 10, thought. So, in introducing alpha function, Bion picked out two of the factors in the reality principle that Freud described—attention and notation. Thus alpha function has a significant affinity with the as-if function. Then to these he added splitting and projective identification.

Some clinical material: Edward's deficit

We can briefly test the concept of an as-if function to see if it works in practice. Segal's (1950) vivid clinical material from her original case, Edward, gave the data on which Segal initially based her theory of concrete symbolic equation (Segal, 1957). It is therefore ideal to see how well the revised model—the splitting-off of a specific as-if function (rather than just the separation problem of projective identification)—could serve to explain these data. If this revision has as much explanatory power in practice as her original model, then it could be the preferred variation since it reduces the complexity that Segal's conceptions gathered over the years. If this deficit can explain an example observed before the as-if model had been proposed, then that is strong evidence for it, because it is spotted in material not intended to reveal it.

Edward's mind had psychotic periods of functioning in which the reality principle was disturbed. Segal gave an illustration: "[H]e felt that his own hallucinations were in everybody's mind. At times the boundary between the internal and external world seemed completely obliterated" (Segal, 1950, p. 269). The phantasy that aspects of his mind are in someone else's was exactly the projective process Klein had described in 1946, and what Segal wished to give evidence for. The confusion is between self and other. At the time, Segal described the mechanism thus:

> When he hallucinated, he felt that the voices he heard were ubiquitous. He would say "All prisoners hear voices", or, speaking of shock treatment, "The doctors were so maddened by voices that they tried to stop them by killing the poor patients". (Segal, 1950, p. 269)

Segal gave these examples to show the pattern of projective identification and how the clinical material demonstrated the confusion of his own identity (ego) with other patients and with doctors. The material showed the loss of differentiation effected by projective identification. She then said she "interpreted to him repeatedly" (Segal, 1950, p. 269):

> On my suggesting that being in the hospital was like being a prisoner, and being like a prisoner meant to him being actually

> imprisoned, he seemed relieved and said it was so, but would I please keep it secret. (p. 269)

So, Segal conveyed, repeatedly, that the hospital was *like* a prison, rather than that it was a prison. When Segal interpreted Edward's equation (not representation), the response was an appreciable change. The change appeared to bring back the missing function; he said "It was so", which supported the accuracy of her interpretation.

So, Edward's belief had changed; he no longer believed that he was a prisoner—he could know the hospital was not a prison, even though the experience remained of a prison. The interpretations had a clear effect. They brought back the as-if capacity to see the hospital as-if it were a prison. He could then see it was so, and that one thing represented another—the hospital was then as if a prison. This was different from the conviction that the hospital actually was a prison. The effect of the interpretation was that he could again see something as if it were something else. Saussure's line had been drawn in again.

Here the clinical process effected a change, and he could regain a capacity to represent. This elucidation of the problem made Edward feel understood, it seems. And that sense of being understood restored his sense of reality, undoing the equation. He could then make a move towards understanding for himself how one thing (the hospital) could represent another (a prison). So, his capacity to represent was not forever overridden by the confusion of a projective identification. The interpretation based on Segal's own capacity for the as-if function brought back Edward's capacity to represent, and therefore the distinction between the hospital and a prison.

Segal understood that Edward believed the hospital to be an actual prison—a symbolic equation. She could make sense of this, and thus preserve the reality for him. It was Segal who could make the distinction first; the symbol was only as if the real thing—the hospital was only as if a prison. Then having performed this as-if function for him, his mind once again showed the ability to grasp the distinction. With his analyst performing this function, he could then re-introject that function. He could see the as-if quality for himself.

This appears to be a process in which Segal took on the role of restoring the function of seeing things as-if. She performed this ego-function, formulated the reality (it is a hospital) and acknowledged how it was as if a prison. Her interpretation worked as a replacement of Edward's lost function. If Edward had fragmented his own as-if functioning, the analyst then performed the function Edward had lost.

However, he needed it to be kept secret—this is interesting. Why a secret? What does he mean? To answer that we would need more material. However, it is possible that, at an unconscious level, keeping it secret could be understood as the need to keep it split off. His own capacity to represent with a symbol had to be kept separate from the rest of his ego/mind. This contrasts with Segal's capacity to keep the as-if ego-function in her mind; that is, she could keep up this double form of reality that is necessary for symbol-formation. Despite the speculative nature of this explanation, we could claim that there is an adequate fit between the as-if explanation and the original data. It suggests that a model based on the loss of that ego-function adds a significant element to Segal's original explanation based only on projective identification. It is not about splitting off *some* part of the ego; it is a specific part that is split off. It adds an answer to the question: What is split off and projected?

Conclusion

We have pursued the argument that the as-if function of the ego is an "integrated kind of splitting" of the personality. Symbols depend on a tolerance of this dual attitude to reality, a "functional" conflict, as it were. The two sides of the conflict hold together; but they split apart in psychosis, in the fetishist, and in other disturbances of symbol-formation. The hypothesis is that ordinarily the ego has a capacity to keep up this state of juggling with both a denial and an acceptance of reality. The ego holds both in balance with each other. It is of course true that the ego has to face many conflicts and to decide between them, without falling apart. In the case of the conflict in symbol-formation it does not make a decision between the two alternatives but keeps both in mind. However, in the case of losing the capacity to balance and to juggle successfully with the conflict, the personality splits and does fall apart.

In the course of these reflections, the focus of attention has moved from projective identification to splitting of the ego, and then to a third variable, the particular ego-function that is split off. The "as-if function" sustains a belief that the symbol is as if it is the thing symbolised, whilst knowing the actual reality. It might seem strange, given Freud's reality principle, that the denial of reality can be functional, but it seems that the achievement of the human mind has been to accomplish this functional and stable conflict. The "as-if" term is unfortunately ambiguous because it may encroach on the term "the as-if personality" (Deutsch, 1942; Britton, 1994), as well as the description of rather false presentations in sessions (e.g. Skogstad, 2003; Mawson, 2004); in which case it risks causing some confusion. Britton reviewed some references to this "half measure", as Freud had called it, but took it as a pathological manoeuvre. In the present proposition, this as-if function is non-pathological. The distinction between the two states of this function will need further investigation.

Freud was certainly interested in representation and symbolisation, and how signifiers may substitute in the sliding sort of way that Lacan described. However, his paper on the two principles of mental functioning seemed to think that the principles—pleasure and reality—were alternatives (Freud, 1911b). Although born into a narcissistic, even solipsistic, world, the human being has to grow wise to its surroundings and accept something much more realistic. He postulated the notion of deferred gratification. But deferred gratification is only one method of coping with reality as it begins to be appreciated. The other method is this functional rejection that allows the creation of a cultural world of symbols as another reality.

The attempt here has been to strengthen Segal's claim that there is an important correspondence between the normal definition of a symbol and the way it is used by psychoanalysts trying to understand abnormal functioning. Her complex theory of concrete symbols based on splitting and projective identification together with the elaboration resulting from critiques described briefly has led to the possible conclusion that the "as-if" ego-function adds a detail to the notion of splitting of the ego and the success of human civilisation.

It seems that by investigating the abnormal manifestations of symbol-formation, as Hanna Segal did, it has been possible to identify the specific ego-function that was necessary for the human species to develop symbolic representations, the accumulation of knowledge and civilised life.

References

Bion, W. R. (1957). Differentiation of the psychotic from non-psychotic personalities. *International Journal of Psychoanalysis, 38*(3/4). Reprinted in W. R. Bion, *Second Thoughts* (pp. 43–64) .New York: Jason Aronson, 1967.

Bion, W. R. (1959). Attacks on linking, *International Journal of Psychoanalysis, 40*: 308–315. Reprinted in W. R. Bion, *Second Thoughts* (pp. 93–109). New York: Jason Aronson, 1967.

Bion W. R. (1962a). A theory of thinking. *International Journal of Psychoanalysis, 43*: 306–310. Republished in W. R. Bion, *Second Thoughts*. London: Heinemann, 1967; and in E. Bott Spillius (Ed.,), *Melanie Klein, Today, Volume 1*. London: Routledge, 1988.

Bion, W. R. (1962b). *Learning from Experience*. London: Heinemann.

Bion, W. R. (1970). *Attention and Interpretation*. London: Tavistock.

Bion, W. R. (1967). Notes on memory and desire. *Psychoanalytic Forum, 2*: 271–280. Reprinted in E. Bott Spillius (Ed.), *Melanie Klein Today, Volume 2* (pp. 17–21). London: Routledge, 1988.

Britton, R. (1994). The blindness of the seeing eye: Inverse symmetry as a defense against reality. *Psychoanalytic Inquiry, 14*: 365–378.

Burling, R. (2005). *The Talking Ape: How language Evolved*. Oxford: Oxford University Press.

Caper, R. (1999). *Immaterial Facts: Freud's Discovery of Psychic Reality and Klein's Development of His Work*. London: Routledge.

Coleridge, Samuel Taylor (1817). *Biographia Literaria*. London: Dent, 1997.

Deacon, T. (1997). *The Symbolic Species*. London: Penguin.

Deutsch, H. (1942). Some forms of emotional disturbance and their relationship to schizophrenia. *Psychoanalytic Quarterly, 11*: 301–321.

Freud, S. (1911b). Formulations on the two principles of mental functioning. *S. E., 12*: 213–226. London: Hogarth.

Freud, S. (1911c). Psycho-analytic notes on an autobiographical account of a case of paranoia (dementia paranoides). *S. E., 12*: 3–82. London: Hogarth.

Freud, S. (1927e). Fetishism. *S. E., 21*: 147–158.

Freud, S. (1940a). *An Outline of Psycho-analysis*. *S. E., 23*: 139–208. London: Hogarth.

Hinshelwood, R. D. (2018). Symbolic equation and symbolic representation: An appraisal of Hanna Segal's work. *British Journal of Psychotherapy, 34*: 342–357.

Holland, N. N. (1979). Hermia's dream. *Annals of Psychoanalysis, 7*: 369–389.

Jones, E. (1916). The theory of symbolism. In: *Papers on Psychoanalysis*. London: Ballière, Tyndale & Cox, 1918.

Klein, M. (1946). Notes on some schizoid mechanisms. *International Journal of Psychoanalysis, 27*: 99–110. Republished in M. Klein, P. Heimann, S. Isaacs & and J. Riviere, *Developments in Psycho-Analysis* (pp. 292–320). London: Hogarth, 1952.

Konrad, E-M., & Petraschka, T. (2018). The paradox of fiction—A brief introduction into recent developments, open questions, and current areas of research, including a comprehensive bibliography from 1975 to 2018. *Journal of Literary Theory, 12*: 193–203.

Mawson, C. (2004). Pseudo-free association: The sophisticated analytic patient and "as-if" relating. *British Journal of Psychotherapy, 18*: 509–522.

Paskow, A (2004). *The Paradoxes of Art: A Phenomenological Investigation.* Cambridge: Cambridge University Press.

de Saussure, F. (1916). *Course in General Linguistics.* New York: Columbia University Press, 1959.

Segal, H. (1950). Some aspects of the analysis of a schizophrenic. *International Journal of Psychoanalysis, 31*: 268–278. Republished in *The Works of Hanna Segal.* London: Free Association, 1981; and in E. Bott Spillius (Ed.), *Melanie Klein Today, Volume 1.* London: Routledge, 1988.

Segal, H. (1957). Notes on symbol formation. *International Journal of Psychoanalysis, 38*: 391–397.
Republished in *The Works of Hanna Segal.* London: Free Association, 1981; and in E. Bott Spillius (Ed.), *Melanie Klein Today, Volume 1.* London: Routledge, 1988.

Segal, H. (1978). On symbolism. *International Journal of Psychoanalysis, 59*: 315–319.

Segal, H. (1998). "The importance of symbol-formation in the development of the ego"—in context. *Journal of Child Psychotherapy, 24*: 349–357.

Segal, H. (2007). Symbolic equation and symbols. In: *Yesterday, Today and Tomorrow* (pp. 111–113). London: Routledge.

Skogstad, W. (2003). Internal and external reality in in-patient psychotherapy: Working with severely disturbed patients at the Cassel Hospital. *Psychoanalytic Psychotherapy, 17*(2): 97–118.

Tullmann, K., & Buckwalter, W. (2014). Does the paradox of fiction exist? *Erkenntnis, 79*: 779–796.

Discussion of Part III

GC: This part starts with a paper that directly follows from the one on social defences against nuclear war (Chapter 5). A way to sustain these defences is by attacking thinking. Here the attack on thinking is described in two independent moves. On the one hand, ideas are modified into becoming ideologies and, on the other, identities embody reified conceptions of being (both individual and collective) which are thought of as immutable and rigid so as to become devoid of life. It is the combined effect of ideological anti-thinking and its congealment into collective identities that allows the projection of parts of "our" unwanted selves into "them" and targeting the "other" for destruction in conflict and in wars. A number of questions came to me while reading the papers in this part. Let me proceed in order.

Alienation and depersonalisation and the impact of a social group

I would like to ask you first about the relationship between (intra-) individual processes and inter-individual, group, social, and political dynamics. You once wrote to me that the concepts of alienation and depersonalisation "express a distortion, not of the world around us but of our representation of ourselves as we appear to ourselves". I made a note of this and now this seems to be a good way to start us on the papers we just read. These words seem to hint at something more than a "convergence" of understanding. Rather, beyond the use of different terms, the same meaning is observed.

RDH: Yes, I think there is a common meaning to the experience of personal depletion. We talk of feeling reduced in ourselves, something like humiliation, say; or we say we are "going to pieces" as if there is no longer a coherence that holds all of ourselves together. What I was getting at is that the common experience is the beginning of building a model to understand how that experience came about. And the model is multiple, two models (at least)—a social causation or an individual dynamic causation. Indeed, their incompatibility, at least at first glance, implies a coming apart cognitively. The demand for a theory of everything is that the whole body of meanings are coherent. In the first paper, there is a different approach. If there is a state of mind that is fragmented—we are "in pieces"—then socially enforced ideas can be welcome to give, as it were, a sticking plaster to hold the pieces together. The point is based on the view that powerful anxiety arises from a feeling that one is unstable in oneself. And then social attitudes can help to stabilise our selves in a rigid way.

GC: In light of the papers we just read, these matters take new, wider, and deeper meanings. In the first of the three papers in this part, for instance, in which you reflect on the deformation of ideas into ideology you write that "when ideas become overvalued" they become ideologies. How are aspects of depersonalisation and alienation at play in this process? I do not imagine that expressing a clear causality is where your work takes you, but you seem to draw links between depersonalised/alienated individuals in regressed groups and their susceptibility to ideological drifts, to the modification of ideas into ideologies (and perhaps vice versa as ideologies modify the creative aspects of the personality). Indeed, in Chapter 6 you link these processes to false consciousness and to how ideologies empty groups of their vitality by replacing their primary task and petrify their identity.

RDH: I do think that the distinction Ron Britton and John Steiner (1994) made is very powerful. Pressures felt by the analyst to produce an interpretation can feel very great and we may need them for many reasons. There are three obvious reasons. First, we wish to show to ourselves that we are competent at our job; second, we may have internal provocateurs taken in from a supervisor, or even our analyst, that prod us to do what they would do; and third, there is pressure from our patient who comes with powerful needs for relief which may be conveyed unconsciously right now. And when he/she makes an implicit demand we either enlighten them urgently on what is happening or alternatively we collude with them to establish a defensive avoidance of what they feel is intolerable and are demanding assistance with. This, of course, only provides a clinical model, but the pressures in groups, organisations, and politics can, I suspect, provoke exactly the same rushed, unthought clutching at ideas and solutions.

GC: Before returning to the depletion of the ego, I would like to ask you one or two more things which I think help me and our readers situate your thinking on groups further. When you write about the difference between generative vs destructive groups you refer to some of the key features of the latter. Among them, that in destructive groups we can observe "spreading a contagion of emotion". Do you mean by this that in work groups decision-making and the division of labour happen through deliberative processes devoid of emotion, or, on the other hand, you rather refer to different ways in which emotions spread in those groups or, alternatively, to the nature of the emotions in both groups?

RDH: I think my most persisting concern is that in the "destructive" groups, apparently convincing rational communications are subjected to interference by hidden unconscious emotional experiences. Of course, deliberative processes are full of conscious emotions. It is the unconscious emotions that can trip us up. They are repressed and it is especially those split off which interfere unseen. Within groups the dispersal around the group of painful experiences leads to a demoralisation of the whole group

GC: From a psychoanalytic perspective you write that both theory and clinical practice alert us to a kind of false knowledge akin to the one discussed in political theory as false consciousness. You suggest that what is false consciousness in groups manifests itself as neurosis in individuals and that, in turn, neurotic false truth in individuals is ideology in groups. I am curious to ask you whether you associate other personality structures and truth regimes to comparable social organisation and their prevalent truth regimes. I wonder, for instance, when an ideology is acted out in extreme, totalitarian, forms of anti-politics. For instance, you write in the same paper (Chapter 6), with Freud, that momentary convergence of ego and ego-ideal generates triumphant manic euphoria and, I would add, subsequent potentially low melancholic depression that may prevent political action voiding individuals and groups of both a sense of (their) reality and of agency.

RDH: OK, that is a realistic addition since depression is usually what is behind, or beneath, manic euphoria, and we are saying that group dynamics in the form of political triumph and failure follow that bipolar path that the individuals tread. Political parties and movements slump into despair often with leaders attempting a rhetoric of triumphal success to restore morale and energy. I have taken as key the personality structure described by Rosenfeld (1971) as akin to the mafia, that bullying force in society. But within the personality it becomes a self-bullying, a repudiation of weakness and vulnerability though adopting a callous and dismissively domineering attitude.

GC: A side question to this, yet one I find very important is the following: Can the opposite be said too, that is, that a neurotic individual is so because she is caught in an ideological group? This, I imagine, might have important implication to which we might return later when we discuss the possible convergences between political and psychoanalytic action.

RDH: Well, my enduring concern is that an individual can become entrapped in an ideology, but under certain conditions. The condition is that the external group hits on an unconscious need of that individual. A powerful political movement may appeal to individuals with an inner sense of a helpless or powerless self, for instance. My example in Chapter 6 of Hitler's proclaiming German supremacy needed to hit upon the population's desperate humiliation of defeat in the First World War and the economic depression of the 1920s and 1930s.

GC: When you address the issue of leadership, for instance in Chapter 6, you write of the difference between a leadership that represents the group ideal vs a leader that "alternatively … may substitute for the ideal".

The foundations of this theorisation, which I find a crucial contribution to the leadership debate, is discussed in Chapter 8 under the rubric of symbolic representation and symbolic equation. I think this is a unique contribution and this link is not fully expressed in the papers. I am sure that the readers of this book would enjoy as much as I would if you could say more about this link between symbol and world and between leader and group.

RDH: Well, you are right I have not brought out clearly enough perhaps that the leader may exist in two different relations to the group. It is perhaps a more recent theoretical conception that I have started to think about and not yet completely thought through. So, thanks for making the link with Chapter 8 so clear. The leader may represent the group, and especially its task, even if that is only a social one, the task being hospitality. But the group may feel the task *is* the leader. To some extent the Nuremberg rallies were for everyone to *be* Hitler. He, in person, was the point of their being there. They were not just supporters of his policies. The conscious process of assessing and supporting, or liking and disliking his policies were secondary. The primary experience is existential—to *be* a Hitler supporter.

GC: It might be worth returning to, and delving a bit further into, how the depletion of the ego "causes" distortions of perceptions and beliefs that drive individual actions, which in turn establish and crystallise social differences in a mutually reinforcing way. Consolidating the understanding of this process would clarify further the relation between a depleted ego and the distortions of perceptions and beliefs, which prevent the political negotiation of differences (of opinion and will). Could you also say what your thoughts are on the relation between social differences and internal distortions in relation to the formation of political opinion and will?

RDH: On the first point about the depletion of the ego and the distortions of perception, I describe two processes. The first is the loss of a specific function and Chapter 8 concerns a specific function I call the "as-if" function, which allows us to use substitutes, symbols, representations as if they were the real thing. The loss of that function results in serious communication problems with oneself in the first instance, and then with others. Ultimately it hinders the perception of reality. The second process is composed of various pressures from inside oneself and from outside that convey a loss of coherence, a self-fragmentation. This is a potential crisis that demands stability, and a clinging to whatever might offer stability including a rigid identification with something that feels powerful and permanent, like a group, or a leader.

These two factors frequently occur together. Damage to the reality principle is self-inflicted, as it is motivated to avoid some feature of the real external world that creates conflict and anxiety. Moreover, if the avoided experience is the existential anxiety, then a depletion through splitting off a function will enhance the anxiety. An everyday example is the following: consider someone going to a lecture with a large audience of mostly unrecognised people. As noted in the papers in Part II, the impact of a large anonymous group is to arouse existential anxiety about one's own identity, and a sense of increasing anonymity. So, it is a familiar occurrence, I think, that, after the speaker's presentation there is often a significant silence before someone collects themselves together to contribute or ask a question. The members of the audience are there because of their interest in the topic, but when they have a chance, they do not speak of their interest (at least not at first). I can describe the unconscious dynamics like this: the silence seems to occur because the members of the audience feel out of their depth and cannot match the presenter's level of debate. One can see this as a process in which the audience identify so strongly through a projective identification that he *becomes* their capacity for intelligent debate (they lose number ten of the listed ego-functions—experimental action). They for a moment are depleted of their capacity to think. The audience needs a short period of time to recover their own capacity. That recovery usually happens, and a discussion starts up. In the case of the Nuremberg Rally, with a much greater sense of depletion and across the entire nation with a destroyed army and culture, etc., the recovery is seriously inhibited as a recovery means a flooding with the collective national disaster echoing in their own sense of existential loss of self.

The social setting creates a separation of the speaker and the spoken-to with an associated separation of the thoughtful vocal functions of the audience being passed over to the lecturer whose sense of enhancement increases and invites a view of himself as the wisdom in the room—not that he has a wisdom he brings but that he *is* the wisdom in the room. The main point is the unconscious relations with the speaker or leader and its contrasting possibilities. On the one hand, the speaker in a hall, standing maybe on a platform, invites not just an exchange of ideas, a process such as reading a book in a library or in one's sitting room, but an identification process in which one is no longer one's own "self". The setting and performance establish an identity shift. The thoughts of the speaker *are* the thoughts of the audience. Though he may offer them for consideration and thought, the shift is that they become unthought, unquestioned, and a pervading equation of identity, at least temporarily. Similarly, the social relations of factory production (and its relations), where the economic exploitation of a worker's products mean just that same weakening of the self that an academic audience feels, or a defeated nation feels. The worker feels his "self" is going to pieces as his product is removed. Ultimately, the removal of the work product is comparable to the removal of the academic's sense of being an intellectual. The two patterns come together. That weakening leads to a sense of not being able to fully assert his own interests either in the factory or the lecture theatre once these social relations capture the internal dynamics. The difference is that the audience are eventually given a space to recover themselves; the factory worker hardly ever. I have to say, I am considering this convergence of the Segal-defined problem with symbol-formation (1957) and the socially provoked relations between a leader and followers as I write it now. Such a new idea needs perhaps time to ferment and to blossom.

Freedom and autonomy

Matters of freedom and free choice are interesting in relation to this kind of social determinism. Full-scale freedom is impossible for a "group animal" whose success has been the capacity for collaboration with each other. Freedom can therefore be overplayed as an uncontaminated aim. Bion once described how the human being is a group animal at war with his groupishness. The reality is that freedom has to be tempered by collaboration, since it is equally true the human animal needs a group to maximise the human capacity to make appropriate changes in reality. It is through that collaboration with others that we have achieved freedom from hunger and from many diseases, and so many other advantages, technical and cultural. Though the Bible says that service to God is perfect freedom, we should be aware that whatever service to God means, service to our compatriots and cultures promotes a freedom that may not be completely perfect but is more free than going it alone; the freedom from hunger or from illness requires a devotion to a mutual give-and-take collaboration. Freedom and liberty have suffered from being too closely linked to the weaponised meaning of "democracy". It is also contaminated by the equally unbalanced emphasis on competition in our contemporary environment which has been labelled anarcho-capitalism. As much freedom as possible needs to be allowed that can live with the give-and-take imperative of collaboration. Clearly, there is a contradiction in the social ideal of free choice if there is also a binding commitment to the (social science) account of the individual shaped into social conformity.

GC: Thinking further about some aspects of free will, extreme versions of identity choice—by individuals (and groups) in search of a unique, one could say radical, authenticity—seem to lead to forms of acute depersonalisation, to the loss of the self in the abyss of choice or to forms of rigid and brittle identity constructs. I think of this situation as leaning on the edge of the abyss of absolute choice. From a belief (an illusion) in the absolute possibility of self-determination, paradoxical outcomes ensue, including flight, paralysis, or radical conformism. Even a kind of conformism in a generalised attempt to be radically unique, authentic, oneself. It is my proposition that, in the political engagement with others, this process can be escaped, but it has to be a transformative engagement, rather than a mere enactment of social dictates underpinned by a transactional attitude to the other(s) considered as the means to one's own ends. I think that the distinction between action and enactment explored by psychoanalysis and observed in the clinical practice can add insight in assessing the political nature or otherwise of collective engagements including around the issues of identity politics, ideology, and racism that you discuss in your papers.

RDH: These are very important points. When is conformism to a group role oppressive, and when is it a creative possibility for both individual and group? Your reference to the abyss of choice is apt and alarmingly graphic. Choice does put one in the headlights, and up for a burden of responsibility, or worse. What's worse?—perhaps a damning annihilation of one's character or person. Evasion and avoidance, despite its weakening effect through projection, can often seem unquestionably and irresistibly preferable. So, much depends on unconscious dynamics and, as much as anything, the context of a collective group dynamic or evasion. Ideology may give itself significance if it gives a moral aspect to the function demanded. For instance, a positive value may have been given to engine drivers of trains that transported to Auschwitz trucks packed with Jews like animals. These are group assignments to functional roles. Such requirements support the splitting off of functions in the individual—such as empathy. Another example, at the beginning of the twenty-first century, might be the so-called "climate-deniers", whose capacity for judgements based on reality has been split off under pressures of certain campaign groups playing on the intolerable sense of annihilation which desperately needs denying. Social roles with restricted individual functioning and socially triggered splitting off of significant functions have a significant impact on the sense of personal identity. And that enhances the existential anxiety about losing one's self. The restitution of the ego is a compelling necessity, and often then through the rigid identification *with* something more stable, with some idea, or some idea-proclaiming person.

One of the major impacts of a social group is that the ego-functions can be shared out between members of a group. This allows a kind of mental division of labour, often unconsciously negotiated. For instance, a single member can take on the function of leadership, or someone takes the guilty role, the scapegoat, and so on. This is of great importance. If the division amongst the group members is not handled carefully the experience can be one of depletion—or we could say, exploitation, as in Lukács' (1923) description of "labour process". But where a special function is consciously appreciated and valued, as by analogy a team of builders with bricklayers, electricians, carpenters, etc., such depletion is compensated by the especial valuing of individual talents and traits. In the mental realm, we could consider a marriage where function of fertility, maternal preoccupation, material provision and protection, home-making, and so on can be negotiated and assigned between the partners. The sense of a weakening of oneself can be counteracted by the strengthening gained from a group membership which supplies a clear view of reality and the individual's place (identity) in it. On the other hand, a strict role-assignment supplied by an ideological culture can seem to fill a gap in identity, or at least plaster it over.

Losing parts of the ego delivered into other persons does not have to be immediately designated pathological since it is so common amongst all of us. But the difference between an ordinary division of labour and an unconscious dumping parts of the self into each other (or extracting) needs reflecting on in a political context. Division of labour has been of great advantage enabling complex cultures. So, a conscious division of ego-functions offers advantages creating important social roles, such as leadership. We put great responsibility into the people we vote for. And indeed into those we don't vote for if our party loses an election. We lodge in them considerable power to make decisions and carry them out, however unsuited they might be as in some non-democratic systems (like an inherited monarchy, or sustained by coercive threats). Whatever the political system, autonomy and responsibility are yielded up to government. This distortion of one's self is a deeply unconscious aspect of politics only psychoanalysts understand.

GC: In your 2000 paper "Alienation" (not part of the present collection), you discuss alienating social relations in mental health settings to raise issues of responsible choice as opposed to the limitation of the autonomy of patients in some clinical contexts. You also discuss the illusion of choice in market-based care that is, in fact, limited to consumer responses to advertising and enforced by psychological technologies. The articulation of alienation, autonomy, and care offers important insights for a healthier, more creative, understanding of human relationships.

RDH: Perhaps I am being a bit restrictive here—restricting the notion of action to exerting the power of alienating and commodifying persons. Possibly I have emphasised this because of the particular neoliberal regime I live and work in. It is a culture that stresses the trading of commodities of all kinds, and which takes possession of commodities and people in terms of abstract value (money) rather than (or at least minimising) their personal value. The introduction of a financial incentive is an introduction of a conflict of interest, a wanton introduction of a conflict of interest, I would say. Action is torn between, say, healthcare and profit, leading to pressures towards costly treatments, or even non-costly ones where money supervenes of over necessity. A long time ago, I came across the following:

> That any sane nation, having observed that you could provide for the supply of bread by giving bakers a pecuniary interest in baking for you, should go on to give a surgeon a pecuniary interest in cutting off your leg, is enough to make one despair of political humanity.

This began the introductory essay by George Bernard Shaw to his play *The Doctor's Dilemma* of 1906. It set a target for the social provision of health achieved some forty years later. We have, it seems to me, to be ethically careful to eliminate conflicts of interest rather than enhance them.

It is the distortion of considered activity that we need to be alert to, and to those cultivated methods of distortion. That is where psychoanalysis can insert a clarifying view on interests and conflicts that otherwise remain misty.

Unconscious dynamics in social groups

GC: The division of mental labour you refer to happens unconsciously in groups. In your papers, you show how these group dynamics result in the creation of a collective unconscious dynamic. You mean this in a way not to suggest, I think, that the group has an unconscious, a collective unconscious, but rather that group members are all involved in dynamics of which they are not aware and to which they contribute unconsciously. These dynamics establish a division of mental labour that is somehow reflected in the role distributions that you refer to (leaders, scapegoats, etc.) but do not reflect only the conscious dynamics of normative and institutional "appointments". An understanding of those unconscious dynamics allows us to better appreciate why groups appoint specific members for certain roles. In particular, it could help us understand behaviours apparently at odds with stated goals and intentions and predicated on unconscious feelings that the members themselves (individually and collectively) deny or disavow. Can you say a bit more about these dynamics and the importance of a psychoanalytic contribution to the study and the life of groups, including whole polities?

RDH: Unconscious role-assignment is related to the affect flow in social networks featured in the papers in Part II. Arising from observations of a therapy group, Wilfred Bion noted:

> Some contributions [a member] is prepared to make as coming unmistakably from himself, but there are others which he would like to make anonymously … then the foundations are laid for a successful system of evasion and denial … because the hostility of the individuals was being contributed to the group anonymously that each member could quite sincerely deny that he felt hostile. (Bion, 1948, pp. 491–492)

Bion was probably trying to elaborate Le Bon's idea of "contagion", which he would have encountered in Freud's examination of the idea in 1921. To accept and contribute to a group atmosphere—of panic, of idealisation, of violent hatred—an individual takes on the developing atmosphere in the group and enhances it in a constantly circulating process. The individual's contributions to a group culture must, in some circumstances be denied and rendered unconscious in him, Bion claimed. For instance, individuals may wish to deny their aggression. Bion's earliest views were that we are all endowed with assumptions basic to human beings in groups. For instance, disposing of dependence, or of the fear and rage behind fight or flight, and the abject obeisance to a messianic presence. Later he modified this (Bion, 1955) to bring it into line with the psychoanalytic anxiety–defence structure of repression, splitting, and the unconscious. So his espousal of these mechanisms and of projective identification had modified the basic assumptions to explain the unconscious structure of anxiety and defence, rather than his earlier espousal of Trotter's inherent and inherited features of the mind.

The collectivising of group anxiety and defences has two main forms. Elliott Jaques (1955) described common anxieties that we all feel, such as the sadness and guilt of mourning giving rise to the social ceremony of a funeral. The other form is an organisation with a specific task that arouses an anxiety common to all in the workplace. The classic example of the latter is the common anxiety felt by nurses in caring for their patients who might often overwhelm a nurse with their pain, their surgery, or mutilation, or ultimately death as Isabel Menzies Lyth (Menzies, 1960) pointed out (see Chapter 5). Such deep levels of the unconscious contain denied phantasies of hatred and aggression towards others, including the wish to see them dead. Hence a nurse must concentrate considerable mental energy to keep such phantasies denied and unconscious.

GC: Chapter 7 continues the work set out in Chapter 6 but shifts the focus from the ego-ideal, here discussed at length, to that of the ego-destructive superego. This conception has proven fertile and clinically illuminating in the consulting room; you make it work in the social context. You describe at length the way in which a very harsh superego, based on the ego-ideal, can have devastating effects on individual development, preventing it, in fact, generating at times addictive mental states to a condition of near death. You write that you "hypothesise that these brutalising internal psychic relations of the pathological organisation can become hooks within the individual on which external prejudicial relations are hung". Can you say more about this mechanism? I ask you this because elsewhere you seem less optimistic about the extension of analyses of the personality into the social. More in detail, if a leader can represent a group ideal or substitute for it, what kind of leadership (individual, collective, or ideological) can illustrate the working of a comparable anti-political (you very poignantly call it "anti-human") agency to the ego-destructive superego?

RDH: I think I had in mind Rosenfeld's idea of an internal mafia gang that subverts the whole personality with grave condemnations of dependency, and a superior idealisation of omnipotence of the self. Such internal role-playing reverberates with social structures (an actual brutalising gang). Although a more benign moral superego can resonate with a judicial court in the social dimension. In the same way, an internal autonomy can resonate with a political leader. I agree, there is also a certain pessimism about the way cultural forms, attitudes, practices can hook onto states of mind in individuals, such as the individuals in the clinical examples of Chapter 7. The crucial point is that a cultural influence needs to find an internal psychodynamic correspondence before it can be effective.

Depersonalisation as a group dynamic

GC: The process of patients' depersonalisation in a hospital as studied by Menzies Lyth, connects with alienation in commodity production as you described it above. Here, nurses and doctors distance themselves from their anxieties and, in the process (and to achieve this), they deny the humanity of the patients that have been entrusted to their care. Processes of alienation on the assembly line and on the ward seem to have some similarities. Here the depersonalisation happens in the mind of the nurse who pushes away from her the anxiety that she feels would otherwise overwhelm her (and perhaps harm the patient too). To do this, she constructs the patients as a commodity to which her labour is applied. On the assembly line something similar happens, so that the worker can be exploited and the fruit of her work taken away from her. It is not immediately evident in Menzies Lyth's work that nurses may be themselves at the receiving end of processes of dehumanisation by health services structured around strict performance and efficiency targets. These reflections are more evident in your work on turning psychiatry upside down, as you mentioned before.

RDH: Yes, that's right. The defensive indifference to the humanity of patients in hospital is not restricted to nurses, just that the nursing service was the Menzies Lyth's research project. A hospital is an entire institution dedicated to life-and-death or sanity-and-madness, and no one, at any level, is immune from the potential infection of emotions about suffering, death, and madness. We should not be shocked that the work of administration and management is also beset with a similar potential to depersonalise patients and the clinical staff, as you say. Though managerial staff may reduce the work of a hospital to statistics, and especially financial ones, there is always the deeper level of anxiety that they too need to face about deaths, waiting lists, and so on as well as the survival of the institution in terms of budgets and expenditure. This is also true, of course, about a factory, where in a competitive economy, financial survival means everything; but, of course, it is only the death of the factory that is at risk, and not the death of actual persons. It is true, of course, that the survival of the factory can always be felt in terms of the death of the mother that holds you in her arms. And an identification with the factory (as opposed to simply belonging to the workforce) can easily touch on worries about one's own death. It may be, too, that the factory product is concerned with death; what is it like, for instance, for people working in a factory making armaments that are obviously intended for killing?

But you are right that in the factory it is the worker who is depersonalised and in the ward, it is the patient, the "raw material" of the working nurse. I suppose that, faced with the working task, nobody is immune from a degree of depersonalisation and loss of ego-functions. In the factory, it would be likely that the factory owner and managers lose their empathy for the workers they exploit.

GC: These processes of extraction of properties of the human self, the subtraction of parts of patients' and workers' humanity until, in extreme cases, the whole of it is removed, relate to and are matched by similar process of misrepresentation by the worker and the nurse. These are processes that take place in close connection and form, at times, excruciating escalations of deprivation of one's and other human beings' very humanity. I find that a description of this process could be useful here. As the patient is approached with efficient coldness by the nurse and doctor, she may feel less and less able to recognise her own humanity, falling in further helplessness, which in turn is met by further curt "professionalism". This dynamic is common in many contexts, including between teachers and pupils, experts and clients of many kinds, politicians and citizens, and perhaps too, between psychoanalysts and their patients in extremely difficult clinical situations.

RDH: Yes, I think the impact of the coldness as you aptly call it, a curt professionalism, can be very powerful with people who already harbour an insecure, weakened, or threatened sense of themselves (i.e. with a depleted ego). And don't forget the army, and the custodial side of the justice system. Meeting it in any institution—whether a rather unwelcoming atmosphere in a hotel, or the downright dismissiveness of a benefits office, and so on. It suggests there can be widespread tensions in many working teams. I have sometimes wondered when waiting patiently (or passively and inhumanly) in the many queues in an airport, how easily we give up out autonomy and regress to become sheep! And on a more gruesome scale, how Nazis herded Jews into and off trains on their way to the extermination chambers.

I have come to recognise that one of the most important ego-functions relevant to political life, debate, and action, is empathy, a key element of humanity, the capacity to feel for others. I could comment on my own blank numbness during and after a visit I made to Auschwitz. I felt an indifference whilst actually there on the same ground that those exterminated prisoners trod. I think of a case illustrating the loss of this kind of experiencing reported by Melanie Klein in 1946 ("Notes on some schizoid mechanisms”). It was a man who arrived for his session in an angry mood. After a while, the analyst interpreted the anger and particularly pointed out anger towards herself. Confronted with that recognition, his mood abruptly changed and he felt a blankness of his mind, and no emotions; he said “Nothing matters any more.” Though this was transitory, as it turned out, he had for a moment had an almost catastrophic loss of his capacity to experience his own intentions, emotions, and much of his self, and especially his concern for things that had mattered. In technical terms he had split off a major function and lost it. It was not repressed, because we know that repressed material surfaces in disguised form. This man felt blank and had lost his capacity to have any emotional life. Blankness and indifference replaced his lost experiences and empathy. This clinical event demonstrates the capacity of a human being to lose a central plank of their humanity.

It seems to me that this particular function is especially vulnerable in political life. Blank indifference towards others, or towards groups of others with certain characteristics, ethnicity, and gender are currently important identifiers. This occurrence is internal to the individual but available as a “hook” for key social attitudes, including racism, as illustrated on Chapter 7.

GC: The above clinical example shows the relation between individual experiences of self and others, their role and behaviour in groups, and, hence, the individual contribution to the life of the group. The dynamic moves in both directions. As Bion noticed, individuals are politicised (i.e. they are made into full humans) in groups. In a way that is congruent with Freud’s (1911b) thinking in the “Two principles”, and reminiscent of Klein’s and Bion’s thinking on effective action and reactive, unthinking, acting-outs (between working through and repeating), one could say that the sphere of the social is the precipitate of, and drives, reactive, stereotypical, and habitual behaviour, whereas political action is a thoughtful, reality-based, and collectively negotiated response to both individual and group needs (as they arise in relations between individuals and between them and their environment). I think the point you make above on Klein’s patient supports a similar view. What are your thoughts about this?

RDH: The important thing we are considering is that the effective political thought is often intruded upon by the influence of unconscious anxieties and defensiveness that can throw the political reasoning off course. Psychoanalysis has sought various ways of understanding the specific uniqueness of our nature—our "species-being" as Marx (1867 [1976]) and Feuerbach described it. And Bion did think that humans are group animals, though ambivalently so. Freud (1921c), too, agreed and claimed that psychoanalysis though an individual psychology was equally a social psychology! Your notion of social behaviour as antithetical to political behaviour is interesting. I am not sure that social behaviour is always dominated by unconscious dynamics. It depends where one draws the line between social and political. I tend to think that all interaction (including social) between people has a political tone to it, while you seem to say that political action is enhancing unless it is interfered with by social unconscious forces.

GC: I see that this would require further clarifications on my part, but this is not the place, as we will discuss this in greater detail after reading the next part of this collection. Instead, following from what you just said and sort of nudging you in the direction of some of my dearest interests, let me ask you this in relation to your work on Segal's theory of symbolism (Chapter 8). Is there a kind of "political equation", analogous to the symbolic equations that denote pre-, a-, non-, and anti-political behaviours in organisations (of the individual personality, of the group, and of society, including global society)? Can populism be conceived of as a malaise of collective thinking? How can we detect drift towards more or less totalitarian forms of thinking and rule? How can we address or even prevent the most radical drifts?

RDH: That is a very interesting thought—the leader who can be a representative of the group or can be a symbolic equation identified with by his followers. It is certainly something to take away and think about. I tend to think of populism as a perfect example of Lukács' "false consciousness", as we have discussed earlier. It is a set of attitudes that arise out of points of view manipulated across the class divide. It is, in particular, connected to an insistent and intense national pride; I would then agree that a kind of equation is made between a personal identity and the lauded national identity, and relies on the depleted sense of the individual selves on a mass scale.

GC: In the context of Chapter 6, you show how internal hooks and external prejudices reinforce each other. What does this say about the nature of the "political–psychological" action you invoke (and only suggest, without fully spelling out)?

RDH: Well, it is crucial to consider whether the kind of psychological appraisals we have been engaging on can be translated into relevant and effective political debate and action. My concern is whether the understanding of the unconscious and its interference in the conscious political debates and passions could ever become commonly accepted and familiar. I think it has to, and if it is not possible, my concern is that our current civilisation will totter to its demise. The difficulty in handling the continuing outbreaks of war that could so easily topple over into a worldwide nuclear conflict, and the bitter contests in taking seriously the climate emergency, as well as the underlying escalating inequalities that turn increasing numbers of persons into alienated commodities all point to a blood-spilling final act. So the consciousness-raising about the unconscious seems long-delayed and desperately urgent. The question is how to proceed with such a rescue operation.

GC: On these worrying notes, I think it is fitting to break our conversation here and to read the next and final set of chapters. There the point is made that—given our current local and global circumstances and the dangers you warn about, of humanity toppling itself to its demise—it is imperative to act to arrest these trends. How can we best do this? What can psychoanalysis contribute to a theory of political action? I very much look forward to thinking with you about whether political action can be made to resonate, converge, or dialogue with the psychoanalytic literature on the theory of technique and on therapeutic action.

References

Bion, W. R. (1948). Experiences in groups: II. *Human Relations*, 1: 487–496. Republished in W. R. Bion, *Experiences in Groups and Other Papers* (pp. 41–58). London: Tavistock, 1961.

Bion, W. R. (1955). Group dynamics: A review. In: M. Klein, P. Heimann, & R. Money-Kyrle (Eds.), *New Directions in Psychoanalysis* (pp. 440–477). London: Hogarth. Republished in W. R. Bion, *The Complete Works Vol. IV* (pp. 207–245).

Britton, R., & Steiner, J. (1994). Interpretation: Selected fact or overvalued idea? *International Journal of Psychoanalysis, 75*: 1069–1078.

Freud, S. (1911b). Formulations on the two principles of mental functioning. *S. E., 12*: 213–226. London: Hogarth.

Freud, S. (1921c). *Group Psychology and the Analysis of the Ego. S. E., 18*: 67–143. London: Hogarth.

Hinshelwood, R. D. (2018). Symbolic equation and symbolic representation: An appraisal of the Hanna Segal's work. *British Journal of Psychotherapy, 34*: 342–357.

Hinshelwood, R. D. (2000). Alienation: Social relations and therapeutic relations. *Psychoanalytic Studies, 2*(1): 21–22.

Jaques, E. (1955). Social systems as a defence against persecutory and depressive anxiety. In: M. Klein, P. Heimann & R. Money-Kyrle (Eds.), *New Directions in Psychoanalysis* (pp. 478–498). London: Tavistock.

Klein, M. (1946). Notes on some schizoid mechanisms. *International Journal of Psychoanalysis, 27*: 99–110. Republished in M. Klein, P. Heimann, S. Isaacs & and J. Riviere, *Developments in Psycho-Analysis* (pp. 292–320). London: Hogarth, 1952.

Lukács, G. (1923). *History and Class Consciousness.* Cambridge, MA: MIT Press, 1971.

Marx, K. (1867). *Capital.* London: Penguin, 1976.

Menzies, I. (1960). A case-study in the functioning of social systems as a defence against anxiety: A report on a study of the nursing service of a general hospital. *Human Relations, 13*(2): 95–121.

Rosenfeld, H. (1971). A clinical approach to the psychoanalytic theory of the life and death instincts: An investigation into the aggressive aspects of narcissism. *International Journal of Psychoanalysis, 52*: 169–178. Republished in E. Bott Spillius (Ed.), *Melanie Klein Today, Volume 1.* London: Routledge, 1988.

Segal, H. (1957). Notes on symbol formation. *International Journal of Psychoanalysis, 38*: 391–397.

Part IV

How do we “take action”?

The papers in this part are more recent and return to the nature of the experience of alienation. They discuss some of the contemporary issues including the way democracy is designated in the West as being in increasing crisis. That crisis would be caused by both a threat from other large-scale economies, including China, as well as by an internal despair within the election-oriented countries of the West where a populism has gathered increasing strength across a wider range of countries.

The part starts with an examination of a "localised" form of alienation that occurs within a professional form of practice in mental health. This exemplifies how, at the unconscious level, parts of persons are transferred around a group (building on the descriptions in Part II). The interchange that locates health and illness in separate subgroups (staff and patients respectively in a mental institution), can be seen to be comparable to the exchange systems by which some become wealthy and others impoverished. Though the latter is a material (or quasi-material) distribution in terms of money, it has unconscious roots that act in part as determinants for the comparable redistribution of parts of the personality. These exchange systems have the capacity to become permanent cycles (vicious cycles).

So, Chapter 9 discusses reflection as the primary mode of psychoanalytic thought. Can it be a form of action in politics as well? Chapter 10 expresses concerns at the most recent historical development, which has brought money as an abstract system of value to the fore. It now threatens to become a superordinate value system that dominates over ordinary values and virtues. Chapter 11, a very recent contribution, reflects on political and psychoanalytical action grounding them both in Freud's conception of experimental action that he framed in opposition to the mere discharge of motor function aimed at alleviating anxiety.

CHAPTER 9

Is reflection an action?

Introduction

In 2015 David Morgan ran a remarkable series of seminars at the London Institute of Psychoanalysis on "The Political Mind". These have become an annual event to demonstrate the relevance of psychoanalytic thought for understanding political issues and policies. I was fortunate to be asked to contribute a seminar and chose a topic that has bothered me for a long time. Politics aims at a social level to make decisions on behalf of groups of people up to the national level, and even international; the core principle of psychoanalysis is, however, to determine what influence we can have on someone's capacity to think. At first glance, there seems to be little connection between the two aims.

PAPER 9

Reflection or action: And never the twain shall meet*

Introduction

I shall talk about the major problem I see in getting psychoanalysis and politics to communicate together fruitfully. That problem is that the unconscious individual influences and the external social ones are essentially different categories of influence, and can be bridged conceptually only with some difficulty.

Group dynamics and the Labour Party

Back in the 1990s, I was part of a group that worked out some ideas which we might take to the Labour Party. You may remember that the dying regime of the Conservatives, Mrs Thatcher, and John Major was hanging on, and with the election in 1997 coming up the Labour Party was desperate to convince the electorate of its better policies. The idea was whether we could give an account of group dynamics which might be helpful to Labour to understand the way to create a more democratic society. At the time Labour were talking about "the third way"; somewhat vague, but it appeared that it might promote more measured attitudes

* Hinshelwood, R. D. (2017). Reflection or action: And never the twain shall meet. *Psychotherapy and Politics International*, 15: 67–74.

in society suggestive of depressive-position thinking—ambivalence, considerateness towards everyone, and generally a reluctance towards the unrealistic perfectionism of ideologies. It seemed there could be a match between their political rhetoric and the study of unconscious processes. In the event, when we met a couple of people at Labour headquarters, it was clear they were politely indifferent to what we were trying to present. Their interest was whether we had the secret of how to influence the electorate to vote for Labour. They wanted advice on their marketing. There seemed a radical disconnection between our earnest views about a more mature society and their wish for effective market selling-points.

I have thought, over the years, about our naivety. Obviously there is a potential for psychology to be used as an instrument for the manipulation of the public and, after our unfruitful approach, I came across the writing of one of the founders of marketing and public relations in the USA, Edward Bernays, back in the 1920s: "If we understand the mechanism and motives of the group mind, is it not possible to control and regiment the masses according to our will without their knowing about it?" (Bernays, 1928, p. 71). He continued:

> The conscious and intelligent manipulation of the organized habits and opinions of the masses is an important element in democratic society. Those who manipulate this unseen mechanism of society constitute an invisible government which is the true ruling power of our country. (p. 10)

I find this unpalatable. Shamefully, this author, Edward Bernays, a founder of this "invisible government", as he called it, was Freud's nephew. He, like Freud, was interested in the "unseen mechanisms" at work in individuals—but for different purposes.

Political change and psychoanalytic change

The aim of psychoanalysis is to change things. That is what patients want help with. The aim of politics is also to change things. But the changes, and how they are brought about, are completely different. Is that difference bridgeable? Influencing a patient towards some healthy state, and doing the same for society, should not be impossibly different.

After all, a society is made up of people. So, what really is the difference, and how can one inform the other?

Practising psychoanalysts address the determining factors of the unconscious—and how the individual is captured and controlled by them. On the other hand, political attitudes and actions are socially generated, and many would say arise from the economic system. The individual is located at the junction of these two sets of influences, one from inside and one from outside the person. If someone has a phobia for spiders, he is driven by internal factors (his unconscious imagining, say, the web-like embrace of a controlling mother). If someone drives his car on the correct side of the road, it is as a result of social forces—the highway code, police patrol cars, etc.

These are inherently different kinds of influences. How do social and unconscious determinisms fit together? Edward Bernays decided it was simple: the external social category could be used to manipulate the individual's interior unconscious choices. Well, for me that is not good enough, and I am interested in whether there are other ways by which these two categories of influences can be combined in our understanding (Hinshelwood, 1996). There are also strong ethical requirements involving paternalism and autonomy (Hinshelwood, 1997).

Labour process

Something that troubles people when they think about it, although they don't think about it much because it is not so easy to grasp, is what is called "labour process". I'll try to explain *my* understanding.

Let's consider a worker in a factory. The worker has necessary costs that go into sustaining his life. This can be quantified in terms of money—he is paid what he needs to survive and live. Each day he is paid that wage and, in exchange, he provides a day's work. The factory has other expenses: the raw materials, tools, and machines, the cost of the factory itself, some administration, banking charges, and so on. Together these are the manufacturing costs.

If the man is making, shall we say, nails in the factory, then a certain number of nails at the market price will roughly equate with the manufacturing costs, that is, the worker's wage plus the correct proportion of the other costs.

Then, if the factory is a successful one, the worker will be making his quantity of nails in less than a full day. And so, for the rest of his working day, he will be making more nails than he costs. Now, under this system of hired labour, the extra nails will belong, not to him, the worker, but to the factory—and its owner, who is a person or an enterprise that has bought the whole day's work from him. Much of labour relations turns on the ownership of the extra number of nails that the worker has made over and above the manufacturing costs.

This is a system that does not apply just to factory work, but also to a slave society or any society where the owner of the product is not the worker who supplied the hours of work. It contrasts with a society based on self-employed land-workers, craftsmen, or professionals. They own what they produce. This system of overproducing, as it seems, with the accumulation of products, is especially characteristic of the capitalist mode of production.

Incidentally, the concentrated effort on systems to maximise the accumulation of products that appear to be independent of their makers may have made an impact on other cultures. The anthropologist C. A. Gregory attributed the phenomenon known as the potlatch to the arrival of Western explorers and merchants in New Guinea. The potlatch is a ritual requiring a seemingly bizarre accumulation of goods that are circulated apparently aimlessly around the tribal community. Of course, there are other explanations, but it is possible that these tribes mirror for us the bizarre nature of our system of production which drastically divides production and ownership, and which has been foisted onto other cultures as a model of mature civilisation.

Alienation

The unease we feel about the labour system needs some understanding. In our society there appears to have been an historical development of a particular bond between the producer and the products that emerge from his work. For instance, since the humanistic age of the Renaissance, painters have signed their own pictures. That tells a story of how the bond between the individual producer and his opus has become an especially significant feature of Western cultures.

So it is of interest that the division of the worker from the product of his work is also, paradoxically, so characteristic of our modern age.

This culturally enforced division of product from producer is especially significant in manual work. The factory worker's labour is physical so he therefore has a particular bodily closeness to his product; there is an intimate connection between the worker and his product. The sale of his working hours removes the ownership of what is felt to be connected to him, and is, in his experience, a part of him. It is not too fanciful to accept that what we physically create is closely identified with us—indeed, what we intellectually create, like this paper, is closely identified with me, and vice versa. I know that I am seen, to a considerable extent, to be the person who has written certain things. Or, an artist, say Francis Bacon, is identified with the paintings he produces. In fact, a painting of his may be referred to as "a Francis Bacon", meaning one of his pictures.

Marx seemed especially angry about this labour process which rips the product from the worker, like a new-born baby from its mother. Long before his classic book *Das Kapital* (1867), we can read his humane ranting about this. In 1844 he was writing his notebooks, which were published as the *Economic and Philosophic Manuscripts*. There he dealt with the unfairness of this separation of the producer from his product:

> The object that labour produces, its product, stands opposed to it as something alien, as a power independent of the producer. The product of labour is labour embodied and made material in an object ... this realisation of labour appears as loss of reality for the worker, objectification as loss of and bondage to the object, and appropriation as estrangement, as alienation. (Marx, 1844 [1975, p. 324])

If the work product is disconnected from the producer, then the producer is disconnected to some degree from what is felt to be him. He becomes a lesser person as these aspects of himself are removed, or, as Marx said, "The worker becomes poorer the more wealth he produces" (ibid., p. 323). He becomes poorer in a psychological sense. This is a psychological understanding, not something that we would normally go to Karl Marx for, although the origins of Marx's thinking was in Hegel's philosophy of mind.

Many years ago (Hinshelwood, 1983) I was struck by a parallel kind of description to be found in the psychoanalytic literature. For example,

"In such fantasies products of the body and parts of the self are felt to be split off, projected into mother, and to be continuing their existence there" (Klein, 1955, p. 142).

No surprise that this comes from Melanie Klein describing the mechanism of splitting of the ego, or self, and subsequent projective identification of that divided part of the self into some other. Klein "referred to the weakening and impoverishment of the ego resulting from excessive splitting and projective identification" (Klein, 1946, p. 104). For the idea of alienation, it would seem that splitting is central because the object—that is the product of the worker—"stands opposed" to him, and it is projected, "alien" and "independent", yet it retains an identity with the worker—it is labour embodied. In other words, products identified with the person's (worker's) body are felt to have become separated off, alienated as a characteristic of someone else.

In that paper of mine, now thirty years ago [Chapter 1 in this volume], I looked carefully at the way Marx described what he called "alienation" and I made a comparison with the psychoanalytic phenomena of splitting and projection. I found striking similarities between the way alienation is experienced and the way splitting and projective identification are experienced.

Implicit in this comparison is a particular view of the relations between social influences from the wider culture and the individual level of personal experience and unconscious mechanisms. We know that alienation is conceptualised as having its origins in the mode of production, whilst its counterpart, splitting and projective identification, have their origins in the unconscious need to deal with an anxiety—the fear of annihilation, or a fear for survival. The alienation from the ownership of the product, on one hand, and the mechanisms of splitting and projective identification, on the other, converge in this case—the outside social influences and the inner mechanisms coincide.

Self-perpetuating systems

Where policies and politics play on already existing psychological mechanisms they may succeed handsomely. We know that psychological mechanisms are defences aimed at managing anxiety by avoiding it and, like all defence mechanisms, as Freud showed, they are usually imperfect and cause further effects known as symptoms. This is the case, no less, with the mechanisms of splitting and projective identification: they are aimed at avoiding fears regarding annihilation and personal survival. However, splitting will enhance the feeling of going to pieces, and projective identification will impoverish the ego. The conscious anxiety may be avoided, but at the same time it is actually unconsciously enhanced. As a result, the defence mechanisms are driven even harder—that is, splitting and projective identification are sustained, a vicious circle is created. In effect the mechanisms of splitting and projective identification allow the social process of alienation. And the redistribution of ownership of the products of labour becomes stabilised as a self-perpetuating system resting on the vicious circle of anxiety and defence.

Another vicious circle also occurs, as projective identification has another aim: it is a means of denying separation; projective identification establishes a merging with the person into whom some part of the self is projected. So projecting some part of the self into the factory or its owner inevitably promotes a sense of solidarity in the worker towards the owners into whom the worker has projected his products. Moreover, the reality situation in which the product is actually removed in a concrete way, separated and sold from the factory, must enhance the painful feelings of separation which the projective identification was intended to deny. Thus the anxiety of separation is enhanced, which further drives the projective identification to deny the separation.

Both these are enduring social-psychological dynamics, which underpin the alienation and allow it to endure, significantly impoverishing the egos of the workers. The alienation and solidarity are stabilised by resting on these enduring psychodynamic cycles.

One aspect of the success of the neoliberal emphasis on monetary value is that survival of the individual is increasingly felt as financial survival. The aim is in part to motivate people through a fear for their survival. This motivating strategy raises the survival anxiety for the individual and for working organisations, playing on the fears of the worker who already feels impoverished in himself and has sought solidarity through merging with the organisation.

Indeed, today such a large proportion of personal identity is constructed through consumer activity—that is, what you buy is what you are, and therefore if you can't buy you can't exist! Again it provides, and stabilises, the inner psychodynamic cycles just described.

Financial survival plays into the anxieties about ego-survival, and add to the drive for the characteristic defences.

The social influences of monetary values and financial survival have become so welded to the internal unconscious survival anxiety of the paranoid–schizoid position that they tend to dominate ordinary human values in certain work and other commercial zones of social life. Human values are left to exist in the more restricted field of the family and personal relations. We are allowed to be generous, grateful, honest, concerned, etc., within the family. But outside that, only monetary value counts as financial survival and is almost equated with personal and social survival.

One contribution we, as psychoanalysts, can make to the political sphere is to increase the understanding of how social processes embodied in a political policy must inevitably have an important unconscious dimension—so, the policy needs to access the personality dynamics of individuals. As psychoanalysts, we could give to political debates an awareness of the anxieties that policies might play upon and the defences that could establish vicious circles within individuals' unconscious dynamics.

It is not enough to take a high-minded position about this; we need to help increase understanding of why people go along thoughtlessly with quite disastrous policies. In the example described above—the occurrence of alienation at work—social influence and psychological mechanisms converge and work together in self-sustaining cycles.

But policies do not always find a suitable internal dynamic. Social policies are not all-powerful and they can be successful only insofar as they can play upon unconscious mechanisms they are able to activate. Psychology then becomes a limiting condition of political economy. Only when there is a clear interaction between the social forces and the unconscious cycling of anxiety and defence can a stable political economy arise.

Interpreting society

We need to find such models of interaction between social relations and psychodynamics. Otherwise it is so easy for us psychoanalysts to approach society or social institutions as if they were individuals. To equate a social organisation with the individual mind risks leaving out the very valid social, historical, political forces that act on organisations and create cultures. Much of those obvious social influences are conscious and not unconscious dynamics.

I am thinking of the campaign started by psychoanalysts in the 1980s, Psychoanalytic Psychotherapists Against Nuclear War (PPANW). It was led by Hanna Segal's special interest, expressed in her paper "Silence is the real crime" (Segal, 1987). She suggested that individual defence mechanisms seemed to be aggregated and she talked of regression during wartime from the depressive position to paranoid–schizoid functioning. As her campaign was largely ineffectual, it seems that there were serious limitations to this kind of individualistic political approach; the problem only disappeared with a political solution, the collapse of the cold war in 1990. I would suggest that attributing individual dynamics to social and political issues, without at least some assessment of their interaction with social factors, risks psychoanalysis becoming irrelevant to politicians.

Freud did something similar in *Totem and Taboo* (1912–13), interpreting whole societies in terms of the psychodynamics of the Oedipus complex. He had relied on outdated texts such as Frazer's *The Golden Bough* (Frazer, 1890) so that anthropologists contemporary with Freud such as W. H. R. Rivers, Elliott Smith, and Bronisław Malinovski easily dismissed Freud as a positive danger! Malinovski described psychoanalysis as "an infection … of the neighbouring fields of science—notably that of anthropology, folklore and sociology" (Malinowski, 1923, p. 650).

The imperative is to understand how social attitudes and policies resonate with unconscious processes, notably anxiety and defence, deep within individuals. This is easier said than done, and there is a place for some persistent thinking about these reverberating social-psychological dynamics of the kind I have illustrated.[1]

I would like to refer to Dave Bell's (1996) point of view insofar as I understand it. Like me, he has come to the conclusion that such action is not based so much upon fighting politically for certain parties or policies, but more on a distinction at a meta-level. The distinction he

[1] Since this paper was originally published in 2017, a more detailed and elaborated set of reflections has been developed in a book titled *Unconscious Politics* (Hinshelwood, 2024).

uses is the Kleinian one between paranoid–schizoid and depressive functioning. Institutions that demand depressive position functioning are likely on the whole to represent more mature functioning than paranoid–schizoid functioning institutions. Thus the NHS, for instance, is an establishment devoted to concern for others—the core element of the depressive position. Perhaps incidentally it could be a factor in why the NHS is always in the front line politically as a key issue in neoliberal policy-making. We need to support with ordinary political action those institutions that embody concern as opposed to self-survival.

This type of action is not just in order to support specific policies; instead it is an engagement with social values—taking profits vs making a contribution, survival vs concern, collaboration vs competitive survival. As psychoanalysts, we must touch on the unconscious substratum of those policies as they affect the individual. There is a policy, to save the NHS, but it is based on an estimation of the unconscious values of the depressive position as well as the conscious arguments that we might or might not agree with. Of course, unconscious personal survival is involved in the anxiety about the NHS; however, crucially, fear needs to be tempered by concern, not defensiveness.

Ethical politics

So I am touching on an ethical dimension of pursuing policies as well as the merely pragmatic one of simply winning. This prompts a big question: What are the more ethical means of doing politics and what are the less ethical ones? It seems to me that the ethics of politics in a representative democracy turns on the issue of autonomy and paternalism. Much is said of the importance of personal autonomy in our society but the fact is that there cannot always be a respect for decisions made by a common vote.

It was an extremely technical decision whether in 2008 the British Government should rescue the Northern Rock Building Society or allow it to collapse. And even experts might disagree—the United States government followed different advice at the time and allowed Lehmann Brothers to go bankrupt. These are extremely difficult decisions that need expertise way beyond you or me. We need our politicians to decide things for us. This is a paternalism and it overrides autonomy of the individual. If we really want a participant democracy, paternalism is not necessarily bad—most of us should not be involved in such delicate decisions as to whether to rescue a financial institution or not. Only after the event do we, the general public, know what should have been done. It had to be left to those with deep knowledge and long experience of economics and even they make mistakes, mistakes that could probably not have been avoided even in a fuller democracy. In fact, it is the point about a representative democracy as opposed to a consensus democracy; sometimes we need experts in positions of power to make decisions for us.

If paternalism is not always good—for instance, what Edward Snowden revealed about the United States National Security Agency and the UK government's communication headquarters (GCHQ) (see the Courage Foundation, 2016, https://couragefound.org/category/edward-snowden/)—then we need to understand when it is good and how to tell the difference. Looking from a psychoanalytic perspective here, when we face such situations, we in effect put certain decisions into the hands of others, a form of projection. In some sense we become impoverished by losing that degree of autonomy we give over to an expert. It is the same as agreeing to a surgeon operating on our unconscious body: we give up our autonomy and place all the decision-making in his expert hands. This is now beyond the scope of this paper; the crucial issue is that such a projective strategy is (a) realistic; (b) the expert is genuine and (c) temporary. If those conditions are met, we can say it is a form of autonomy to engage in that projection (I have explored forms of ethical action in my book *Therapy or Coercion*, 1997).

Where the projections are not realistic and in line with human values, or where they are not temporary, then they approximate to the labour process. Impoverishing the man who makes nails has its ethical equivalent in a process which impoverishes a person's autonomy as well as his identity and financial possessions.

Conclusion

I have tried to describe some psychoanalytic reflections on politics and where psychoanalysts might position themselves. Psychoanalysis is the only discipline that can supply an understanding of the unconscious processes of the individual and how they get played out in social forms. But we have to be careful to recognise that our contributions as psychoanalysts only stretch as far as those unconscious aspects. We will all have our favourite policies and parties, with perfectly valid conscious reasons for supporting them. It is not really valid for us to simply argue psychoanalytically in favour of such consciously adopted policies—this is reminiscent of the Labour Party in 1997 wanting to exploit group dynamics for their manipulative marketing. Our contribution needs to draw attention to the underlying unconscious issues, the vicious circles, the level of understanding, etc. that affect not just policies but the political process itself—which of them are, or are not, being mobilised by the conscious policies and debates.

To some extent these are seriously incomplete reflections and may be invalid. But we need, and I believe we have the conceptual resources to deal with, the complex interaction of the double influence of society and the unconscious, which intersect in politics. We do need, in my view, to contribute the possibilities of psychodynamic reflection whilst taking action.

Acknowledgement

This paper is based on a talk given at the Institute of Psychoanalysis in London, in June 2015, as part of the Political Mind seminars.

References

Bell, D. (1996). Primitive mind of state. *Psychoanalytic Psychotherapy, 10*: 45–57.

Bernays, E. (1928). *Propaganda*. New York: Liveright.

Freud, S. (1912–13). *Totem and Taboo. S. E., 13*: 1–162. London. Hogarth.

Frazer, J. (1980). *The Golden Bough*. London: Macmillan.

Hinshelwood, R. D. (1983). Projective identification and Marx's concept of Man. *International Review of Psycho-Analysis, 16*: 221–226.

Hinshelwood, R. D. (1996). Convergences with psycho-analysis. In: I. Parker & R. Spiers (Eds.), *Psychology and Marxism* (pp. 93–104). London: Pluto.

Hinshelwood, R. D. (1997). *Therapy or Coercion*. London: Free Association.

Hinshelwood, R. D. (2024). *Unconscious Politics*. London: Karnac.

Klein, M. (1946). Notes on some schizoid mechanisms. *International Journal of Psychoanalysis, 27*: 99–110. Republished in M. Klein, P. Heimann, S. Isaacs

& and J. Riviere, *Developments in Psycho-Analysis* (pp. 292–320). London: Hogarth, 1952 and in *The Writings of Melanie Klein, Volume 3* (pp. 1–24). London: Hogarth, 1975.

Klein, M. (1955). On identification. In: *The Writings of Melanie Klein, Volume 3* (pp. 141–175). London: Hogarth.

Malinowski, B. (1923). Psychoanalysis and anthropology. *Nature*, *112*: 650–651.

Marx, K. (1867). *Capital*. London: Penguin, 1975.

Marx, K. (1844). Economic and philosophical manuscripts. In: *Early Writings* (pp. 279–400). London: Penguin, 1975.

Segal, H. (1987). Silence is the real crime. *International Review of Psycho-Analysis*, *14*: 3–12.

CHAPTER 10

Democracy weaponised

Introduction

The word "democracy" was weaponised for fifty years during the cold war period to challenge "communism", similarly used as a contrast. The implications of freedom for everybody is a gross exaggeration and this paper attempts to reflect on a few of the false claims and the more sensible reality of what a democracy could be. In the debate about what can be done politically with psychoanalysis, this paper attempts to explore the unconscious elements that distort the term "democracy" and render it idealised as a weapon of propaganda, and the ensuing, and unrecognised, consequences of such distortions.

PAPER 10

The disappointment of democracy*

Many forms of Government have been tried, and will be tried in this world of sin and woe. No one pretends that democracy is perfect or all-wise. Indeed it has been said that democracy is the worst form of Government except for all those other forms that have been tried from time to time.

—Winston S. Churchill, *Hansard*, 11 November, 1947

Indeed, Churchill was wrong in saying no one pretends that democracy is perfect. His pronouncement full of English irony acknowledges that there are many failings of democracy. And its lesson must be that we should not be taken in by claims for its perfection. However, reservations about democracy do not sit well with the familiar triumphalism of the dominating view in Western democracies, where there is an ideological need to portray democracy as the ideal state of man in society. Such rhetorical claims for democracy have increasingly created an ideal, no less. This occurred in the course of its becoming an ideological weapon in the cold war with "communism" (first Russia, and then China). So today we are left with the expectation that all good

* Hinshelwood, R. D. (2021). The disappointment of democracy. *Free Associations: Psychoanalysis and Culture, Media, Groups, Politics, 83*: 2047–2062

comes from democracy. However, nothing is perfect and yet we tend to yearn for it. Due to this, the reality of democracy can feel disappointing. Rhetoric and reality are not friends.

In this paper, it is claimed that amongst the discontents of civilisation, a disappointment arising from democracy itself is at times inevitable. An attempt will be made to pinpoint various disappointments with our current notion of democracy, and the implication that a vigilance for failures is a necessary antidote to idealisation. A selection of the disappointments will be discussed with the plea that modern democracy certainly needs systems of accountability much more than empty promises of freedom.

Democracy as freedom or accountability

The rhetorical equation is that idealised democracy is a freedom that leads to quite unreal expectations if we do not question it. Unreal expectations can only fail, and so deliver disappointment. As perfect freedom for all, democracy is patently illogical, since the basic gift of human beings is that we have developed a civilisation comparable to no other biological species, in which we depend utterly on cooperation with each other. It does not mean the freedom from the pressure of other people; rather a give and take. We do need others and we co-operate with them, so we do not just take our freedom, but we are taken from as well. It is inevitable that democracy cannot deliver on the promises of the rhetoric. Civilisation relies on people adjusting to each other; leaders demand acquiescence from followers, and are thus dependent on followers, etc. Civilisation relies on most people most of the time accepting authority from elsewhere, from outside themselves.

Democracy cannot equate with the freedom promised. The defence of "freedom" has powered the conservative thinking that democracy can release all restraint on everybody. The sovereign individual has the right to make his own choices. Such exaggeration appears seductive, and can become exaggerated. In the book *The Sovereign Individual*, by the ex-editor of *The Times*, William Rees-Mogg, we can read, for instance: "The government's capacity to tax ultimately depends on the same vulnerabilities [in the ordinary individual] as do private shakedowns and extortion" (Davidson & Rees-Mogg, p. 154). Taxing is wrong because it removes the freedom of choice of the owner of money. The imposition on the rich to provide health or education for everyone curtails the freedom of successful entrepreneurs. Obstructing them makes democracy suspect. As a result, increasing inequality, with feudal levels of poverty, are quite acceptable.

That indifference in the fabric of our contemporary culture is known as neoliberalism and harks back to eighteenth-century Britain and the Dickensian nineteenth century. The "State" is now hated as a result of the belief that it infringes on our imaginary rights to use our money as we wish, especially to invest in entrepreneurial ventures. At present, the balance is decidedly in favour of the individual freedom from restrictions rather than solidarity of the individual with his community. The extreme constriction on the lives of so many in poverty, and their needs for collegial respect and even assistance in times of need, has receded into the distance. Despair amongst the many without entrepreneurial gifts develops, and anger overtakes them, at the very same time as the media glorifies celebrities living lives to be admired by all.

The rhetoric and the media express the principle that having a wish automatically gets you what you want. In reality, democracy allows only one wish—expressed in a vote every few years. There is indeed a freedom to vote. It was a freedom won slowly, but now universal suffrage exists in Western society. However, such a very restricted view of democracy is impractical without an informed assessment of what government has, and has not, achieved—of which more below.

Voting does not mean "getting"—not necessarily. And in fact, only a proportion win the vote—the majority is not everyone. There is, then, a proportion that is less than the majority who do not win and have to cope with having no freedom to receive what they want. They are disappointed. So, actually, a significant number of people have to be disappointed, which does not square with the idealising promise in Western cultures.

That relentless demand for the ideal may be encouraged by the shopping mall, and by TV advertising where every individual can choose for himself. The result is that the consumer culture becomes the pattern for political demands.

Disappointment and unconscious dynamics

The necessary fact of disappointment for some, or many, in a voting system is easily ignored. If it is dismissed or underestimated at the conscious level, it will inevitably lead to anxiety or resentment in some hidden form. The losers in a vote are expected to abide by the result without demur, as the will of the majority. That means, of course, without *conscious* demur. But there are serious possibilities of unconscious dynamics carrying the bitterness in other, equally unseen, directions. Then, disappointment can emerge from hiding as a collective angst.

Accountability

For instance, the Declaration of Independence of the thirteen states was about freedom from Britain. The Declaration nowhere mentions the word "democracy". A key clause is: "That whenever any Form of Government becomes destructive of these ends [life, liberty, and the pursuit of happiness], it is the Right of the People to alter or to abolish it, and to institute new Government" (written by Thomas Jefferson in 1776). In other words, government has to be held accountable, according to agreed principles. The real purpose of democracy is that it be a system of accountability. And not of individual freedoms. From ancient Athens, Pericles' rivalry with Cimon was not for the freedom of the demos, of the people. It was about an accountability they fought out in a court of law. Declaring independence and freedom has become confused with democracy. In reality (and in practice) democracy means an authority that is answerable to those who they make decisions for. This was the core element of England's own "declaration of independence", the Magna Carta, in 1215, when similarly the ruling elite took steps to oversee King John's management of the monarch's taxes and financial affairs.

Taking authority means taking on responsibilities, and in a democracy, that means being held responsible—or accountable. Ultimately, democratic voting signs off on the accountability of a government. There is no perfection to be found in running the country, and mistakes will always be made. A relatively forgiving accountability is necessary, together with a necessary transparency. People do make mistakes, even when in authority—"to err is human". Accountability means the openness of authorities to being questioned, to having their decisions re-examined by anyone else (Przeworski et al., 1999). It is a big request, to which authorities are not always willing to acquiesce. A government's achievement has to be subjected to a critical review, but may feel like being found out for failures. Many governments understandably may prefer a simple periodic voting system which can downplay a detailed reviewing system.

Democracy is therefore a very limited freedom—the freedom to vote for or against an elected person or government on the basis of their performance and future programme. This is certainly an improvement on, shall we say, a mediaeval system where assassination was a common method of dealing with leaders who lost the approval of some significant power in their land. Allowing losers to go on living is an improvement, and a more civilised method of accountability.

Democracy and protest

The logic, however, is that if democracy is ideal, then any reconsideration or accountability must puncture the ideal of perfection. There is a temptation, therefore, for protests and protestors to be identified as insurgency and terrorists. When it comes to an ideal, then, in the extreme, it becomes a religious form of good vs bad; any criticism of God must be devilish.

Mistakes, guilt, and forgiveness

A complex issue exists between any authority that fails, and those who are disadvantaged by the failures. The idea of a "forgiveness" for mistakes is very foreign—or at least unspoken—in political systems. This perhaps quite unconscious dimension links authority with guilt. Those in authority have to take responsibility for their decisions, and that includes the responsibility for imperfect decisions, which will inevitably be taken. The painful feeling of guilt is internally damaging and potentially punitive. There is a sense in which voting is a kind of jury system.

It can be a considerable relief for many in an electorate to assign blame to authorities who disappoint them. We all have our superegos to appease, and one means is to become someone else's judge. But the reverse, too—some authorities can assign culpability to their populace. A blame game is such a human aptitude and can flare up as an infectious dispute between couples and groups and parties, up to the international level of cold wars and hot ones.

Informed accountability could, if well conducted, have the objective of gauging the mistakes and successes, and assessing a balance that could allow a level of mistakes. Of course, such an accountability will always be subjected to influences from unconscious sources, including the need for a scapegoating blame, and for ideologies, as well as naked self-interest. Such an aim seems a long way off, and it is consigned to the shadows by the idealising rhetoric of freedom for everyone.

Democracy and inequality

A second confusion is that democracy enshrines equality for all within a nation. When there is inequality, there is another source of disappointment. Democracy has not delivered on yet another promise. So, inequality—inequality of money and power—introduces all sorts of complications, jealousy, envy, incompetent elites, hidden guilt, self-justifying self-interest, and more. But these disadvantages cannot be an argument for a complete equality. Equality in every respect will never be achieved. But the impossibility of full equality is not an argument for an unrestrained promotion of the opposite, of inequality. Inequality for the sake of it has had a massive impact on Western societies, which has taken us back to mediaeval levels. Like freedom, inequality is a distraction from accountability.

One longstanding argument for the benefits of inequality dates from the eighteenth century. Indifference to poverty and the damage of sustained impoverishment to human lives is still justified on the basis of this antique argument. Adam Smith's (1776) idea of the "invisible hand" promoted the entrepreneurial society as inevitable, and justified by the "trickle-down" argument—as the richer spend their money on the products and services the poor can provide, so the wealth is distributed amongst the poor. So, having a wealthy class will benefit the poorer labourers as a secondary effect. This argument was dominant in the rhetoric favouring tax cuts for the wealthy in the Reaganomics of the 1990s. But there is no evidence that such a policy has benefitted the poor. The trickle-down effect has little economic impact (Persky et al., 2004; Dabla-Norris et al., 2015; Hope & Limberg 2020). But such research has not provoked much thought; it does not work effectively against idealisation.

If the wealthy impoverish the impoverished, they are morally guilty by most standards. So, they need arguments such as the rhetoric of "trickle-down" in order to hide the guilt, the conscious guilt, that would come from a reasoned judgement about inequality. And the wealthy do have the means to fund media justifications of their own ideologies. The arguments of "trickle-down" and the "invisible hand" are the let-out arguments, which spare the elite from the evidence of research and accountability. It is an effective (unconscious) dynamic system to hide the real consequences.

Of course, economics has moved on since the eighteenth century. For instance, one alternative to the invisible hand would be a visible one—Keynesian economics would promote the State as the investor through "deficit spending". The national budget could directly promote industry, and jobs and the rehabilitation of the impoverished when necessary. Its effectiveness was partially confirmed by Roosevelt's New Deal in the depression of the 1930s in the USA. However, that view was disputed in the 1970s by claims an even-better effect could be achieved by an expansion of the money supply. It is a sophisticated argument by which those on the wealthier rungs of the ladder could soak up the extra money and (hopefully) trickle it down. This is the primary debate that insists on enhancing the idea of the entrepreneurial freedom of individuals (through tax cuts) and against the State's direction of investment. Today, the policy that the state should manage only the money supply is now a dominant one enhancing the freedom of individuals.

Democracy and corruption

The emphasis on money joined with the idealisation of freedom and now justifies the freedom to accumulate money, for the apparent good of all. In effect, it promotes only freedom for some. And inevitably, the impossibility of it for others—a disappointment for those with less inherited wealth and privilege, those with less talent, or opportunity, and so on.

Money has entered the system of values in society—supposedly, the more you have, the more benefit to everyone else. Therefore, anyone should accumulate money. With the economic arguments briefly recounted above, money has acquired a moral value beyond simple wealth. Banking facilities and financial institutions have responded to this by focusing on money with, it seems, other values stepping down to a secondary place. London, for instance, is a major centre for laundering the finances from corruption and the illicit drug trade (Burgis, 2016). Ethical values and money values appear to be on a collision course. When one considers the laundering of so-called "dirty" money, one has to recognise that its moral value can trump the ordinary human values of morality, notably honesty, and fairness. So, if the value of making money has superseded the other, more ethical, values then it is entirely reasonable for financiers to follow the dominant value. Can one reasonably condemn individuals for corruption when the context of cultural values places money as the highest moral good?

It is, of course, very different in private life with relatives, friends, and acquaintances. There, ordinary human values of honesty, consideration, loyalty, and fairness, etc. still dominate. So, from one point of view, the values of bankers, financiers, hedge fund managers, and their colleagues are reasonable, but from another cultural angle it is corruption. This is a fault-line in contemporary culture. Should the value of money ever win in a contest with honesty? And should it win a contest over consideration of others (drug dealing, for instance), or over unfair bargaining against the poor in the Western nations or in the poor countries (systematic impoverishment)?

If democracy means freedom, then such value judgements are an individual's business. But if democracy is about accountability, then human values should not be replaced. The fact that corruption on a scale that is evidently increasing rapidly implies that accountability is disappointingly failing in some sectors of society.

If it is genuinely the case that freedom to make money is a superordinate value in some sectors, then we might go back to the thesis that emerged in the meticulous study by Edward Gibbon of the decline and fall of Rome (Gibbon, 1772–1789). Gibbon's conclusions were that Rome succumbed because of a decline in "civic virtue". It might be argued that the ascendant valuation of money today relegates normal human values to a secondary position, and is expressed in an equivalent decline of virtue in public life. In a nutshell, private accumulation of wealth has become a loss of civic virtue.

Underlying unconscious dynamics and anxieties

The overvaluation of freedom of the individual and, in particular, of their freedom to make money, gives democracy an awkward and impractical shape. Some people have a special need to set scaffolding around their self-esteem to build it up, and that is something money can supply if its high social and moral value is culturally pervasive. In the end, it is only a superficial support to the ego, but such superficiality is likely to fend off a disappointment (consciously). However, it is likely to continue in a hidden way to drive the build-up of money as a moral value. That self-sustaining set of attitudes points towards hidden motives, promoted by unconscious pressures. It then takes a psychoanalytic sensibility to give a picture of the unconscious cultural narrative that has captured people collectively.

The value of money needs, like all mistakes, to be understood in its unconscious and its self-sustaining qualities. Similarly, the prejudices based on gender, race, and religion are likely to be forever prevalent. Human beings notice these kinds of difference, and inevitably we make value judgements. Without judgement, we are out of touch with reality. Humans will make judgements according to unconscious principles as well as conscious ones. The unconscious aspects of the politics of diversity has certainly been exposed (Davids, 2002, 2011; Hinshelwood, 2007 [Chapter 7]) but cannot be further detailed here. We may have to say that, similar to equality in wealth, it may never be possible to achieve bias-free politics, only a vigilant minimisation to counteract exploitation.

Freedom as a defence

The possibility, for which there is some evidence, is that the bitterness of disappointment is not necessarily owned by those who most feel it. Because the idealisation of democratic freedom leads to an unacknowledged bitterness for many, it can be ignored by those who win an election. If not acknowledged, such feelings can later emerge in unrecognised forms. One typical method is a group dynamic in which resentment is disowned and projected into other segments of the community, often those with more overt claims for resentment; for instance, those poor and exploited who are not free to choose their position in society and may be further used for a kind of psychosocial exploitation. They can be used to express (indeed feel) the projected disappointment, resentment, and bitterness on behalf of others in society. That kind of displacement into other people, groups, and issues is hard to follow, of course. For instance, the impoverished, those deeply disappointed with themselves, with their place in society, and the endless reductions in public provision, can turn their ire towards other races.

Another instance might be the intellectual class turning their disappointment towards the referendum on leaving the EU in 2016. Such rational people (of whom I would count myself as one) have a deep respect for the process of voting and have to deal with their emotional state in the face of a mandate they don't or can't agree with. They too can divest themselves of their painful feelings by condemning the gullible people who are so irrational as to believe in and to promote oversimplification, lying, and so on.

What could be a better means of coping than to split off that emotionalism and instead find the disappointment in disgruntled elements in other segments of society. Thus, the prejudiced and hate-carrying members of society are good emotional receptacles. They can act out impulses on behalf not only of themselves, but also on behalf of rational people who repudiate their own more angry emotionalism.

Wealth as a defence

The other distorting and defensive ideology in current Western culture is that of inequality and its pale rationalisation in the trickle-down effect. That rationalisation is conscious and shallow, impervious to evidence and reason because people need the rationalising in order to cover their unconscious pain of guilt and shame at their own responsibility for impoverishing and exploiting others.

However, wealth does not only lead to guilt. It can have a profoundly stabilising effect on the wealthy man or woman. In a culture where individuality is highly prized, this can then combine with the ideology of what the highest value is. The cultural expectation of the most valuable individuals can be their possession of the largest amount of wealth. Such a view is not consciously reasoned out but can nevertheless be powerfully felt unconsciously by those pained by self-doubt. The boost given to feeling doubt about oneself makes wealth an important defence. This is expressed, in the West, in the view that "having something" has taken over from the sense of "being someone" (Fromm, 1976). This may be very different from other cultures where "being" is connected much more with a sense of belonging to a family, culture, or group. In the West, property belonging to the self can provide a major boost for many fragile people. In the end, their despair about themselves undermines a benign civic society.

Money, as well as gender, race, etc., can be important distinctions useful for giving implicit and unconscious valuation to prop up a fragile and unstable sense of self. But in a culture devoted to the individual, these differing valuations can be used in the underground, unconscious zone to combat the self-uncertainty through designating different others as having lower value.

Participation, representation, sortition

Democracies are affected by other unconscious concerns, not least are the relations with authority. Authorities who make decisions for us are always significant and constitute the central idea of democratic institutions. In part, our deepest experience of authority is evolved from the early relations with parents. The capacity, seen in the process of development, is to use authorities in important ways that preserve the sense of self. But, importantly, it is largely without conscious awareness.

Unconscious authority

Unlike parental authority, people in democracies can participate in choosing the authorities, whether they decide to participate in voting or not. Nevertheless, the chosen representatives are given authority of a parental kind. Authority is thus loved as if a parental protection, as well as feared for the threat of condemnation. Each of us, as an individual, carries within ourselves that sense of authority, often expressed as their level of self-confidence. In groups, we also see authority exemplified in others. And we can exemplify authority for others with our own confidence. These aspects of ourselves draw a great deal on unconscious sources. Freud himself regarded this internal form as derived from the Oedipus complex, which he saw as a general template for the development of human subjects and for personal authority derived from loved-but-hated parents. That relationship is complex: we identify with them, and at the same time murder or are murdered by them. Such relations and conflicts are played out by each of us in our own varying ways in the world of politics, and the debates it provides. Careful reasoning fights against this undergrowth of complex feelings. And we need other minds to debate with in order to find our way through.

The various individuals' experiences at this unconscious level will match or not match with the actual situation in political life and political process. Familiar idealisations and guilt may emerge in the guise of reasoned conscious debate, but they are underpinned by unconscious certainty that obstructs the debate and stands as needed ideologies.

Alternatively, it may be a great relief to externalise all authority, requiring someone else to decide the really important issues. That process offers an escape from responsibility, and our democratic system of representatives invites an escape in practice. Responsibility may need to be escaped for various reasons, in particular it threatens to deliver guilt if things go wrong, as they sometimes will. Then, for some people, the guilt can be very internally punishing (often unconsciously) and felt in terms of cruel criticism. The easy temptation is to grant authority to someone else so that blame and an aggrieved vengeance can adhere to them rather than to oneself. One variation in the unconscious dumping of responsibility and guilt onto others is not to vote for representatives at all. Then we can deny any responsibility for politics and the governance.

An even more promising and prevalent method of coping with authority is to recognise oneself publicly as a victim of the government or of the system. This locates responsibility and guilt very firmly in place—with those who have power. Even a demand that the powerful relinquish power puts the power in the hands of those who are required to relinquish it. It can be very hard to distinguish true victims of an authority from some who feel that being victimised is preferable to feeling responsible.

Giving responsibility

Most democracies are representative, although there are other forms. A participatory democracy, in contrast, relies on everyone to contribute to all decisions, via referendums, for instance. It is, however, unwieldy as a general method of decision-making for large groups or nations. Even with occasional referendums, there are difficulties, particularly for getting a wide-enough spread of reliable information and deliberation on the issues. All decisions rely completely on information being accurate and distributed and digested by all the constituents.

It has recently emerged that there is a surprising degree of resistance to information and to uncertainty as a necessary condition which must pervade debate and discussion. It is necessary to see other points of view that inevitably arouses challenge to one's own. The perverse attraction of improbable conspiracy theories has drawn a mass following of people with hidden and unconscious bitterness and existential threats. Exposing their destructive fear and intentions, located at an unconscious level, has hardly yet been contemplated. It may in many cases result from the rhetoric that promises freedom, only to result in a disappointing lack of it. But, such a hypothesis regarding the unconscious emergence of frustration in the social media requires research.

A further experiment in democracy is to gather a random assignment of representatives. Called sortition, it resembles the appointing of a jury in a law court. These constitute "citizens assemblies" and provide an opportunity for properly presented points of view in the debate, with a summary of evidence for each side. They tend to be largish groups of, say 100, in order to capture a sample representation. However, it is known that very powerful dynamics of insecurity arise in groups as large as this (Kreeger, 1975). Processes of identity and its loss can make it difficult to think and debate even if assemblies are well run.

In conclusion

Freedom, and in particular the current freedom to accumulate money, has taken over as a fundamental but erroneous actor in democratic governance. Strong rhetoric to that effect sustains such cultural distortions and in part does so probably for the guilt-free benefit of the wealthy classes. It is a cultural achievement to have created such a loyalty to this contemporary notion of democracy.

An attempt has been made to unpick the argument for democracy as freedom. Our dependence on each other is the solid brickwork of civilisations, and gives the lie to democracy as freedom from the encroachment of others. That rhetoric promises inevitable disappointment, and it gives cover for various forms of exploitation, and of the corruption of social values.

A number of ways in which the rhetoric of freedom in the guise of democracy disappoints, damages, and corrupts civil and social life in Western culture have been discussed. The conclusion must therefore be a strong plea for changing our focus of attention. Instead, we could claim that accountability is really the core. Accountability, too, has many problems, and they are little addressed publicly, especially as the distracting rhetoric of freedom consigns accountability to the shadows. The necessity for, and the problems of, an adequate, informed system of accountability needs to be foregrounded urgently for the rescue of Western civic and sociopolitical life. But more than anything, we should keep in mind that like human beings themselves, there is no perfection to be idealised. We need always to be open to imperfections and the disappointments and grievances that they inevitably give rise too, and then to assess such failures in balanced ways.

References

Burgis, T. (2016). Dark money: London's dirty secret. *Financial Times*, 11 May, 2016.

Dabla-Norris, E., Kochhar, K., Suphaphiphat, N., Ricka, F., & Tsounta, E. (2015). *Causes and Consequences of Income Inequality: A Global Perspective*. International Monetary Fund, https://www.imf.org/en/Publications/Staff-Discussion-Notes/Issues/2016/12/31/Causes-and-Consequences-of-Income-Inequality-A-Global-Perspective-42986

Davids, F. (2002). September 11th 2001: Some thoughts on racism and religious prejudice as an obstacle. *British Journal of Psychotherapy*, *18*: 361–366.

Davids, F. (2011). *Internal Racism: A Psychoanalytic Approach to Race and Difference*. London: Palgrave Macmillan.

Davidson, J., & Rees-Mogg, W. (1997). *The Sovereign Individual*. New York: Simon & Schuster.

Fromm, E. (1976). *To Have or to Be*. New York: Harper Row.

Gibbon, E. (1772–1789). *The History of the Decline and Fall of the Roman Empire*. London: Penguin, 2000 (abridged).

Hinshelwood, R. D. (2007). Intolerance and the intolerable: The case of racism. *Psychoanalysis, Culture and Society*, *12*: 1–20.

Hope, D., & Limberg, J. (2020). The economic consequences of major tax cuts for the rich. London: International Inequalities Institute (LSE).

Kreeger, L. (1975). *The Large Group*. London: Constable.

Persky, J., Felzenshtain, D., & Carlson, V. L. (2004). Does "trickle down" work? Economic development strategies and job chains in local labor markets. Kalamazoo, MI: W. E. Upjohn Institute.

Przeworski, A., Stokes, S. C., & Manin, B. (1999). *Democracy, Accountability, and Representation*. Cambridge: Cambridge University Press.

Smith, A. (1776). *The Wealth of Nations*. London: Penguin. 1982.

CHAPTER 11

The inexistence of debate

Introduction

The most recent paper in this collection was a contribution to the Political Mind seminar series in 2023. It continues my own move from attempting the synthesis of social science and psychoanalysis to teasing out the contribution psychoanalysts might make to political *action*. However there is a vital similarity to be explored. I was interested to discover the importance of Freud's philosophy teacher, Franz Brentano. This paper relies a lot on the interchange of "inexistent" objects that can be attended to by one or more minds. This kind of attention is a prerequisite for political discussion. Debate is the vital fore-runner of political action, and psychoanalysis can be seen to have an important role in understanding the details of how debate can be had effectively or not.

PAPER 11

Political action, psychoanalytic action*

[A]nimals that live politically are those that have any kind of activity in common.

—Aristotle, *Politics*, Book 1, section 1253a

The central point of our whole series of Political Mind seminars is that psychoanalysis and the unconscious human mind has a really important relevance for political thinking and action. And of course, this has been a thread of intellectual life all through the twentieth century. That long tradition, however, has not really produced a consensus. Here I want to put forward some basic considerations., and a conceptual model based on Freud claiming how psychoanalysis can offer political action.

Political debates and decisions on the one hand, and psychoanalytic practice on the other, appear very different kinds of activity. One is in the social domain and the other is in the internal world of

* Unpublished presentation to the Political Mind seminar series, 2023.

the individual. That seems to make them very diverse. I can quote John Strachey:

> Nor is there the least doubt that these sciences [Marxism and psychoanalysis] are directly opposites. The question is, are they dialectical opposites? (Strachey, 1937, p. 7)

John Strachey was a writer and later a member of the Clement Atlee government in 1940s Britain (Thomas, 1973). He was a one-time member of the communist party (in the 1930s), a beneficiary of a personal psychoanalysis, and a cousin of James Strachey, the translator of Freud. Strachey's question would seem well founded: Are they dialectical opposites? It expresses the almost irreconcilable differences between social science explanations and psychoanalytic ones. Should we give up on their relevance for each other?

Experimental action

So let me to take you through a train of thought; it is set out in detail and with more consequences in a book recently published (Hinshelwood, 2024). I start with Freud, more than a century ago. It comes in his spin-off paper that resulted from his examination of the Schreber case. Freud (1911c) had described how Schreber had dismantled reality in his own mind. This put Freud onto a description of the "reality principle" in "Formulations on the two principles of mental functioning", published in the same year (Freud, 1911b). He described a number of ego-functions brought into play to form the reality principle [see also Chapter 8] including: distance perception, attention, notation/memory, judgement (true/false), appropriate change of reality. And then, the final function he described like this:

> Restraint upon motor discharge … was provided by means of the process of thinking … It is essentially an experimental kind of acting. (Freud, 1911b, p. 221)

He explained this:

> [M]otor discharge, which, under the dominance of the pleasure principle, had served as a means of unburdening the mental

> apparatus of accretions of stimuli … was now employed in the appropriate alteration of reality … (p. 221)

This is one of the most significant steps in the development of human mentality. It is a move away from immediate "knee-jerk" reactions to satisfy a stimulus, such as hunger, or sexual stimuli, which are the impulsive responses typical of animals. Instead, human beings insert a moment of no motor action. In that moment, the "stimuli" are then held as thoughts. They become an experimental kind of action in the mind.

Can we note Freud's notion of action *in* the mind while I digress for a moment. In 1875, Freud was a medical student, and he attended the lectures of a philosopher in the University of Vienna. This was Franz Brentano, who provided a basis for the development of phenomenology; that is, the study of the nature of those things that exist *within* the mind (see Kriegel, 2017). They were termed by Brentano *inexistent* objects. Freud attended Brentano's lectures at the same time as Husserl, an originator of phenomenology. Being a study of how things sensed in material reality are processed to become experiences in the mind, phenomenology is exactly the focus of the reality principle and how reality can be distorted and reconstructed.

In fact, Freud's enthusiasm for Brentano even made him consider for a moment changing from his medical studies to a PhD in philosophy (this can be found in his correspondence with his student friend, Eduard Silberstein, published in 1992).

The importance of Brentano is that what exists in the mind does not have to exist in the real external world. The objects in the mind are "inexistent"; they are not non-existent. When I talk to you of Freud, he is *in* my mind. He exists there as some sort of entity with specific meanings and attributes as an object I attend to in my mind. As a result, these representations can be manipulated with our thoughts to form experiments that are not really enacted. In fact, Freud experimented in his mind with doing a PhD in philosophy. That was real in his mind in 1875, even though he did not do a PhD in philosophy. Today, we might include the mental activity we call "thought experiments".

Inexistent objects exist as mental representations, not "real" in a material sense. But, they *are* real in our own experience. And they do not just exist there, they are active and create dramas as in dreams. There is a world of internal action we experience in our minds as imagined narratives and dramas played out between objects. In contemporary object relations theory they are now called "unconscious phantasy". They are composed partly of memories, of the recognition of actual external objects out there, together with imagined objects.

Freud later said:

> Thinking is an experimental action carried out with small amounts of energy, in the same way as a general shifts small figures about on a map before setting his large bodies of troops in motion. (Freud, 1933a, p. 89)

And interestingly we can find an exactly comparable view expressed nearly a century before Freud, but in the field of social and political science:

> [M]any a human architect is put to shame by the skill with which a bee constructs her cell. But what distinguishes the worst architect from the best of bees is that the architect builds the cell in his mind before he constructs it in wax. (Marx, 1867 [1975, p. 284])

So, our minds work in this way, to construct a view of some structure or action that does not exist, does not *yet* exist, but could exist in the material reality. This is not just about constructing buildings, of course. but about developing our society as well. Thus, political debate goes on in this domain of experimental action, with these inexistent objects, interior to our minds. We could envision a society without racial prejudice, for instance. Thus, it is the first step in political action.

This also approximates to a psychoanalytic action when we make an interpretation. Instead of acting out, we speak about a set of internal inexistent objects, for instance the elements of a dream. By directing a patient's attention to the meaning of a dream, an analyst is acting upon inexistent objects, those that exist in the mind. Indeed, when a patient tells us a dream, he is also acting upon the analyst's mind by putting inexistent objects there, and in relation to each other, as narratives known as unconscious phantasies. We can direct attention to these inexistent objects for specific reasons.

This leads on to an important aspect of inexistent objects that Freud did not go on to develop in these philosophical terms.

Interpersonal inexistence

Individuals can have different experiences of the reality they share. The inexistent objects in two (or more) minds may be different. We can direct not only our own attention to them, but to other people's as well. When I speak to you of Brentano, I invite you to have an impression, even an image, of the man 150 years ago who so impressed Freud. I can point your attention to certain objects which I might think are in your mind—such as Freud; or I can point your attention to an inexistent object that I think may not be there, such as Brentano. There is an interpersonal dimension to the action with inexistent objects.

So, I am postulating a collaborative interaction in that inexistent world in the mind. And I suggest it is the basis of ordinary discourse between human beings. We invite attention of others to objects in our own mind. And also we can place such objects for attention in other people's minds. It is so ordinary and is the basis of what I am doing now with objects in your mind, as you read these very words.

So collaborative experimental action occurs between minds. But I want to extend this one more step. This collaborative action of directing each other's attention can be just an enjoyable conversation. But it can also be something different. Minds can collaborate in experimental action for thinking to be "employed in the appropriate alteration of reality", as Freud put it in the quote I started with. At this point, I believe we have reached a description of political debate. It is interpersonal experimental action then transferred to actual external reality. Whether the external reality is the material world, and issues like the environment, or whether it is the cultural reality of the way we live together, political debate engages our attention with the inexistent worlds we each have in our minds, which then collaborate in that appropriate alteration of reality.

So collaborative thought becomes politics—not just experimental thinking but experimental thinking *together*. There has to be a transfer of inexistent objects from one mind to another and back again. We call this simply talking and listening to each other. I am moving my inexistent objects that exist in my mind into yours—or I am trying to. And you the reader—some of you, perhaps—are trying to receive these inexistent objects.

Going back for a moment to Freud's description of the ego-functions that make up the reality principle, it is clear one of the other ego-functions is very important; the function of "attention". We focus our attention on some inexistent object. The architect attends to the building he is creating in his mind. His attention is directed inwardly (and Brentano called this "intention"—an inward attention).

Public opinion

The architect will also focus the attention of his builders, bricklayers, electricians, and so on. And politicians do the same. They focus our attention on, for example, Vladimir Putin and create an evil object in our minds (at least they do so in the West). But that directed attention aims to prepare the way for some specific actual action, one that goes beyond thinking. The UK might send a battalion of tanks to the Ukraine (as an illustration from the early 2020s). That actual action in external reality has to be prepared for by directing attention in the inexistent world within the minds of the public. Directing the attention of a politician's constituents is a first step before actual action, then directing the attention of other politicians.

So, in our social world we not only focus our own attention, we try to focus each other's attention. There are various ways in which we direct each other's attention. We can point with the finger (something, by the way, that even the higher primates have difficulty in doing). Or we turn our gaze towards something, and some would say we as humans have evolved, biologically, the whites of our eyes in order to facilitate being able to follow each other's direction of gaze.

But the most effective way that humans have developed for pointing at *inexistent* things is to use language, the capacity to represent thoughts in my mind that can be transferred into your mind—it is the study of semiotics. I don't want to go too deeply into that, but just to get across the idea that we direct the attention to these internal inexistent objects through language to create an exchange, we can call a debate. Language is a pointing system that extends the capacity of finger-pointing or gazing.

Directing attention

I have been speaking of course of a society aiming to be a democracy as we understand it in the West. But in fact, a similar pattern does apply to more authoritarian or totalitarian regimes. There is a difference, of course. But the difference lies in the means used to direct attention. In an authoritarian system, attention is directed by manipulation, threats, and coercion. There is a dimension of difference here, which runs between persuasion, on one hand, and manipulation/coercion on the other. In a democracy there is a tendency to prioritise persuasion rather than coercion—though manipulation is not at all unknown, and I think of the writings of Edward Bernays (see Chapter 9), and the "hidden persuaders" that Vance Packard wrote about, back in 1957. The difference is not either/or, but a dimension of variation and balance, a mixture of manipulation and persuasion.

I have gone through this elaborate set of points in order to claim that the difference between political action and psychoanalytic action is not a direct opposition—politics in the external world and psychoanalysis in the internal world. The internal experimental action and our attempts to direct other's attention is fundamental to political debating.

Relevance of psychoanalytic action to politics

Now, I should like to question how psychoanalytic understanding can contribute to politics. The upshot of the argument so far in this paper is that the contribution is likely to be limited to the initial step of political debate, whether that is persuasion, manipulation, or coercion.

There are two particular areas we might focus on:

- First, the particular ego-function in which the more animal sequence of motor action proceeds from stimulus to satisfaction;
- And second, once thinking has been accomplished, the complex phenomena of inexistent objects psychoanalysts know as highly determined by unconscious factors not necessarily relevant for appropriate alteration of external reality.

I propose to consider both these problems with an example of each.

Failure of inhibition of motor action

The last of Freud's ego functions that constitute the reality principle can fail; that is, motor action that discharges the response to a stimulus may not be adequately inhibited. For instance, I might follow the impulse to buy a cheap burger when hungry rather than stop and think that

I am trying to diet a bit and keep my weight down. Or it might be to follow the impulse to punch someone in a bar on Saturday night rather than take stock of his provocation and attempt at least to see his point of view. In the analytic setting, a reversion to more reflex action is behind the phenomenon of acting out.

This implies a process in which an ego-function is put out of action. Freud described this kind of possibility in his paper on fetishism (Freud, 1927e), where the ego is split and in one part, at least, the capacity to recognise reality is lost. Splitting of this kind, which depletes the ego, was taken up by several British analysts in the 1930s, including Edward Glover (1939), and Marjorie Brierley (1937), and eventually, of course, by Melanie Klein with her influential paper on schizoid mechanisms in 1946.

I have contributed, elsewhere, to a special journal issue edited by Era Loewenstein on this kind of loss of function as an explanation of populism of all kinds (Hinshelwood, 2023). Within social groups, Freud (1930a) said a "narcissism of minor differences" tends to operate. A group gets together by identifying themselves as different from some other group. The difference may be very minor and completely without significance. Nevertheless, emotionally, the difference can be felt powerfully to sustain a significant *feeling* of superiority. In a class-based society, notably Western democratic societies with large and increasing inequality of wealth and opportunity, two specific classes seem to emerge with that kind of emotional significance. On the one hand are the wealthy, with a superior education, and on the other, the impoverished, with a more limited education and sophistication. The difference is often marked by the different newspapers and media aimed at each class.

I identify a consequential difference in the nature of the superiority felt by each class over the other. The educated wealthy see the impoverished as lacking in the capacity to think clearly and contribute importantly to political debate and decisions. In other words, they imagine that the impoverished class is not adequately making the transition Freud noted—from reflex motor action to thinking as experimental action. They are often believed to require the hidden persuasion by the class that is well educated and capable of the necessary thinking required for political decisions. This was explicit in Bernays, as noted, but also by Einstein in his correspondence with Freud on warfare (see Chapter 5).

On the other hand, those in the class of the impoverished find themselves identified as not thoughtful people and accept it, but do so in such a way as to create their own sense of superiority by flaunting their capacity for impulsive emotional judgements and action. As one English politician speaking for them said: "I think the people of this country have had enough of experts with organisations with acronyms saying that they know what is best" (Michael Gove quoted in Mance, 2016). The wealthy educated are condemned for their "we know best" attitudes. And it would be claimed that anyone can know the answers without recourse to specialist knowledge and thought. There is here a simple denial of the importance of the move from motor action to careful forethought, and, in effect, an idealisation of human emotionalism.

How far this goes to explain the full extent of populism across the voting democracies may be debated, but it is the kind of pattern of implicit, unconscious dynamics that I am trying to illustrate. It arises from the tendency of one group to split off its emotionalism, and the other to split off its capacity for experimental thinking before action.

Unconscious interference in collaborative experimental action

The second area we need to concentrate on is the unconscious interference in our conscious debate. Political, and in fact any other, debate is conducted at a conscious level, and mostly by means of representations. Those representations are the actualisation, usually in words, of the inexistent objects that comprise experimental action.

More concretely, the general deploys his toy soldiers in order to experiment in his mind about how to deploy the real army. The toys actualise on the map what will be real. Such a mentally actualised battle is the nature of a chess match. We engage with the battle through the pieces on the chess board. Let us suppose, for example, that one chess player has particular gender issues stemming from whatever unconscious dynamics, so that, inexplicably, in game after game, he gets his queen taken by his opponent: not a very good strategy and it leads to a persistent low performance in his play. This might be an absurd example, but it is in order to demonstrate the interplay between unconscious dynamics that are not relevant in experimental action. It is an interference in the capacity for thought. Whilst it has been argued here that the capacity for thought has been a defining characteristic of human beings and our success technologically, the example demonstrates that there are pitfalls, since the unconscious dynamics cannot be allowed for—precisely because they are unconscious. That, it seems, is the point where psychoanalysis could apply some leverage.

Let me take a more realistic example. One profoundly important and influential capacity of the human mind is to notice differences, and then to make judgements of good vs bad. The facility with which we can revise differences to become oppositions is quite extraordinary. Typically, skin colour is required to serve as a marker of moral, cultural, even financial value, even though such assignment of superiority to some races and inferiority to others is changeable from one historical period to another. Skin colour is both quite irrelevant as a judgement of value but also very common. Something so irrelevant capturing the evaluative judgement so effectively and persistently suggests unknown causes. In other words, it is the unconscious dynamics that surface as the deeply held, and even murderous, racist beliefs. The significant point here is that to take action to abolish such prejudice may need more than conscious political strategies. Or, to put it the other way, conscious strategies to eliminate racist views may be ineffective unless a psychoanalytic understanding of the unconscious is brought into play.

We might in this context consider the current state of racism in the Metropolitan Police. This has been under formal research since the early 1980s, nearly half a century. The racist culture was brought to light explicitly by the co-called Bristol Seminars in 1991 when all black officers of the Met were mandated to discuss their experiences. It's over thirty years since those discussions, and they revealed the common experiences such as "racial slurs in their stations or finding racist graffiti on their lockers or faeces in their helmets" (Muir, 2021). Little has been achieved except that the abuse is not so overt. In fact, the Casey Review (2023) found the Metropolitan Police to be racist, sexist, and homophobic. In fact, it has now become so bad and so hidden by a culture of denial, according to the report, that the force may need to be disbanded altogether, and restarted. There seems to be no evidence of even slight improvement since 1991. And that failure of progress has been in the context of increasing public awareness of the problem for three or four decades. Such a sustained institutional culture strongly suggests hidden forces that keep it going against the conscious awareness that the problem of police prejudice needs to be effectively tackled.

I don't want to stress overconfidently a psychoanalytic position on this. So, more tentatively I might suggest a few points—in fact, three steps. First, it seems to me important that given the human propensity for turning differences into oppositions we are *none of us* immune from just this kind of prejudice. That might be the most difficult step to undo. The second step would be that in a racist social culture we imbibe the prejudice every day in all kinds of hidden and unconscious ways.

We might therefore start from the position that we are all racist. It is really unlikely that we can be non-racist.

Moreover, this may be true of the Black races as well as the white. What we could, however, strive to be, is anti-racist. In other words, a third step would be to recognise *in all of us* a conflict we need to own. That conflict is, whether we like it or not, that we are embedded in a racist culture and at the same time we are opposed to that aspect of our very own culture. That puts us all in a personal conflict over a culture that probably runs very deep in us. We need to own such a personal conflict rather than claim a righteous innocence. It needs acknowledging, perhaps as a fourth step, to refrain from converting the conflict into a blame-game with another group. Typically, we need to resist the projective defensiveness that the problem is in someone else. And here I suggest that there are two temptations: one is to see another culture as external, Black culture say, and see the conflict not in ourselves but between white culture and Black culture (our racist side); or second, we see ourselves in opposition to racism and to racists and critical of other white people who are overtly racist (our anti-racism).

Whatever our own conscious awareness of these dynamics (which may be very little, as they are unconscious), it is a start to know at least we do have such a dynamic unconscious conflict within all of us which tempts us to externalise it as criticism of some other persons and groups.

Conclusion

In conclusion, I am suggesting that there is a place for psychoanalytic action within political action. And especially following on the past illustration, there is a need to carefully consider what unconscious issues might be necessary to tackle, and then how to do it.

The question of what issues we psychoanalysts might give assistance to, can be answered by saying that we could consider that certain intractable issues will be found to have unconscious determinants that make them intractable because they cannot be effectively addressed by conscious debate. That may not be easily accepted by politicians and the public. How to tackle such unconscious interference may be even more difficult since it involves, for example in the case of racism as I have conceptualised it, an acknowledgement by many ordinary people of their own complicity in some social process they would prefer to deny, as the Metropolitan Police have done for decades.

Finally, and perhaps sadly, I suggest the place for psychoanalytic understanding is limited. We should refrain from wide-ranging discourses on all sorts of political issues that often reflect more our own political position rather than a targeted intervention at the unconscious level of debate. I realise I may be contentious here, but we need to avoid the danger that we slip into making a value judgement about the difference between psychoanalysts and non-analysts such that we assign a superiority to one side … though I won't suggest which side that might be!

References

Brierley, M. (1937). Affects in theory and practice. *International Journal of Psychoanalysis*, *18*: 256–268.

Casey, L. (2023). *Final Report: An Independent Review into the Standards of Behaviour and Internal Culture of the Metropolitan Police Service*. https://www.met.police.uk/

Freud, S. (1911b). Formulations on the two principles of mental functioning. *S. E.*, *22*: 213–226. London: Hogarth.

Freud, S. (1911c). Psycho-analytic notes on an autobiographical account of a case of paranoia (dementia paranoides). *S. E.*, *12*: 3–82. London: Hogarth.

Freud, S. (1927). Fetishism. *S. E.*, *21*: 147–158. London Hogarth.

Freud, S. (1930a). *Civilization and its Discontents. S. E., 21*: 59–145. London: Hogarth.

Freud, S. (1933a). *New Introductory Lectures on Psycho-Analysis. S. E., 22.* London: Hogarth.

Freud, S. (1933b). *Why War?* S. E., *22*: 197–215. London: Hogarth.

Freud, S. (1992). *The Letters of Sigmund Freud to Eduard Silberstein, 1871–1881.* Cambridge, MA: Harvard University Press.

Glover, E. (1939). The psycho-analysis of affects. *International Journal of Psychoanalysis, 20*: 299–307.

Hinshelwood, R. D. (2023). Populism: The politics of emotions. *Psychoanalytic Inquiry, 43*: 110–118.

Hinshelwood, R. D. (2024). *Unconscious Politics*. London: Karnac.

Klein, M. (1946). Notes on some schizoid mechanisms. *International Journal of Psychoanalysis, 27*: 99–110. Republished in M. Klein, P. Heimann, S. Isaacs & and J. Riviere, *Developments in Psycho-Analysis* (pp. 292–320). London: Hogarth, 1952; and in *The Writings of Melanie Klein, Volume 3* (pp. 1–24). London: Hogarth, 1975.

Kriegel, K. (Ed.,) (2017). *The Routledge Handbook of Franz Brentano and the Brentano School.* New York: Routledge.

Mance, H. (2016). Britain has had enough of experts. *Financial Times*. 3 June, 2013.

Marx, K. (1867). *Capital.* London: Penguin, 1976.

Muir, H. (2021). Black and blue: The secret lives of BAME police officers. *The Guardian*, 7 February, 2021. https://www.theguardian.com/uk-news/2021/feb/07/black-and-blue-the-secret-lives-of-bame-police-officers

Packard, V. (1957). *The Hidden Persuaders*. New York: David Mackay.

Strachey, J. (1937). Introduction. In: R. Osborn, *Freud and Marx.* London: Gollancz.

Thomas, H. (1973). *John Strachey*. London: Eyre Methuen.

Discussion of Part IV

GC: The papers we have just read focus on current matters of political relevance in their often separated aspects, both practical and theoretical. You discuss democracy, action, and reflection, and the relationship between political and psychoanalytic action aimed at alleviating mental suffering and alienation. In a way congruent to the formulation we saw in Part III in Chapter 6, you study here the possible dynamics of a "political psychological" action. What struck me in this last set of papers was that the foundations of collective life are in symbol-formation. Relatedly, the challenges to collective living come from the various pathologies of thinking, such as symbolic equations, ideological untruths, and more radical enactments and anti-political (very poignantly, you called them anti-human) activity. The paper on symbolism, it seems to me, helps the reader ground your work until then, and since, in the papers we just read on reflection and on political, psychoanalytic, and experimental action. In that paper you showed how the psychoanalyst could stand for, and then allow, the patient to re-introject the symbolic function, allowing him to see the difference between feeling, as in the case of Segal's patient, that he was entrapped in a jail and realising, instead, that actually he was an inpatient in a hospital, which he experienced as if like a prison. Would you say that there can be a political function that could be played by individuals and groups resembling this therapeutic action in the clinical setting? I ask you this because I would also like to hear your thoughts on a theory of political action in relation to psychoanalytic theories of therapeutic action and technique.

RDH: I think that is the big question. The big issue is that the unconscious exists to contain the intolerable, and the result is that facing the dynamics of the unconscious cannot be tolerated! Only slowly over the years or in a specific setting (a therapeutic or group therapeutic one) can the anxieties and conflicts be gradually resolved. Can such a process be promoted on the scale of a large population? It may perhaps only occur when there has been a national catastrophe, and I am thinking of the cultural surge towards regret, guilt, and reparation in Germany after the Second World War (Figlio, 2018). It is indeed the biggest of questions not answered in this book—how to address the unconscious dynamics that disturbed the heart of a civilisation pushing us towards decline and collapse.

So in relation to your question—is there something in political debate that is comparable to a psychoanalytic interpretation?—I don't think it has been invented yet. And if it ever will be, then it will be resisted, as are psychoanalytic interpretations. I see the best hope is perhaps to avoid simplistic dos-and-don'ts, such as the so-called woke phenomenon of advising people not to use certain words or express certain opinions. In fact, as with the racist example in the last chapter (Chapter 11), it is better if we all accept our inherent potential to be racist in a racist society rather than criticise others for their racism as if we were innocent ourselves. It is not just the Metropolitan Police who are racist; rather the racist tone of white society has infiltrated the police. I might add that it could be just as well for non-white people to own their racism as well, and avoid posing as innocent victims—but that implies that racism is a mutual interaction of guilt between oppositional groups. Or am I being unfair and naive?

GC: As we have read in your papers and as we have discussed so far, there is a long tradition of engagement between psychoanalysis, political thought, and public commitment. How are we to make sense of these relations? Do they entail—as some seem to imply and others just as adamantly seem to reject—a kind of militant attitude in the consulting room? Alternatively, would these relations point towards public engagements by individual psychoanalysts, their organised groups, and the national and international institutions of psychoanalysis intervening in the public sphere? Is this separation of domains—the private one of the consulting room and the public of the public sphere—convincing or itself unsatisfying?

RDH: Yes, this is the question the book heads towards from the beginning. I don't know if we are going to come out with a clear and practical answer. I think as psychoanalysts it has never been very clear what the relations are between three things: (i) the internal dynamics of the people we are working with, (ii) their politics which may show up in the free associations and other material they bring, and (iii) our own political commitments which can be judged very strongly to be correct in our own minds. Perhaps it is a good moment, not too late, to confide a little of my own political commitments and wonder aloud how that intrudes as interference or creatively into psychoanalytic work. My own concern is with the ownership of private property, and especially the ownership of other persons, not just slaves, but peasants or waged employees, depending on which phase of history one is concerned with; and in addition taking possession of parts of someone's ego as in projection and projective identification. I have some hesitancy over single-issue politics, which, however distressing, seems as though they might be a concern merely with symptoms rather than the causes. Training as a doctor, though many years ago, one learned that treating symptoms is not necessarily treating the cause of the symptom. And the Enlightenment project of the eighteenth century was, in part, to understand that difference—to understand causal determinism. This is not to say that gender, religion, race, and ethnicity and the power relations involved in those differences are not important or distressing. But it could be like saying pain-killers for a broken bone are all that is needed, when we know actually it is necessary to reset the fracture. Similarly, we are interested in the way a person lives out ancient issues in the present—either as a result of regression to a trauma, or as current deep unconscious phantasies. Those originating experiences need exposing. But if we go back to origins of experiences, maybe in preverbal life experience, how did politics impact on that? Or how much does that impact on the way we commit ourselves to a political view of action now? I am not giving an answer to these questions right now.

You raise an interesting possibility, that analysts take a public stance to establish an understanding of unconscious processes and their social consequences. I don't know how effective that would be. I know Susie Orbach had a regular column in—was it *The Observer*?—and I once discussed such a possibility with Alan Rusbridger, editor of *The Guardian* at the time (his brother is an analyst), though my suggestion was not taken up. I don't have any evidence of how much such a contribution would be useful. Maybe we should think about the social media. Perhaps these discussions should move to become podcasts?

A possible (normative/analytical) relationship

GC: Let me return, for a further moment, to the consulting room. The former understanding, perhaps a misunderstanding—that you refer to when you wonder how the political affects the earliest preverbal phases in a person's life—has often concerned psychoanalysts who consider the consulting room as a space separate from the sphere of the political in somewhat similar ways perhaps as the beginnings of the infant's life and her relationship with her carers. In the consulting room, therefore, political issues (whatever we understand as political issues, and this understanding is perhaps the crux of the matter) should not be discussed directly so that they avoid becoming screens, pretexts, sources of denial, or a kind of psychic retreat, in other words an obstacle to psychoanalysis. Yet, as you show, those matters are inevitably present to the consciousness of both patient and analyst and may have been fed to the infant since very early on as part of her earliest and most meaningful relationships.

RDH: Yes, it is widely felt that political practice and psychoanalytic practice can only interfere with each other. Of course, that is potentially a realistic problem, just like any commitment of the analyst's. At the same time, we can understand that we may not be able to prevent such interferences playing upon the analysis or the analyst.

I have a particular problem here. For over a year I have been supervisor of an international group of left-wing therapists who call themselves the Red Clinic. They provide affordable treatments, and it is clear that people who find their way to one of these therapists do so because of a search for a politically compatible therapist. However, the place of politics in the actual material that comes up is very, very small.

I am not sure if this is my inadequacy as leader of the supervision or if the political dimension, which must have been a factor in the process of selecting a therapist, just becomes irrelevant, as patients concentrate on intensely personal and intimate issues. I persist with this practical work, in order to try to penetrate towards some understanding of the absence of political issues and phantasies which must be important to both parties—perhaps not spoken because there is a silent agreement on the politics they share. I can say that reading through this discussion and your thoughts, I do feel I could go back to the Red Clinic sessions with some further stimulus for thinking.

GC: Let's consider also, for a moment, the work of psychoanalysis outside of the consulting room. A wide enough part of the psychoanalytic movement appreciates, indeed even advocates, public commitments by psychoanalysts and their institutions as it is illustrated by the IPA commitment towards psychoanalysis in the community and psychoanalysis in the world as championed by its latest two presidents (the first two women ever to lead the IPA). I find that this kind of approach to politics and psychoanalysis rests perhaps on a limited conception of the political as restricted to the sphere of the state (perhaps augmented by the sphere of civil society) and to decision-making mechanisms and conflicts around the management of the public thing (the *res publica*). Feminist activists and intellectuals have extended greatly the scope of politics. They claimed that, "the personal is political". I think this statement has been expanded further by psychoanalysis, as one would paraphrase the feminist slogan by saying, "the psychic is political". I find, therefore, that we could think of psychoanalytic action as inherently political, though not in the restricted understanding of the political as referring to professional politics related to the government of the state. Such action would be opposed to enactments and acting outs in ways that we are familiar with and have been theorised extensively by psychoanalysts.

RDH: Yes, we used to say, the personal is political. And it is interesting to expand to psychoanalysis as "the psyche is political". I think that political issues do invade everywhere. Just in terms of power, we think of the power of the analyst to intrude into the deepest levels of the mind. Is this a political power? It is not easy to say. Certainly, the analysand seeks the analyst's power of influence; but, at the same time, we know, it is a matter of great resistance, as it is a threat that his defences will be penetrated, and all his horrors and spooks will be let out like Pandora's box. How much does the analyst exert his power to intrude? And is that political?

There is a profound division of labour in the analytic setting, as explored in Chapter 9. So, one could ask the question the other way around—How could a division of labour not be political? The analyst for instance takes over the analysand's function of enquiry, when following Freud's instruction, and the analysand suspends all judgement on what he says.

Except of course the analysand does not. He interrupts his free associations with defences, known in the analytic session as "resistance". An analytic treatment proceeds by reducing resistance and enables the analysand to achieve more compliance with his associations. But this becomes complicated, and we need to distinguish between compliance and collaboration. With compliance, authority is ceded to the analyst, while in collaboration there is a negotiated kind of sharing. We meet a similar issue in medicine when a patient signs a form to agree to a medical procedure. This is merely a conscious agreement, and unconscious factors involved in giving over authority to the doctor are inevitably ignored. A psychoanalytic treatment explores this kind of exchange at the unconscious level, and any initial agreement between analyst and analysand at a conscious level cannot really be meaningful, nor is it a valid agreement at the level of unconscious exchange at which the work will be done.

GC: Here, you look at the political (or potentially otherwise) relationship between analyst and patient due to their power differentials. There is also another way in which I can think of the expression "the psychic is political", maybe two … Bion came to describe the human mind as a group. In that group, political dynamics are inevitably expressed in relation to any instance of decision-making for action (or inaction) by the mental collective as the actor, as it were. Rosenfeld as well (which you also commented on in your recent comprehensive introduction to his work), in his oft-quoted reference to a certain mind dynamic as that of an individual bullied by a mafia gang, reduces the dramatic interaction of the mental group to anti-political dynamics expressing the brutal law of the strongest. Presumably, establishing a more genuinely political dynamic among (psychic) group members could be a way to express the outcome of a successful analysis.

And the idea that a successful analysis establishes the domain of politics within the internal mental group is again consistent with Bion's conception, to which we have already made reference, of politics as the highest form of human collective endeavour. In Chapter 10, you return to a subject dear to you, perhaps one of the leitmotifs of this collection, the convergence between psychoanalysis and sociopolitical disciplines. Here the emphasis is their unique focus on action. The quality of psychoanalytic action that you describe in this paper revolves around its drive "towards truth, validity, and authenticity". The way I understand this is that therapeutic action and (or as) political action can be thought of as convergent conceptualisations of a certain (creative, generative) relationship between individuals and of individuals with their environments which appreciate the role of unconscious dynamics in both individuals and groups. I wonder what your thoughts are on this way of looking at politics in the mind, and thus looking at the (unconscious) mind itself as a (potentially) political field.

RDH: Yes, I agree, we can consider the internal object relations as a form of political activity and exchange. And as you say, it is interesting that Rosenfeld used the analogy of a coercive authority, the mafia, to characterise disturbed personalities. The crucial issues in our debate, however, are twofold: (i) the externalisation of that internal coercive politics into the actual world of social politics; and (ii) the processes by which that externalisation is coordinated or collaborated between numbers of separate individuals. As so much of this book has investigated, the exchange of mental phenomena, emotions, and ideas, appears to be a bedrock process on which actual social politics must be founded.

And in relation to something I mentioned earlier, it is worth considering here again that I posit a hypothetical link between the exchange of mental health and of financial wealth. They appear equivalent systems of exchange. The social relations of production can remove a key element of the person who produces (as Harry Braverman elaborated about the labour process). It is a process not just of power but of the power to reduce the humanity of persons. It is a commodification of persons, and then an ownership, a possession, of them or of a part of them. Then the question might be whether that kind of taking possession of someone and alienating them from themselves is a feature of psychoanalysis. Or whether the opposite is the case, that through psychoanalysis an individual is able to recover alienated parts of herself. Some people would criticise psychoanalysis for its intrusion into the unconscious and to lay it bare according to the analyst's map of the mind, which appears to be a potentially powerful coercion. That could be seen as just such an act of alienation or of appropriation of the analysand's knowledge of the mind. Erich Fromm (1971), in his early essays, *The Crisis of Psychoanalysis*, was extremely conscious of that kind of invasion and did castigate psychoanalytic practice as mechanical. And to some extent it was. Freud's structural model—energy circulating in the mental "apparatus"—does reduce persons to machine-like causality. It can remove the sense of purpose and meaning, and we become in that mould persons alienated from our own psychology. Personally, I think it is a corruption of psychoanalysis and I agree with Fromm's criticisms. But I would say alienation does not necessarily characterise psychoanalysis. And in fact, there has been a swing away from this energy model towards prioritising relationships, knowing, and meanings.

Also, perhaps you are right to insist that there is a healthy form of politics that is truthful, valid, and authentic, whilst I keep on bashing away at the corruption of an unhealthy politics which is intransigently ideological or blatantly self-seeking with all the manipulative and coercive strategies those alternative aims employ. It sometimes seems as though you would have another word to designate the form of politics that I think of as corrupt. I would say that when a corrupt politics (in my terms, as above) is conscious, it is simply criminal, and when it is an unconscious deviation, it is psychoanalytic territory that requires an understanding of the anxiety-defence structure and investigates it, writ large as group dynamics.

I would like to add a thought or two on authenticity. I recently wrote a book on "alive moments" in a psychoanalytic practice, the term "alive moments" being taken from Elizabeth Spillius. The point is that dead moments can be very common. Spillius considered it a key sign if there was a sense of alive contact, even if it was an angry one. Something had gone deep. I have come to think of authenticity as an important element in a psychoanalytic practice. It is not always easy to find, and that tells us how difficult the work is. In a sense, patients come to us because they are already alienated from themselves—either through repressing some painful, personal experience from their conscious minds, or by splitting off ego-functions, which have generated painful experiences. It is then quite difficult to gain an authentic contact with what they have, understandably, disposed of. But that is the job we have decided to spend our lives doing!

It is perhaps important that human beings, probably unlike animals, can alienate themselves from themselves. Because of that propensity, it seems we are therefore vulnerable to the exploitation of that facility by external pressures. I would say that certain kinds of political regimes probably build on self-alienation and create persons as depleted entities more resembling commodities we buy from the supermarket shelves. This is a really important aspect of power—to deplete persons and alienate them as commodities in a culture centred on trade, commodity exchange, and values that are abstract rather than human. And I can give a quote that you may know from an anthropologist:

> [There is a] logical opposition between gifts (relations between non-aliens by means of inalienable things) and commodities (relations between aliens by means of alienable things). (Gregory, 1997, pp. 52–53)

In the extreme, exchanging Christmas presents is radically different from trading goods. One is an exchange supporting personal relationships, and the other is using relationships to support commodity trading. What this amounts to is the similarity of the power of alienation in both politics and in psychoanalysis; just as we can see the importance of authenticity and the alive moment in human connections in politics and psychoanalysis.

GC: Another aspect of the relationship between political action and psychoanalytic action that I am interested in is the following. Can we imagine a convergence, to use your term, between the two that can contribute to a theory of political action with the literature and the experience developed over decades by psychoanalysts on the theory of psychoanalytic technique and on therapeutic (and anti-therapeutic) action? More precisely, you wrote a fascinating paper on "The Kleinian theory of therapeutic action" (2007) that we could not collect here but that I think would have been very apt and useful. There you distinguish three kinds of change that occur in patients during a psychoanalysis, but consider only the one directly achieved by psychoanalysis. Moreover, you discuss transference and countertransference, and finally the use of interpretation from different theoretical perspectives. Earlier in our discussion you referred to an aspect of the possible convergence between political action and psychoanalytic action when you stressed that symptomatic approaches are palliative at best but at worst can make the "patient" worse (you spoke about aspirins for broken bones). Can you say something more about whether, and in that case how, psychoanalytic approaches to clinical practice can contribute to developing a theory of political practice?

RDH: Well, you ask the crucial question, and I have described the two problems, that first, we have no over arching model of psychodynamics and of society, and second that psychoanalytic work is not "active" in the sense that politics is. But you raise an interesting point earlier in this discussion about the internal world of an individual being a group and thus implying we as analysts may have to consider if there is a kind of politics of the group of internal objects. It is a pretty unexplored territory, but as we would agree that Rosenfeld's idea of a kind of internal mafia gang seems as though it is a beginning shot at some thinking, we could explore it. Perhaps another book, Giuseppe?—one day, maybe.

GC: You write that psychoanalysis is or can be subversive; this statement recurs in several papers in one form or another. Consider for instance what you write in "Convergences" (Chapter 2) about a potentially revolutionary psychoanalysis. You relate this in a very vivid way to the relationship between modes of production and personality structures. In your 1983 paper you write that the mutually reinforcing development of capitalism and narcissistic personality structures resemble "an endlessly turning spiral". In the 1996 papers you strikingly and vividly show how the roots of narcissism (of the particular kind that found fertile ground in contemporary capitalism) are in a culture of control over one's identity defined by an ideal of "stability, continuity, and permanence". You describe this spiral as what I think of as an unstoppable escalation that needs to be arrested as it "is not self-limiting". You write that "to step out of this rolling momentum may well seem to some people to require a revolution". You return to similar questions in your 1996 paper. You write, "[p]sychoanalysis can only be revolutionary if it has a much wider effect on self-consciousness, in other words, on the false consciousness of whole classes—or on whole particulate liberatory movements—feminism or anti-racism as well as political liberation". I am very interested in these matters, among other reasons because I have participated in and I also studied social movements for much of my life and often noted dynamics that you indicate as false consciousness limiting the political efficacy of these collective actors and causing depression and hopelessness to their members. Can you say something about this? In particular, what do you mean by "step out" (as opposed to arresting the vicious revolving of the spiral) and what do you make of the revolutionary calls of "some people"?

RDH: Perhaps "step out" was a poor choice of expression. I meant stepping off the unstoppable round-about. As Marx, and Lukács, would say, it is coming to recognise the way one has unquestioningly accepted the unspoken assumptions on which social institutions and our daily life run. In contemporary terms it is called "raising consciousness" and comes directly from Lukács pointing to the falsity that entangles us so easily. About revolution, I am not sure how much I am a revolutionary. I say there has to be this revolution in perception of our society, of competitive commodification and accumulation of money (abstract capital), but at the same time revolution tempts people into that simplistic good–bad, righteousness-vs-blame state which leads people to simply dig themselves into a self-assigned purity. The anti-racist needs to acknowledge his own racism which he cannot have avoided in our racialist society. He cannot be non-racist; he can only be anti-racist and thus in conflict with himself as much as his political opponents.

The revolutionary quality of psychoanalysis was apparent early on in its history. Reich was the most extreme exponent, but only represented Freud's implicit revolution in the place to be given to sexuality. It is revolution first in one's own understanding of oneself, the throwing over of the defensive convictions about oneself. But there is that long-standing view that psychoanalysis implies an overthrowing of cultural attitudes such as the prudishness about sex. However, as psychoanalysis has developed, it has exposed various other falsenesses in society (or at least Western society)—such as the rigid sense of self/identity which psychoanalysis now shows to be fluid and extremely flexible and compliant to the social group. Further, in my view, it can expose the inauthenticity of much of the culture of the advanced countries where so much is valued in terms of impersonal monetary value, and at least since the days of slavery, persons have been easily, and perhaps increasingly, seen as commodities rather than persons. So I think there is a continuing place of psychoanalysis as a counter-cultural influence. I am now bordering on giving aspects of my own political conviction—so, RDH, stop!

GC: You also ask, "What then is the scope for a *negative practice*?" It is not enough that psychoanalytic practice liberates the individual; and often, incidentally, it does not. "Psychoanalysis can only be revolutionary if it has a much wider effect on self-consciousness; in other words on the false consciousnesses of whole classes—or on whole particulate liberatory movements—feminism or anti-racism, as well as political liberation". There are two aspects to my question. First, what do you mean exactly when you stress the revolutionary potential of psychoanalysis? The second matter, perhaps even more poignant, is that you recognise psychoanalysis' most revolutionary contribution to emancipation and social justice as its "negative practice". Can you say something more about this negative practice, perhaps a negative emancipatory practice?

RDH: Within a social culture that is focused on trading commodities, there is the risk of psychoanalysis descending to a mechanical and impersonal level, and we can see it as culturally driven. At the same time psychoanalysis could operate in the opposite direction—the personification, or re-personification of persons. In other words, there may be a choice of actions we can take as psychoanalysts. When is it mechanistic, as Fromm (1976) argued, and when is it alive? Thus, there is a choice of actions that can be taken by psychoanalysts and by politicians in relation to the social culture. They may conform to the mechanistic commodification or they may challenge it.

My reference to "negative practice" is a reference to Marcuse and critical theory that aims to question and critique as many assumptions in cultural discourse and political dialogue as can be exposed. And psychoanalysis could be an important instrument for such exposure. For example, if our culture sustains a politics of commodification, then psychoanalysts could be doing the same and commodifying our patients, as much psychiatry does. But in fact, we have the option to do the opposite. We can subvert that kind of commodification. We can restore the personal to what patients have alienated themselves from, in themselves. This challenges the prevailing culture of alienation, and we could promote a radicalisation of psychiatry in the same direction.

So, I agree psychoanalysis can be "revolutionary" in the sense of counter-cultural. It could expose the falseness of false consciousness, for instance. In that sense it critically negates the falsity. My view has been grounded, for instance, in the clinging to an ideological system that is seductive of many individuals who have a self-uncertainty. We all do to some extent, but some of us have a more uncertain and wobbly sense of self, which needs external support. That support can be found in crusading intransigence and righteousness—ideology, in effect. To tackle such dynamics requires some subtlety. One cannot go straight ahead and challenge the ideology because challenging will enhance the self-uncertainty that has to be avoided, and then an even stricter ideological commitment will be defended. The current "Prevent" programme in the UK, aimed at "preventing" the grooming of new members for terrorist organisations, seems to be coming under criticism for the over-simple strategy of simply making a logical challenge to the grooming. Psychoanalysis would prescribe a different approach focused on the underlying existential anxiety. That is, to help potential victims to establish a more stable sense of self.

GC: I wonder whether, when thinking about the subversive possibilities afforded by psychoanalysis, something can be referred back to the early days in the formation of the mind. Perhaps, then, I could invite you to offer your thoughts on the questions you opened up earlier. You said, "if we go back to origins of experiences, maybe in preverbal life experience, how did politics impact on that? Or how much does that impact on the way we commit ourselves to a political view of action now?" And, I wish to add, what if those early moments failed to inspire in us the subversive ability to be ourselves?

RDH: The impact of our neoliberal culture on our earliest phases of development must be difficult to assess. Indeed, the impact of any culture must be difficult to assess. And I don't know if we can do justice to that question here. Any cultural influence presumably comes through the handling of a baby by its carer, as I mentioned earlier in our conversation (Discussion, Part I) with reference to Noreen Giffney's, *The Culture-Breast in Psychoanalysis*. As Bion remarked, the baby at the breast sucks not just milk but also love. And with love, do other personal attitudes come, dissolved as it were in the milk? For instance, is the use of a bottle to feed an infant instead of the breast some sort of primitive communication to the baby about our culture of mechanical communities and of commodities?

GC: I wish to return to one more matter you briefly mentioned above which, it seems to me, constitutes the heart of political action, something that we could call (paraphrasing Freud's expression "the return of the repressed"), the retrieval of the projected. Could you say something more about what you have in mind when you suggest that political responsibility "involves 'taking' on responsibilities that others leave to their politicians"?

RDH: I think this question perhaps points to a hole in the last paper (Chapter 11) on the limitations in the general understanding of "democracy". Responsibility, including political responsibility, is potentially a burdensome obligation, not least because when things go wrong (as inevitably they do at times) those responsible are at risk of criticism and guilt, from others outside (and from inside) themselves. It is, in a representative democracy, a temptation to use a voting system to discharge and abandon all responsibility and leave it to the politicians. Indeed, it gives the voter an opportunity to take the role of a guilt-free criticiser. It is a projection, as you suggest.

But, it is an abdication of one's autonomy and a depleting kind of amputation of a significant element of oneself. It needs to be contrasted with a different kind of projection which we might call delegation, in which one does not abdicate responsibility but retains the responsibility at least for having participated in a voting democracy. That act of voting retains a responsibility (difficult when one's own party has lost!); it is the responsibility to track the government's achievements (and its flaws) and call it to account. This is discussed to some extent in Chapter 11. If you like, this could be called retrieving the projected. Though it does have a rather different function—more an integrative effect, than symptom-formation.

GC: I wish to turn now to a theme of great currency, democracy, from the perspective of the paper "Reflection or action" (Chapter 9). You distinguish between "participant democracy", "representative democracy", and "consensual democracy". How do you think of the differences between them?

RDH: I might start with the point in the last entry, that democracy can be used to dump responsibility on others and remain guilt-free by setting up a potentially blaming relationship with the government. This contrasts with retaining a responsibility for giving over political authority to the government. One of the big failings of a voting system is that there are losers, and their disappointment can so easily feed into a blame-game with a dumping of all responsibility, whereas a well-informed and questioning responsibility needs to be retained. We vote for representatives and the system is thus a representative democracy. The government should always attempt to garner as much consensus across its population, but it will of course never be complete.

I have wondered about participant democracy where everyone has an opportunity to have their say, and I have been very involved in therapeutic communities where the whole community meets with everyone participating. But this can only work with relatively small groups, up to a maximum of one hundred perhaps. It is certainly not possible on a national level. With the spread of very extensive social media on smartphones it is possible to facilitate widespread discussion, but it remains completely without responsibility, and much of it seems an expression of the joy of being completely responsibility-free for what one says.

I have wondered about sortition, or citizens assemblies where chosen groups of representatives of the public gather to discuss specific issues on which they are well-informed, much as MPs need to be informed. They can decide specific issues and thus go much further than merely voting for individual representatives. In some countries the outcomes can be binding on the government. On occasions the UK parliament has used a citizens assembly for advice (an example is https://www.parliament.uk/get-involved/committees/climate-assembly-uk/about-citizens-assemblies/). One could imagine this being an improvement on mere voting, although its effectiveness must depend on the selection of persons, as well as the composition of the packs of information. In short, there needs to be a retrenchment that can return a useful and measured meaning to the term "democracy" and rescue it from its current weaponised use/misuse. This means a radical assessment of the problems and failings as well as the importance of its collaborative principles.

GC: I would like to ask you to expand on the relationship between populism and democracy and the relationship between democracy and rationality. Your link between the two might seem to deny the role of emotions in politics. Emotional work, I find, is necessary in managing the radical uncertainty which is constitutive of our human condition and which is inherent to democracy as a political system that has replaced the routes to stipulated certainty allowed by the divine law and the monarch.

RDH: Of course, politics is an arena of the emotions as much as rationality. The requirement to act with the determined hatred and violence of a soldier at war is just such a situation. To drive one's car with a consideration for pedestrians who want to cross the road is equally a situation requiring emotion (a human concern) and a reasoning that takes in all the variables—speed, braking distance, road conditions (if it is wet, for instance), and the rest. Where psychoanalysis enters the drama of life is when the emotions are not on the surface and are kept hidden for the reasons that psychoanalysts understand. One of those problematic experiences which can enter unseen to distort is the uncertainty about so much of life, as you suggest. Most of the acts we commit in the course of every day of our lives do not come with an evidence base as might be required of a practising doctor; and so, not even with a probability, let alone a certainty. The result is, therefore, that at every turn there is a risk of failure, inadequacy, mistakes, and harm. Certainty would be a delicious luxury! Claims for it are therefore understandable. But they are really very obstructive.

Claims for democracy are built on a certainty it is the best of all politics—no question about it. But stepping back a bit, we have to acknowledge it is a word that has been weaponised ever since 1945, if not long before. Its use is to do damage to opponents. The ability to question what it is, how it could be understood, its nature, the best forms of practice of it, are not raised for general discussion. Yes, there is a sortition movement, a movement for proportional representation, and so on. But these are hampered by the emotional surge towards identifying enemies as non-democratic and then fighting them—righteously. So, populism is, amongst much else, an emotional righteousness, built on nationalism and an identity with, mostly, geographical residence, but also ethnic identity too. It is given a righteousness by irrefutable ideologies, such as "democracy" or "communism", which cannot be thought about except in terms of opponents who attack the right-minded persons in one's own identifiable group/nation. Certainty and righteousness are blood relatives. They have an ancestry rooted in anxiety and not in more thoughtful questioning to the extent that inevitably questioning is undermining and the work of enemies. It is not possible to make headway, I suggest, in resolving populism without an understanding of the driving force of the anxiety that drives unthinking populism. It is an anxiety that is necessarily hidden by populism. And when it comes to hidden anxieties, we might wish to reach for psychoanalysis.

GC: I would like to return to domination and emancipation. Why do people not rebel in the face of domination and exploitation? Why do so many people chose fascism or Trump (or Boris Johnson, Le Pen, Salvini, Orbán, Berlusconi, Modi)? Why do many, even most people, sometimes or often, seem to make decisions contrary to their personal and material well-being, repeating patterns of behaviour that are not conducive to their enjoyment of life? The Frankfurt School, for instance, has trained over decades its analytical tools on the failure to revolt. It may be said that, according to at least one perspective presented by these authors, the structural and political conditions are available for revolt but the psychological configurations of Western societies make them "unprepared" for a revolt. From the point of view of your work on democracy, its pursuit is prevented by the dampening role played by expectations, in particular unrealistic expectations. This resembles something Bion would consider in relation to a pairing basic assumption predicated on the paralysing hope that something or someone redeeming (a Messiah, an ideology) is to be born, is on its or their way. The expectation of a redeeming democracy is just as an opium to the people, a damning hope.

RDH: It is a big and important question: Why do people accept conditions and policies not in their interests? Lukács suggested it was the development of a false consciousness across the classes. Although he was aware of psychoanalysis, he did not use psychoanalytic ideas in his construction of the falsity of consciousness. One element is the cognitive conception of the trickle-down effect—that is, the enrichment of some is a benefit for all. As noted in Chapter 10, formal research into this does not confirm the assertion. However, to protect themselves from guilt, the wealthy need to believe that trickle-down does happen. And it may be that the impoverished people also need to believe that the elite do work in their best interests. However, perhaps a lot more work needs to be done on why these belief systems exist and persist. It is clear, however, that what is behind a false consciousness is something we are not conscious of, and then psychoanalysis is the perspective and the telescope that can inform us on that. In other words, the answer to the question why self-damaging policies are irrationally accepted is that the determinants exist in both the psychoanalytic unconscious and also in the social power of the manipulation.

GC: As with psychoanalysis, we have taken to conceive of the mind in terms of a complex organisation, an organisation of the personality, what would a "democratic" organisation of the personality look like? (Oppression figures large in your papers on the conception of the oppressive superego.)

RDH: Perhaps this goes back to the problem of ideology (Chapter 6). The internal world of the ideologue is restricted to a single point of view that cannot admit of any alternative. And it is similar to your reference to the "internal mafia gang". There is a distinction between possessing an idea that will come in useful, and being possessed by identifying with an idea that becomes a core of one's personal identity. In the latter case, any questioning or doubts about the idea reverberates as doubts about the nature and quality of one's own identity/self. A "democratic internal world" might therefore be one where alternative points of view are not so very threatening and alternatives can be held in mind without feeling too wobbly. In fact, one knows that every story has another side, and such an internal state, at ease with alternatives, is that political animal who embraces the collaboration that "democracy" demands. I am indicating, in effect, the acceptance of diplomacy, a word that comes from the ancient Greek word "diplo", meaning double. The upshot of this point of view is that a person capable of being democratic needs to be free of too much neurotic defensiveness that limits broader forms of experimental action in the mind. Of course, such an individual has to be in the context of a group of individuals accepting of democratic debate and collaborative action.

We can definitely say there is political action not preceded by forethought of this experimental kind. We have knee-jerk reactions to cultural issues—for instance, the pollution of our national identity by immigration feels almost poisonous to some people as if swallowing toxic spiders or such like. In fact, we probably react to many, many cultural stimuli in that reflex way. For instance, when meeting a friend, we almost automatically say "How are you". And then they will reply, "Fine". Such greetings, and also farewells, as well as a vast number of interactions, have quickly in our development become second nature to us, like riding a bicycle. And so it is in more complex interactions in the political domain. For many people it is simply unthinkable to vote for any party other than the one they have always voted for previously.

Much reflex reaction can be instilled from media and propaganda. The cultivation of enemies on an international scale can create loyal reactions deeply felt and lasting a lifetime, and even for several generations, against well-defined enemies: Protestants against Catholics, Christians against infidels, democrats against communists. How many traders in the Kingdom of Benin, or the crews of English (and Portuguese) merchant ships, or plantation owners of the United States and the Caribbean, gave experimental thought to the humanity of those who were traded? Do not such reflex and unthinking actions correspond to the man who thinks he cannot play the violin in public because it is not only like masturbation but actually *is* masturbation?

GC: Justice, social justice, and rights do not figure in your papers. Can you offer your thoughts on these matters, or perhaps only a consideration on their absence from your reflection so far?

RDH: About justice, yes, we have not said much about that. Perhaps it is as well. Again we have to scrub off social meanings that adhere like dirt to the term. One of the incentives of the justice system is that all people will be criminal if given the chance and all need a magistrate's court sitting metaphorically on their shoulder. Proudly, the system proclaims that "justice is blind", meaning that all are treated equally, from the monarchy-supporting aristocracy to the marginal and impoverished. In practice, the blindness is not actually true for various reasons. One underlying dimension from which to criticise is the position taken here.

Blindly indifferent to the individual, and only judging his overt acts can lead easily to the kind of categorisation we have called alienating or commodifying—or depersonalising: a somewhat sad recourse for regulating society, but understandable if it is accepted that *only* social phenomena provide consideration and concern for each other.

We have come full-circle back to the alienating, commodifying, and depersonalising, and so perhaps we have come to the end, or more precisely to an unfinished end. There are just a few final comments we cannot hold back on that must form our conclusions.

References

Figlio, K. (2018). *Remembering as Reparation: Psychoanalysis and Historical Memory*. London: Palgrave.

Fromm, E. (1971). *The Crisis of Psychoanalysis*. London: Cape.

Fromm, E. (1976). *To Have or to Be?* New York: Harper Row.

Giffney, N. (2021). *The Culture-Breast in Psychoanalysis*. London: Routledge.

Gregory C. A. (1997). *Savage Money: The Anthropology and Politics of Commodity Exchange.* Amsterdam: Harwood Academic.

Hinshelwood, R. D. (2007). The Kleinian theory of therapeutic action. *Psychoanalytic Quarterly, 76* (supplement 1): 1479–1498.

Conclusions

GC: We have now completed a thorough enough reading of your papers (so much more there might be to delve into!) and we had the chance to discuss some of the most inspiring ideas that you developed over the course of your writing career, we reflected on some of their implications, and I invited you to explore further some points that you could not explore further within the frame of these papers. I think that before closing this volume, it would be interesting to reflect on your career as a thinker in hindsight, as it were, and from your present vantage point to consider the development of your thought on political matters in order to draw some concluding thoughts. In fact, I think I would find particularly interesting if, after this excursus through your work, you drew a preliminary balance which then opened up towards your current and future thinking and writing projects. I would like to begin from this: these papers cover a span of five decades, how do you look at the evolution of your thinking over time from your present standpoint?

RDH: This is a project with a beginning and a middle. It commenced early in my life with a political commitment originally to a pacifism that I inherited from an aged great-aunt. She was an ardent socialist and a Peace Pledge Union member. It led me into the Campaign for Nuclear Disarmament in the late 1950s: a common sense approach to the cold war politics that invaded everything from nuclear treaties to the rationing of children's sweets. The lifelong concern has been to understand why good sense never showed many signs of coming out on top. It is easy to say how we should be managing the globe we have inherited as home, but hard to say why the most intelligent of species so mismanages it. This book has, with your very thoughtful help, plotted a course through the development of my own "good sense"—if it is. The conclusion is that we are hardly the most intelligent of species. If we the human species have, in fact, developed a side of consciousness hardly shared with other species, we have not used it to sufficient advantage. We are not the species with consciousness, but the species with an unconscious, it seems. Or to put it more specifically, the computer-model of consciousness, which is most researched by ardent neuropsychological scientists, overlooks the radical step humans have taken. We have developed self-consciousness. Not just that we are conscious of the things we perceive and intuit, but that we are aware, consciously, of our own abilities to represent our world to ourselves. We have, in that sense, a self-consciousness. We are the being that is conscious of being and seeing and hearing and sensing and representing. In other words, we have a sensitivity to ourselves as the entity that is conscious of ourselves. This reciprocation is termed, or can be termed, "subjectivity". We need a science of subjectivity.

And we have one.

It is psychoanalysis. However much psychoanalysis has attempted to mimic objective science to establish its own credibility, nevertheless it remains the listening science. We have the instrument for listening in to subjectivities. And interestingly, it is our own subjective consciousness that can, as they say, reach out to others' subjective experiencing.

So, how should we use it? Our one gift takes us beyond the biological world of animals? Well, in practice, like all efforts to approach the unconscious, we fight it; we resist.

The unfinished ending to the story of this book is that our good common sense would confront how we ignore the interfering unconscious side of our subjectivity. The part that might have been added—if it had been possible—would have plotted a political strategy of attending with "good sense" to that unconscious world which interferes in all we do.

Are we able to confront our mistakes and unconscious "slips", as Freud categorised them. In the unlikely event that we do turn and face these threatening mistakes, what would we tell ourselves? I have a few thoughts.

But an initial precursor question is, whatever could make us do such a good-sense thing as to turn and face what constantly makes us fail? The appalling thought is that we may only do so after a real catastrophe or two to our world, to our species, to our comrade species throughout biology. And on the horizon are a couple of such catastrophes. At the time of writing, we perceive the approach of a new world war fought out with nuclear weapons, and second a climate catastrophe we seem only half-heartedly able to face. And behind these, the argument in my papers is that we might need to consider that there is a common factor underlying the catastrophes we face.

I have postulated that the causal driver is the extraordinary growth in the value of money. I have categorised it as a malignant growth (Hinshelwood, 2024). And it has been growing for millennia. We read in the Bible that the one moment when Jesus' ethics of forgiveness lapsed and he became destructively vengeful was with the moneychangers in the Jerusalem temple. He overturned their tables on which presumably they had carefully arranged their different currencies for exchanging.

Today, it is the hangover of the eighteenth-century view of the marketplace with its sole purpose of competitive trading that has plundered the earth's resources unthinkingly. It has applied competition as the sole factor behind progress, while the neglect of companionable collaboration has increased. Such an imbalance of human competition vs community has tested views about profit and generosity, a mistake that has stuck in our skin like a mosquito's stinging proboscis.

And the ultimate synthesis of these mistakes has been to create a trade in money itself; we make money out of trading money, instead of sticking to money's core role of oiling the trading of useful products.

There is a lost value in the political conditions we face today. There is no balance between collaboration and competition. Trade wars and military wars are the outcome of that imbalance. And the risk in the wholesale commitment to competition is that this civilisation risks dying. No civilisation has lasted for ever, and that may apply to our present one. Most dominant civilisations die from a corruption within. The heart dies and the outer manifestations wither and wrinkle. We can perceive, if we wish—because we have *self*-consciousness—the withering. But its roots will have to involve the embrace of something like the psychoanalyst's knowledge of that which is intolerable to know; that is, the interfering human unconscious.

We have travelled through all our discussions with a notional focus on "alienation", without concentrating on it specifically. Perhaps we have not needed to since the pervading context of our discussion has been psychoanalysis, which more than any other discipline focuses on the authenticity of oneself. That is to say, we recognise psychoanalysis as having the primary concern with a person's sense of himself and his own self-distortions. I've implied that this reflexive self-regard is a specific human mode of experiencing. It is a unique capacity to position our own self as being a point of view, as being *my point of view* from which I survey the world inside and beyond me.

Significant elements of this discourse

First of all, I wanted to clarify as a list the points I consider significant that pervade all the texts and discussions in this book:

- I started with my concerns that we focus on human beings with questions and answers that come from radically different directions. The human being's experience of being a person has two dimensions; we balance ourselves between that world within and with a "non-self" world around us. The individual is a committed member of relations and communities with others and the contest between these two perspectives may be oppositional, complementary, or, as some say, dialectical.
- The logical relations between theories in social science and the broad spectrum of psychologies are less important than the need to keep in focus a holistic view of human beings. I have tried to suggest, gently, that the structure for understanding that convergence is a multifactorial system: (a) the influence of factors from outside the person and within others or in the non-personal environment, together with (b) those factors inherent within the person deriving from inherited traits and the personal meanings of experiences.
- One major element is the fluidity of the individual self which uses and is used by others to dispose of and exchange "parts of the self".

Those exchanged entities are certain mental functions (ego-functions) and the experiences arising from those functions which lead to playing out personal roles in the social world.

- These exchanges, at a very personal level of our identity, are so often not noticed consciously. It is as though they did not affect a core sense of identity fixed perhaps to a particular body. However, those exchanges between persons leads to the fluidity of the ego/self and thus of one's identity. Often, though certainly not always, the function divested from the self is an autonomy that gives our authority over to others.
- The exchanges that I emphasised can occur in extended sequences, referred to here as affect-flow in which felt experience travels through multiple individuals in a working or social group creating some important element of the culture. This affect flow is merely an extension of the idea of "contagion" in groups. It can, however, be observed.
- This fluidity of a contagion/infection at the basic levels of emotion and identity are no less significant than the cognitive exchanges that occur so significantly at a conscious level. The interesting point is that the affective experiences occur so deeply buried in the unconscious of humans. Despite their unconscious recognition only, this fluidity and inconstant composition of functions leads to an equally unconscious experience of fragmentation and incoherence of identity and the self. That painful experience is then reacted to with an unfortunate degree of rigidity and can become a needed equivalence or equation with ideas or a leader—known sociologically as an ideology. This identity that *equates* with the leading idea or person contrasts with a more flexible sense of *belonging*, which allows a comparison of ideas and a co-existence of cultures. Intrusion and coercing an object into others' minds by threats and manipulation—or by persuasion—is the exchange system of a society.
- The contrast between belonging and rigid identity-equation has some similarities to the contrast emphasised here between symbols and symbolic equation. The latter is a feature particularly of a psychotic state. The more ideological form of equation rests, as indicated, on the loss (splitting off) of the function of autonomy

and giving the self over to another—to the extreme end-point of a physical death of oneself. The function lost in psychosis is the ability to recognise reality at all and to reflect on it—I have labelled this the as-if function.

- The loss of representation draws the mind back to the reflex type of function more characteristic of animals. Loss of forethought (implying the inhibition of reflex enactment) is equivalent to the collapse of symbols into the thing symbolised (concrete thinking using symbolic equations)
- Finally, there is inadequate surveying of possible forms of action to determine the unconscious interference with conscious political debate and action.

There seem to be three significant elements to these conclusions. First is the need for empathy and a "crusade" for the idea that all stories have two sides to them. Second is to eradicate conflicts of interest such as health-for-profit or news and information "for-profit", which aggravate the inevitable conflict between self and the social. And third, that the bad opinions we attribute to others are almost always insertions originating in us which we consciously deny, because it either shames us or puts us in conflict *with ourselves.*

You have been so generous, Giuseppe, with your interest in the ideas I have tried to express and you have helped to get that expression clearer. And so, I want to ask you to elaborate on one or two of the points of your own that you have brought up. Engagement with others in this dialectic is the nature of politics, and since one brand of psychoanalysis, the object relations school, is to recognise that, then psychoanalysis *is* politics. If as you have said, identity politics has established that "the personal is political", then psychoanalysis, being the most personal of all professions, draws close to some aspect of politics. I wonder if I have got your point correct and you might reflect on that for us.

GC: I agree, Bob—interest (not only in the sense of having a vested interest, but also just being interested in, curious about, something), generosity, and genuine engagement with and commitment to others are key aspects of politics. Curiosity, in particular, expresses the drive towards creativity and development, Klein's epistemophilic drive. These are key aspects of politics. They are a great deal more than the mere struggle for power, or its (bureaucratic) management, to which politics is often reduced. When these aspects of politics fail or are perverted, they cause its degeneration into anti-politics. Consider for instance, the master–slave dynamics in race, gender, class (and other) relations. These patterns of exploitation and domination are not "natural", they are not related to a Hobbesian state of nature that the human contract aims to counter and discipline, but an active attack on the ability, indeed the existential need, of humans to live together, they are anti-natural (you very poignantly write of humans' "anti-human" behaviours in Chapter 7). As I referred to in passing previously, I even go as far as considering psychoanalysis as (a form of) political action—specifically, psychoanalytic action as political action. In my view, the pursuit of truth is at the core of both politics and psychoanalysis. A search for truth that eschews facile illusions about absolutely "grounded" truths, rather a search for truth that at the same time constructs it within the conflictual contexts inherent to human collective existence. I appreciate that this may appear as though stretching the concept of politics to the point of taking away any of its specificity, However, although this is not the place for me to show all the ways in which my thinking on these matters is still unformed, let me raise two points for consideration. On the one hand, I believe that removing emotions and the unconscious from politics hinders our ability to account for some of the most pernicious dynamics of collective human life, but also for some of the most inspiring as well. On the other hand, I believe, consequently, if politics is about both thinking and conscious and unconscious collective feeling, then what takes place in the consulting room too has either political or anti-political aspects. It is a form of thinking and feeling together, or it fails to achieve that. When it fails to be that, I think, it generates those pathological dynamics whose transformative analysis psychoanalysts aim to inspire. I believe that most psychoanalysts would call clinical practices aiming at achieving or failing to achieve shared thinking and feeling either psychoanalytical or anti-psychoanalytical—please discount, for the sake of a broader conversation, what seems to be formulated in shallow binaries. I do not want to go on for too long about something I am only clumsily groping at, but some of the coordinates of what I am saying here can be found in Bion's formulations about work and basic assumption groups, in his extension of that theory through his analysis of projective identification, and about how projective identification underpins (including in the consulting room), commensal, symbiotic, and parasitic relation. I believe that Bion's foundation of human interactions in projective identification can also shed light on the micro–macro issue central to the social sciences, in so doing allowing us to think the political from the two-person relationship in the consulting room to group and social dynamics. It indeed allows us to formulate both intra- and inter-personal dynamics. This is not much, but it might give you a sense of what I have in mind when I speak about politics. Now, let me turn to your comments on my own thoughts about the relation between identity politics and psychoanalysis, or indeed about my understanding of the mind as a political space, a stage, on which political dynamics are performed between different agencies and between different internal objects.

Let me think about this matter in the terms of your work on ideology, as I understand it. I wonder whether you indicate a way to separate identity politics from identity anti-politics. The latter would pivot on an ideological drift of identity. We would then have, on the one hand an identity as a containing object/space from within which to engage the other in generative relationships and, on the other, we would have an identity as a walled retreat, a citadel perceived to be under attack. Incidentally, I think that what complicates some investigations of identity is the ever-lurking possibility that discrimination turns to incrimination.

These very dynamics of discrimination (i.e. separation from the primary object, identification, and the return of the projected to form an identity) are crucial in the development of the personality and are well documented by psychoanalysis. Difficulties in identity formation, the development of personality difficulties, have often been discussed in terms of organisation of the personality. Personality, identity, here understood as the outcome of internal object relations in which, I would say, anti-politics prevail. Similarly, in the political sphere, the organisation of group identities sometimes sees a prevailing of anti-political ideological dynamics—what Bion called basic assumptions or, later, symbiotic and parasitic object relations (as opposed to commensal).

But, allow me to return to something you said that struck me. What you write about the civilisational outlook we face may sound bleak and even worrisome. You remind me of some of Freud's reflections on a life experience as a psychoanalyst, especially after the First World War, including in his brief epistolary exchange with Albert Einstein on war. And perhaps also some interpretations of Klein's work on primary envy and destructiveness, pointing, it seems to me, towards Freud's thoughts on the death drive, towards their logical conclusion. But you close the reflection above with a clear indication of what could help us see and think through our collective predicaments "something like the psychoanalyst's knowledge on that which is intolerable to know". This reminds me of Bion's remarks on some of the differences between his theory of groups and Freud's. He wrote that he believed that in the end, work dynamics always prevail in groups and in societies at large. Can you continue from here a bit further to perhaps leave me and your reader with some thoughts on what you envisage the role of psychoanalytic knowledge and practice could be and how best to deploy it? I think I am asking you to leave us with some final thoughts on psychoanalysis and political action.

This might be the right moment to address what seems to be not only a summary of what you aim to achieve with your work but a consideration on the innermost core of your conception of the political, if I can put it like this. You spoke about the value of "trying to construct a dimension from alienation to authenticity". Would you say that this formulation indicates the source, object, and aim of the political drive, if I can paraphrase here the Freud of the *Three Essays*?

RDH: You pick out that important dimension—from alienation to authenticity. That may be very clarifying, for myself as well as the readers. Perhaps it is the interaction—the movement along that axis, to and fro, that I come to see as the throbbing life of the social group composed of living individuals—that I'd suggest. Perhaps it is the freedom to move as reality demands, first one way and then back again, as the core of political activity. I emphasise the freedom of that movement, as sometimes it is a real necessity to leave decisions about living and life to others.

I have become acquainted with the notions of "complexity theory" and the self-sustaining cycles that must be the basis for a continuing bodily physiology; and that oscillating continuity may be the potential for understanding the life of a mind as well (Hinshelwood, 2024). It is interesting that although the mind does not at a conscious level demonstrate a cycling rhythm, the brain does. The lasting rhythms observable with ECGs almost makes me think we should stick with the ECGs and understand them, before moving on to the more modern technology of the MRI, which unfortunately only aims to show static connections. But that is speculative … and moving into a whole other area. To gauge how psychoanalysis can extend our thoughts on political action, we need to face that which feels impossible to face, the repressed/split-off unconscious.

You ask about the dimension between alienation and authenticity, and I think that is important to clarify, as you do. However, in my view, our egos, being fluid, often leave others to perform ego-functions for us; for instance, one person drives a car whilst a passenger directs the route (reading a GPS system). This is a division of psychic labour, similar to any physical division of labour. Some psychic functions are performed for the benefit of others who give over their own expertise to an expert, like going to an accountant or a solicitor. The two important points are: (i) the fluidity and the capacity to receive back those functions that are only temporarily donated to others; and (ii) the realistic (vs the unconscious and defensive) need to export functions to others. In politics, the risk is the important, even life-threatening, dumping of psychic functions onto others. We resist receiving them back for fear of the heavy responsibility and potential guilt. I think this fluidity and rigidity dimension exists equally with the alienation-authenticity dimension you have extracted.

In the moment just now, you briefly mentioned your own perspective in which you point to curiosity as "the drive towards creativity and development" and that this epistemophilic drive is bonded with generosity and engagement with others. Because these "softer" feelings coincide in my mind with an authentic engagement, I think we reach similar positions. You eschew "the mere struggle for power, or its (bureaucratic) management" as a reduction of politics, and therefore a misdirection or perversion of the best is us. You inventively use the term "anti-politics". You give examples of this "master–slave" pattern—race, gender, sexuality, religion—which we slip easily into and which undermines our living together as persons.

It is the sensitivity we tend to have to the inflaming response to differences that provokes this descent into power relations that characterise, in my terms, the inauthentic alienation of others we engage with. They lose for us the sense of a personal other to receive our indifferent use of them as commodities; both physical use, as in slavery and wage-labour as well as the psychical use of objects to be valued only in our rigid value systems. They slide for their human value to a use-value in terms of their contribution to abstract value. You call this, aptly, a "degeneration into *anti-politics*".

We can tut-tut about this degeneration of "others", strangers, those who are different and who can be subjected to extreme value judgements. But in my view, only psychoanalysis can give us a grip on *why* difference is so disastrously handled. From Freud, we can see that the dawning awareness of the difference between two parents, coming together in their own affection, is both enormously generative (procreative) and also damningly excluding, almost unforgivably excluding, leading to the primal rage-vs-bliss confusion of infancy (see, for instance, Wilden's *Man and Woman, War and Peace* (1986)). The master–slave dynamic is not, as you say, natural, but it is highly motivated by the painfully sensitive experiences of jealousy and exclusion which have to be rigidly denied/repressed/split off. And so, in this way, we need also to understand the underground turmoil beneath the tut-tutting we do to retaliate by excluding others. The reduction to the inhuman and impersonal power-struggles is your depersonalising equivalent to what I call alienation (or inauthentic).

GC: What I found most interesting in your work is your ongoing and committed engagement with intra-psychic, inter-psychic, and social dynamics considered at the same time. I think, as I mentioned, that some dynamics of the mind can be described in political language and equally some political (and anti-political) dynamics can be described using psychoanalytic language. I do not think this is limited to the level of description. In fact, I think that the language of psychoanalysis and political analysis share a great deal more than a descriptive dimension. I think your papers show precisely that and a number of ways to work with this conception. One aspect that I mentioned earlier and that I would like you to say more about as we draw to an end of this stimulating conversation, refers to certain potentially mind-numbing and even very destructive social dynamics. I have in mind authoritarianism and totalitarianism (and the possible drift from the former to the latter). As populism and forms of anti-politics have seen a dramatic global increase over the past two decades or so, concerns about the prevalence of the authoritarian mind and a potential return to totalitarian societies do not seem too far-fetched. What are your thoughts on this? And what are your thoughts on what could contribute to reverse this global trend?

RDH: At this point I wish to introduce the text of a recent short paper on authoritarianism. The following was presented at the "Psychoanalysis and public sphere" conference in October 2023. It relates to theme of power-politics and a key moment in Freud's writing.

Authoritarianism—From baby to second childhood

R. D. Hinshelwood

In his paper "On narcissism" in 1914, Freud (1914c, p. 91) quotes the English phrase, "His Majesty the Baby". The baby has an almost instinctual impact on others to stop and attend to the baby *as if* a regal authority. Such demands are often felt to have charm and create a warmth, even joy, in both parties when the needs are satisfied. A baby, as a monarch, touches something primitive in us all.

When a baby starts crying for something, the mother (or carer) will immediately be filled with some urgency to go and attend to the baby's immediate need. In 1956 Winnicott called this automatic *complementary* response in mothers a state of "primary maternal preoccupation". Mother has become maximally open to the baby's experience. This is a mutual collaboration of mother and baby to attend to the baby. Winnicott described it as a transient, though benevolent, psychosis lasting a few months after birth.

In 1962, Bion described a similar state he called "reverie"—again a collaborative openness to other people's minds, not only a baby's. Perhaps human beings are particularly susceptible to this kind of majestic demandingness; we are made, as it were, to be particularly acquiescing to others' states of mind. That response may be inevitable. Perhaps it is biological. Mammals attend to their immature young in the same way.

But it is for a varying but limited period of development. Mostly they have a cut-off point when the young are subsequently regarded as adults and treated as rivals, sexual partners, or collaborators in hunting down prey. But, for the human "animal", the care and attention to each other lasts a lifetime. Of course, this care falters at times, although that is another story.

I want to turn Freud's saying on its head. If we consider a baby to be a monarch ruling the household, it also works the other way: a monarch rules his kingdom as if a baby making demands. The higher primates are legendary because we talk of the "alpha male" who is the leader of a troop of gorillas. Dominant and compliant roles are just accepted. Such hierarchical relations arise in herds of horses and many other animals.

It seems unlikely that the human ape is different. Of course, when applied to humans, the term "alpha male" is more akin to a bully. We can find its insistent and punishing demands not only in the social structures of infancy, but also bullying in childhood and often in the CEO of capitalist mega-corporations and many other social forms such as the army and the church. In other words, Freud's aphorism can be taken both ways—not just that the baby is ruler of the household, but that the ruler of a nation can exhibit the demandingness of a newborn baby, to which we inherently comply. The point I am making is that there seems to be a continuity of baby–mother demands into adult political authority where it can be backed by a physical coercion, with threats of, or even actual, abuse, punishment, imprisonment, torture, and execution.

There are several important points about this mutually collaborative but interpersonal state of mind. It is not only coercive. As with the mother–infant, there can be a joyful acceptance of the intrusive demandingness. Dominant and compliant roles are not always coercive. We go to experts, such as a solicitor, for his authority to advise us from his knowledge and experience. Similarly with an accountant as a tax advisor. It is realistic to accept the authority of the expert. Humans can then *resist* this biological reversion when appropriate (and sometimes when not appropriate). However, an authority is not always rigid demanding and coerced; we also seek a different mutuality, a flexible authority, promoting collaboration between the leader or authority and his followers.

Collaboration, whether by coercion or by joyfulness, has been the basis of human civilisation, although we can see historical phases alternating between greater or lesser coercion—such as republican vs imperial Rome. We might agree, though, that coercion has tended to lessen over historical time.

Now, how is psychoanalysis relevant? I suggest that under certain social circumstances individuals identify profoundly with their nation. This goes beyond a thoughtful ordinary belonging. It means an unthinking idealised nation with which a person's own sense of self is deeply united. To some extent this is true of everyone, so that mostly we follow our national football team. But there are other seemingly more desperate forms of identification—a soldier's willing self-sacrifice, a suicide bomber.

What are the conditions that bring out such intense identification. For example, it is generally agreed that Nazism in Germany in the 1930s arose from the sense of national humiliation after the Versailles Treaty in 1919 and was aggravated by the extreme poverty of the economic depression. Both a humiliation of the nation and an impoverishment of the individual across Germany drove an unconscious dynamic led by Hitler's "infantile" authoritarian demand to control Europe. It did two things. First, it rescued the nation from its humiliation of the First World War, and in addition, at an unconscious level, a large segment of impoverished individuals could feel unconsciously a rescuing of their own sense of self.

So, individuals who feel a diminished or annihilated personal *identity* can compensate with a rigid identification, that is, by *becoming* their overvalued nation. I suggest that a widespread personal anxiety can lead unconsciously to a widespread acceptance of a pseudo-superior nation. It conforms to Freud's "narcissism of minor differences", which he elaborated in 1930 just as the German nation was about to elect a coercive but triumphant authoritarianism. It was supported, of course, by the fantasies of profoundly inferior races, notably Jews, but also Poles, gypsies, homosexuals, the mentally ill, and the egalitarian left-wing intellectuals.

Today, a similar potentially authoritarian and nationalistic pseudo-superiority has emerged in various so-called democracies. To be consistent, we would apply the same thinking—a felt sense of national humiliation has led to a pseudo-national superiority. In fact, it can be exemplified by the "Make America Great Again" movement in the USA, and provoked, I understand, by a failing sense of global leadership.

As with Nazism, it leads to populist support for wild belligerence, such as the new US cold war against China. It is not that Trump is the problem; he is at this stage the *expression of a widespread problem*, and a personalisation of it. It is a tempting though dangerous simplification to consciously locate the problem in one place or person when the sense of a loss of self is widespread (and unconscious).

The conclusion is that if social conditions cause a common unconscious fear of annihilation in individuals, they can identify deeply and unthinkingly with a *national* pseudo-superiority. Nationalist identification is not just coercion; but it can be relief and joy, and touches on that *infantile* sense of rescue by a joyfully successful mother.

If this is valid, there is a trap that an opposition party falls into. Any criticism of a government may be heard as an attack on the nation, and therefore a threat to insecure people identified with the nation. If so, then calling the government to account risks stirring up annihilation fears in the individuals. Is there an art to be learned in calling a government to account without threatening the core of identity of those identified with their nation?

GC: Thank you for this, Bob, this reconstruction of the infantile in the group and society is very interesting. Indeed, I am keen to investigate further the permanence of phantasies along the entirety of human life and the recurrence of "positions" (configurations of phantasies and emotions) both in minds and in large human collectives. I think this analysis of authoritarianism—the analysis of Trump as a symptom of an underlying social dynamic, and the relationships between individual and group, and individual and leader—find me in complete agreement. In your turning of Freud's aphorism on its head, the leader does not represent either a caring or a neglecting parent but stands for the shared helplessness and consequent demandingness of the group. Who is then "the adult in the room" as the oft-used expression goes? Different commentators referred in turn, in the Trump case, to the constitution, the judiciary, the administration, congress, the institutions as a whole, experts like Anthony Fauci. Closer to us, how would you analyse the UK circumstances including Brexit and Boris Johnson's government from the "His Majesty the Baby" perspective?

RDH: Well, the "wonderful" British Empire has suffered a long decline in size and status. It may well have taken a toll on many people who had been identified completely with it. Their internal sense of self may have sagged and become depleted. I think of the poor in Britain particularly, the first to suffer from industrialisation leading to complex enduring cultural/class role, and then subsequently the de-industrialisation from the 1980s onwards. And then, second are those born to rule the great Empire and sent, long before maturity, to boarding school, severing them from family identifications. These are the privileged who are also depleted, without a role. Is it far-fetched to consider these depletions of identity to have established intergenerational cultures of depletion for the individual? The compensating national (imperial) identification has now failed them.

GC: An implication of what you say above, that Trump is not the problem but the expression of an underlying problem, is that we are all involved, and I think you may agree with Seamus Heaney's Cassandra's opening lines that there is "No such thing / as innocent / bystanding". I think that this does not only mean that we are all responsible (in our very different and differential ways), but also that we can all contribute (in our different and differential ways) to change the circumstances we find ourselves (implicated) in. Here is where my main interest lies and I think yours too, the *Thesis Eleven* question. In other words, the tension between interpreting the world and changing it, as Marx put it in his "Theses on Feurbach" (1845). You refer to an art of political action that, paraphrasing you a bit, can show its Majesty the Baby that it is naked without threatening and humiliating it and, in turn, all those who projectively identify with it. We are returning here to our previous conversation on political action. I find that your main indication, not to threaten and humiliate the imperial baby and those who identify with it, closely resembles what psychoanalysts speak about when we intimate caution to ourselves as we formulate interpretations so that they are not experienced by the patient as excessively superego-ish. In other words, I think your caution to avoid threatening those identified with their nation personified in an authoritarian leader creates another opportunity for convergence between the therapeutic action of psychoanalysis and the art of politics. So let me ask you now, what is this art of politics? What would make a good enough political artist?

RDH: I think the issue of threat—threat of loss and of depletion—is the central interesting point. As you may also understand, such threats that occur in a personal, and indeed internal way, may often be defended against by psychological forms of splitting of the ego. Alarmingly, this results in a further sense of loss and depletion of the self. So an enduring and self-sustaining sense of being reduced can be set up (see Hinshelwood, 2024). It is not of course as radical as the kind of fragmentation that can occur with psychotic states. But it may be widely occurring in society. Politically, there is then a need for a form of governance that has a degree of empathy for those feeling that kind of internal impoverishment (often associated with actual material poverty). So I think a political system that is very cautious, as you say, about the risk of causing widespread diminishment and humiliation can be very much in demand at times of national crisis.

So, turning the table around, I know you own thoughts about reparation, forgiveness, and emotion is not a strand that is particularly evident in these papers. It might be a really useful final exposition to complement what else we have said. So, what do the intimate and positive feelings have to contribute to a useful form of action in politics?

I think it would be very interesting if you took some space, whatever you need, to lead us through some of the thoughts you have been holding back on about reparation and forgiveness. I might say, perhaps in tune with you, that I do think forgiveness is a very neglected emotional state in psychoanalysis (not to mention in politics and public life)—having said that, we should not overlook the book published only last year on *Psychoanalytic Approaches to Forgiveness and Mental Health* (edited by Ron Britton and Aleksandra Novakovic, 2023); there is also Karl Figlio's (2017) *Reparation as Remembering: Psychoanalysis and Historical Memory*.

GC: Thank you for asking me to think through some of my ideas on the politics of reparation and forgiveness. I will take what I said a little earlier about the internal politics of the mind in relation to (individual and group) identity as my starting point. I will only say very little about reparation and forgiveness because I have only recently started to think about their application to the political sphere and these thoughts are still very much preliminary. Matters of reparations for crimes against humanity and specific groups, for underdevelopment and social ills, have made an important appearance in various debates both in academic and in activists' spaces (and, often enough, in spaces of mutual engagement between scholarly and political actors). Reparations have been advocated for chattel slavery, for the Shoa, for apartheid, and in contexts such as Rwanda, Yugoslavia, Chile, Argentina, Peru, in several iterations of truth-and-reconciliation processes. Reparations have been demanded by First Nations, to redress colonialism, and for a variety of social injustices from class, race, and gender inequality. The range of proposed measures include monetary reparation and deeper processes of transformation aiming not only at repairing the present social fabric and its relationship with the natural sphere but also at creating new contexts and dynamics in which what is to be repaired may not occur again. Recently, a small but growing literature on reparative welfare systems has been developing, drawing both from the legal field, and the theory and practice of international development. These are only a handful of examples of a growing field of interest which finds me very sympathetic.

Whereas these debates centre on reparations, I suggest that the idea of reparation (in the singular) as developed by Klein first— and later in the literature that drew inspiration from her work—can contribute important insights based on clinical experience. Importantly, and to some, provocatively, this literature may contribute to the debate on reparations by putting what is to me a necessary stress on the reparation of the self. Klein, and I agree with her, suggested that the reparation of the damaged internal object and more broadly of the individual's self, were necessary in order for the reparation in relation to the other to have a chance to succeed. Now, I think that the process of reparation does require forgiveness in a mutually sustaining dynamic. For reparation to take place in the internal world, one has to appreciate the damage done, feel guilt, and act upon it. However, if guilt is too powerful, if it is persecutory, it may indeed prevent reparation proper and instead drive what Klein called "manic reparation", an omnipotent defence against actual reparation. When guilt can be felt and borne, the self can forgive itself and draw energy towards the repairing process in a virtuous dynamic. A self that can forgive and repair itself can also accept forgiveness and enact reparations to others. I know this simplifies the matter a great deal, but I hope this conveys sufficiently what I am concerned with here. In a similar vein, earlier in Discussion IV, you focused on the inability to feel empathy for the other as a consequence of the inability to feel empathy for oneself (perhaps feeling unmoved by the demandingness of the baby). This inability to feel empathy for oneself, to experience one's emotions and one's intentions, and, ultimately, to make sense of one's motivations, are directly responsible for the way in which one takes up a role in a group and, more broadly, in society at large. The relationship between the internal world of mental objects and the external objects is often a complex one to make sense of, especially from the vantage point of social and political theory. In other words, what is difficult to make sense of and often ethically to accept is that, if empathy for self and empathy for others are connected, un-empathic and damaging individuals and groups, in order to repair their social relations, would have to repair first their internal world and group dynamics. This invitation of Klein's for reparation is often being misunderstood as follows: that to repair the damage done to others one would have to concentrate on oneself "rather than" onto the damaged individual or group. To be fair, Klein stated that after the genocide of native people in North America, the new settlers repaired the damaged done by repopulating the land they had stolen.

There is a final point I wish to raise, which I referred to previously in our conversation from different perspectives. It is about the relation between clinical experience and the development of clinical action, on the one hand, and, on the other, political thinking and action in reference to groups and societies. I wonder whether, taking further Bion's application (and extension and advancement as well) of Kleinian thinking to groups, we can then extend issues of reparation and forgiveness in the internal world in order to make sense of group and societal dynamics. And if, by the same token, can we use the clinical experience in the consulting room to reflect on political action in conversation with debates on therapeutic (and anti-therapeutic) action. If I may add a point, one very similar conception of anti-therapeutic and anti-political action is framed in both contexts by using the very same concept of collusion (with the dominant part of the personality or with the dominant class in society). But let me ask now about your thoughts on all this. Let me ask you whether you think we could, indeed, translate into the political sphere theories and techniques such as those guiding the analytical work in the consulting room. If that were the case, in some way at least, what could it mean to say that political action would address the tyrannical superego, the subaltern Ego, bring to the fore the underlying anxieties, or confront group defences but without doing so in such a way as to make them stronger? Do you think that Klein's belief (based on her experience) that the analysis of hate would release love (she opposes this to pedagogical—seductive, manipulative—ways to work) could have a meaning analogous in the political sphere? Let me add to my question that I think that this is an attitude that I associate with your thinking that psychiatric and psychoanalytic work can be political action, the action of drawing the human from underneath the symptom, not to allow it (to the extent that it is possible) to be overwhelmed by it. It is the work of having the human break through the de-humanising, the alienating.

RDH: Well, I am not sure if I have quite got the idea of reparation right. You are making an equation of empathy for others with empathy for oneself, which might be the conclusion to draw from Klein's case; her patient should accept his own aggression, not least towards his own ego. In Klein's view, reparation in one domain has a complete equivalence to reparation in the other. Of course, it is possible to be very self-absorbed and in fact relatively indifferent to the actual external person; and indeed mere reparation to an external object may have little impact on the internal situation. The importance for political activity is the resonance between internal and external dramas. One can replace the other, either way; and that fluidity allows for collaboration at the emotional and the unconscious level as well as the purely conscious cognitive level. Figlio's (2017) assumption that reparation requires a memory of the wrongdoing and not just a righteous do-gooding that denies the guilt.

I am sure you are correct in gauging the capacity for making reparation and forgiving oneself depends on the degree to which one feels guilty and the degree to which one feels, as it were, "forgivable". The unforgivable sin exists in all our minds from biblical times and no doubt before. Unconsciously we feel unforgivable when we have no course of action other than to foreclose on the problem by those methods understood by psychoanalysts, that is, to render guilt unconscious (by repression or splitting) and to engage in rigid self-justifications. Although there may be other unconscious attempts to deal with the bad conscience, I am thinking that the easy donation of money might have that quality—financial enrichment is the ultimate value and so making monetary recompense settles the score. To me there is a doubt whether quantity of value (money) can really assuage the qualitative values of guilt, unforgivable sin, and forgiveness. We are culturally caught up in a money culture that provides, to my mind, over-simplistic solutions to grave existential crises.

GC: As we come to the end of this inspiring—wonderful, indeed—conversation and, with it, to the end of this volume, I will only renew to you, Bob, my gratitude for the inspiration that your work has been for me, for the generosity with which you have accepted to work with me on this project, and for the kindness with which you have never held back. Thank you!

RDH: Likewise, thank you, Giuseppe, for this opportunity you have given me to revisit much of this interface between psychoanalysis and politics, and for your untiring interest. I think we have found a great deal in common, a very great deal. It is heartening that a medic from which psychoanalysis sprang and a social scientist (an anthropologist) have found a framework for conversing and even taking forward a shared engagement. I think our discussions promise a productive joining of these two vital disciplines. I hope together we have enabled readers to continue a discussion with themselves as well as with us on the resonances of our personal experiences. It can hardly be more urgent to engage our two disciplines in the issues and crises in present-day politics which we confront every day (or which we avoid!).

References

Bion, W. R. (1962). *Learning from Experience*. London: Heinemann. Republished in *The Complete Works of W. R. Bion, Volume IV* (pp. 263–365). London: Karnac, 2014.

Britton, R., & Novakovic, A. (Eds.) (2023). *Psychoanalytic Approaches to Forgiveness and Mental Health*. London: Routledge.

Figlio, K. (2017). *Reparation as Remembering: Psychoanalysis and Historical Memory*. London: Palgrave Macmillan.

Freud, S. (1914c). On narcissism: An introduction. *S. E., 14*: 68–102. London: Hogarth.

Hinshelwood, R. D. (2024). *Unconscious Politics*. London: Karnac.

Marx, K. (1845). Theses on Feuerbach. In: *Early Writings* (pp. 421–423). London: Penguin, 1975.

Winnicott, D. W. (1956). Primary maternal preoccupation. In: *Through Paediatrics to Psycho-Analysis: Collected Papers* (pp. 300–305). London: Tavistock, 1975.

Wilden, A. (1986). *Man and Woman, War and Peace: The Strategist's Companion*. London: Routledge & Kegan Paul.

Index

Page numbers followed by "n" refer to footnotes.